DICTIONARY OF
MANAGEMENT

DICTIONARY OF MANAGEMENT

R. CHOPRA

ANMOL PUBLICATIONS PVT. LTD.
NEW DELHI - 110 002 (INDIA)

ANMOL PUBLICATIONS PVT. LTD.
H.O.: 4374/4B, Ansari Road, Daryaganj,
New Delhi-110 002 (India)
Ph.: 23278000, 23261597
B.O.: No. 1015, Ist Main Road, BSK IIIrd Stage
IIIrd Phase, IIIrd Block,
Bangalore - 560 085 (India)
Visit us at: www.anmolpublications.com

Dictionary of Management

First Edition, 1990
Reprint 1992, 1993
Revised Edition, 1995
Reprint 1997, 2004, 2005, 2008

PRINTED IN INDIA

Printed at Mehra Offset Press, Delhi.

Preface

The Revised edition of this Dictionary is an effort to keep pace with rapid developments and expanding vocabularies in various aspects of management. It includes terms which have been carefully selected from the various fields of management. Throughout the process of compilation and editing this book my sincere effort was to make the dictionary serve as a ready reference for students who are pursuing management courses in Indian universities and management institutes. It will also be useful for candidates preparing for the qualifying examinations of professional institutions like the Institute of Chartered Accountants, Costs and Works Accounts, Company Secretaries and similar other examinations. This dictionary is expected to serve as a ready reference for professional and practising managers, functional executives, management consultants professional accountants etc.

When a dictionary of this kind is being compiled, it becomes essential to depend upon the work of many authorities and seek the advice of colleagues to all of whom the editor is deeply indebted.

All comments from users on omissions or shortcomings will be highly appreciated.

Editor

A

A and D Rates. Refers to the published rates that apply to freight moving to assembly or consolidation points and from distribution points.

A and S Insurance. Abbreviation of accident and sickness insurance.

AAR. Refers to the initials for against all risks, with special reference to freight insurance. Also, refers to the initials for association of American Railroads.

AB. Abbreviation of Aktiebolag or aktiebolag which literally means share company. A limited company organised according to the laws of Sweden.

Abandonment. In accounting, it refers to the complete retirement of a fixed asset after it is removed from service. There are several legal applications: Abandonment of property means the giving up of all control over it with the intention of relinquishing all claim to it. Loss of property is involuntary: abandonement is a voluntary act. When used in connection with duty or responsibility, abandonement has been synonymous with repudiation.

Abatement

1. An allowance or deduction.
2. Where the estate of a deceased person is insufficient to pay all the legacies in full, the legacies must normally be reduced, or abated, in equal proportions in accordance to the amount available.

Abatement—of—Rent Clause. In a lease, it refers to a provision that the tenant will be released from his obligation to pay rent if the premises are made uninhabitable by such causes as flood or fire.

ABC Control. Also known as selective inventory control. A system of inventory control in which every item carried in stock is assigned a rating of A, B, or C, according to its costliness, with the two-fold aim or of reducing capital investment in inventories and lessening the likelihood of running out of low-cost but did not pay for a TV set she purchased, the defendant might file a counter—claim that the plaintiff's truck damaged her driveway while delivering their cost for a given period (for example, the number of items used during one week multiplied by their unit cost). The most expensive items, constituting perhaps 10 per cent of the period's outlay, have been classed A; the next most expensive, comprising an additional 20 per cent of the period's expenditures, have been classed B; all others are classed C. As they represent a high investment, inventories of A items are kept as low as possible; inventories of B items are also kept low, but with a slightly generator safety margin against depletion; and inventories of C items are much larger and less closely controlled.

ABC Method or Analysis (or Usage-value analysis). Analysis of a range of items *e.g.*, stock levels, customers, sales territories etc. into three groups: A=very important; B=important; C=marginal significance. The object is to sort the total into categories which should be handled and controlled in different ways. In the case of customers, for example, the A customers might be the responsibility of the sales manager and warrant regular visits whilst the C customers whose turnover and potential have been insignificant might not justify regular visits at all. The approach has been closely allied to Pareto's law and eighty-twenty rule.

Ability to Pay. A wage theory which holds that the wage level must be based on a company's ability to pay. Under this theory, wage levels should increase [as profits increase. Those who support this theory rarely recommend the converse, lowering wages as profits decline. Also, a theory of taxation holding that taxes should be based on the taxpayer's ability to pay, the rich paying proportionately more than the poor.

Ab Initio. Latin, "from the beginning" for example: A person who enters upon the land of another with permission and thereafter abuses the permission becomes a trespasser ab initio; that is, he has nullified the permission and is legally regarded as a trespasser from the time he first entered upon the land.

Above Par. As used in the securities market, it refers to a premium price, either paid or quoted, that is higher than the face value of the item.

Above the Line. The term, in relation to business, refers to promotional expenditure incurred by a concern on the sale of its products or services by means of direct advertising through newspapers, radio, television, posters etc. (below-the-line expenditure comprises all other promotional sales expenditure like that incurred by special offers, free samples, and window displays).

Above-the-line Advertising. Any form of advertising for which a commission or fee is payable to a recognized advertising agency operating on behalf of its client(s). Usually press, television, radio, cinema, and posters, sometimes referred to as Theme Advertising.

Above-the-Line Promotion. Term used by marketing men of sales promotion in the form of expenditure on advertising in the press, on television or in other media. The term below-the-line promotion, on the other hand, is used for such forms of sales promotion as reduced price special offers, premiums, and point-of-sale displays.

Absenteeism

1. Refers to the time lost in industrial establishment by avoidable or unavoidable absence of employees.
2. Failure of workers to report for work when they are scheduled to work-especially when caused by un willingness rather than incapacity.

Absolute Advantage. A country is considered to be at absolute advantage if she, with equal quantities of productive factors of production, can produce more of a given product, than another country.

Absolute Advantage, of Law. The principle that a basis for trade exists between nations or regions when each of them, because of natural or acquired advantages, can provide goods or services that the other wants at a lower cost than each could provide for itself. This law accounts for much of the world's trade.

Absolute Component Bar Chart. See bar chart.

Absolute Cross-Elasticity of Demand. Means the absolute change in the quantity of commodity. A demanded which would result from a unit change in the price of B, other factors remaining constant.

Absolute elasticity of Demand. Means the ratio of the change in quantity demanded to the change in price, *i.e,*

$$A.E. = \frac{\text{Change in Demand}}{\text{Change in Price}}$$

Absolute Income-elasticity of Demand. The change in the quantity demanded per unit change in income, all prices and determinants held constant.

Absolute Liability. Legal liability for an act that causes harm, even though the doer of the harm is not at fault.

Absolute Monopoly. It implies that the entire output of a commodity or service is in the hands of a single producer or supplier. However, this condition never takes place because there are alternatives for most of the things or services.

Absolute Value. Synonym magnitude.

Absorption Costing. Procedure for controlling the assignment of indirect or overhead costs to specialized product costing. Many methods are used for assigning overheads including the rate of cost per unit system (obtained by dividing the total overheads for a given cost centre (center) by the number of units produced), the standard cost rate used in conjunction with standard costing, direct materials cost percentage rate, direct wages cost percentage rate, labo(u)r hour rate and machine hour rate.

Abstinence

1. The conduct of a person who either abstains from the unproductive use of what he can command, or designedly prefers the production of remote to that of immediate results.

2. The sacrifice of the present for the sake of future has been called 'abstinence' by economists. However, this term is misunderstood. Therefore, we may better use the term 'waiting' for it.

Abstinence Theory of Interest. According to this theory, interest gained by saving money in an interest-bearing savings account is a reward for not spending the money on goods and services.

Abstraction

1. In real estate, it refers to a method of placing a monetary value on land upon which improvements have been constructed. The value of the improvements is estimated and subtracted from the total. The remainder becomes the value of the land.

2. Method of classifying data by accumulating past experience of information, and applying this knowledge to future decisions.

Abstract of Title. A written document used to determine the ownership of a particular parcel of land. It summarizes the material portions of every deed and other transaction that affect the title of that land, thus representing a history of tis ownership.

Abusive Dismissal. When an employee is dismissed in a way which is technically correct according to his Contract of Employment—for example, by giving the stipulated period of notice—but in such a way that management has abused its power in doing so . Such dismissal can be grounds for appeal to an industrial tribunal and is illegal in many countries.

Accelerated Depreciation. Depreciation of a fixed asset at a faster rate than with straightline depreciation—*e.g.* by using the declining balance method.

Accelerating Premium Bonus Plan/Scheme/System. A premium bonus scheme in which the incentive payment per unit of time saved increases as more time is saved. (Also known as a 'progressive scheme'.)

Accelerating Vocational Training. Training or (usually) retraining which is intended to help adult workers to acquire skills which traditionally have been acquired by apprenticeship in a much shorter period than is usually taken by an apprenticeship. Training programmes of this type are usually government sponsored.

Accelerated vocational learning teaching methods off the job but with a realistic working or industrial environment.

Acceleration Clause. A provision in an agreement for the repayment of a loan by instalments that if a specified number of instalments are not paid then all the outstanding payments are due immediately.

Acceleration Principle. The basic relationship between the change in the level of output and the volume of investment spending is known as the acceleration principle. The capital-output ratio is known as the accelerator. The theory of investment based on this relationship is known as the acceleratory theory.

Accelerator. Relatively small change in demand for consumer goods resulting in a comparatively substantial change in demand for capital plant supplying these goods.

Accelerator Co-efficient. It tells by how much investment will increase given a particular rate of change in consumption or in national income. More simply it is known as accelerator. In terms of formula, it may be put as follows:

$$\text{Accelerator Co-efficient} = \frac{\text{Increment in investment}}{\text{Increment in Income}}$$

Acceptability. Extent of customer approval of package, product, service, as expressed during a survey.

Acceptable Quality Level. In manufacturing, it refers to the level of quality at which components, processes, or finished goods are considered good to be continued without rework, or immediately shippable. The maximum percentage of defectives (or number of defects per 100 units) that will be accepted in the output from a production process.

Acceptance. It is a contract of offer and acceptance. If one person offers to do something for another, the contract is not complete until the offer is accepted. Acceptance must be on the same terms as the offer and must be communicated to be second party. A conditional acceptance is neither equivalent to an offer nor is it an acceptance.

Acceptance word is commonly used as meaning a bill of exchange, that is, the actual bill itself; but an acceptance is really the writing across the face or a bill by which the drawer agrees to the order of the drawer.

Acceptance Bank. Also, accepting house. An organization that specializes in accepting or guaranteering domestic and foreign bills of exchange.

Acceptance Credit. A credit whose terms involve the drawing of time bills needing acceptance either by the bank issuing the credit or by the customer.

Acceptance, Sampling. In quality control, this term refers to a process of sampling that forms the basis for accepting or rejecting a product. For example, an inspector 'might inspect 10 items from every lot of 200. From the number or defects found, the number of defects in the entire shipment can, by statistical inference, be estimated.

Acceptance Test. Made early in the progress of a project, etc., with the object of checking that the finished work will be fit for its purpose.

Accepting House. A financial enterprise whose principal function is facilitation of negotiation of Bills of Exchange either by accepting them or guaranteeing them. Are situated near the central bank and other institutions concerned with the smooth running of the country's financial system. The signature of an established acceptance house on a bill of exchange is a sign of the reliability of that bill and enables the holder to discount it at favourable rates.

Accession Rate. Also, hiring rate. The number of employees added to the payroll during a given period, an important Leading Indicator of future business conditions, may indicate a coming recession; an increase usually heralds the end of a recession. As business improves, companies initially tend to postpone hiring, in order to avoid future layoffs but eventually they do begin to add personnel. Statistics on the accession rate of manufacturing establishments, expressed as a percentage of total employment, are compiled monthly by the Department of Labour of various countries.

Accessorial Service. A transportation service in addition to the linehaul service, usually at an added cost, such as heating, packing, loading and storage.

Access Right

1. The level of access which is granted to users of a system *e.g.*, read a file only, or write to a file.
2. The right of an owner or his authorized agent to enter or leave his property without trespassing.

Access Time

1. The time it takes for information to become available once it has been called for through a control signal.
2. The amount of time a computer takes to locate data on a storage device and make them available to a user. Also, the time interval between a request for data to be stored and actual storage.

Accident. Refers to an event that occurs even though no reasonable person could foresee its occurrence. Due to this, the law holds no person legally responsible for any harm that may result from an accident, unless injury or damage is increased by negligence.

Accident and Sickness Insurance. Intended to reimburse the insured for loss of income or for expenses incurred as a result of an accident or illness. Indemnity or reimbursement through A and S insurance may be purchased by individuals, or through other forms of contracts such as group insurance, disability insurance under a life insurance policy. Workmen's compensation, and medical insurance provided by federal state, and local governments.

Accident Book. A book which almost every employer must keep at each workplace so that any employee can make a record of any personal injury suffered by him as a result of an accident at work. The main purpose of the record is so that an employee can have evidence to support a claim for industrial injuries benefit.

Accident Frequency Rate. Number of lost-time accidents per 100,000 man-hours worked.

Accident Insurance. This is a loosely used term to include personal accident insurance or other forms of insurance in which accident may be a factor, *e.g.*, accidents at sea, accidents on the highway and accidents involving building.

Accommodation Note. A note which is signed by one person as the maker, endorser, or accepter on behalf on another whose credit position is not strong enough to be self-suporting. Usually no consideration gets envolved. The signer acts as guarantor for the note.

Accommodation Party. Someone who signs a bill of exchange either as drawer, accepter or endorser, but receives no value in exchange, *i.e.*, does it to lend his (presumable respected) name as a guarantor that the bill will be paid so that the payee can easily discount it. the payee is, therefore, 'accommodated'.

Accomplishment/Cost Procedure (ACP). Technique for accurately comparing and contrasting cost and results of large-scale projects developed by Stanford University research Unit (US). It is essentially, a management information and reporting system for effectively managing complex projects.

Accord and Satisfaction

1. An agreement that is made an executed in satisfaction of the rights one has acquired under a former contract.
2. Legal term for the making and completion of an agreed variation of a contract. 'Accord' means there must be agreement that the contract be varied. 'Satisfaction' means satisfactory completion of the replacement contract.

Accord and Satisfaction. The legal term for a change in contract, meaning that the parties are in agreement regarding the changes and are satisfied with the new document.

Accountability. Refers to the obligation of an employee or a manager to undertake a task or to fulfil an assignment and to bear responsibility for the effects of his or her effort. In government accounting, the designation of the account or the amount of a disbursing officer's liability.

Accountant. A person trained in accounting who may either be employed by a firm or work independently.

Accountant's Report. See Auditor's Report.

Accountant's Return. Alternative term for return on capital or book rate of return.

Account Conflict. Situation in which an advertising agency or other outside service house is offered a business opportunity which is similar to that of an existing client or account agency handing an automobile account could not thus take on another competing and therefore conflicting client in the same field. The problem can be overcome only partially by having a number of separate account groups. A more satisfactory solution is for there to be a separate company with no more than a financial connection.

Account Executive. In advertising, public relations, brokerage, investment counseling, and similar service industries, the person in direct contact with one or more of the firm's clients. The account executive passes on the clients ideas to others in the firm and presents their results of the firm's work to the client.

Account Group. Sub-unit of an advertising agency, handling a group of clients or accounts. May be fully or partly self-contained.

Accounting Department Manual. This is a manual which outlines the system of accounting, the entries or number of typical transactions in the books and giving sample entries; also outlines the duties of the cashier.

Accounting Machine. Mechanization of routine accounting operations has been a recent innovation. Invoicing, ledger posting, Preparation of statements, cash receipts, debit and credit notes, recording of payments, etc., can now be made by standard mechanical applicances. Accounting machine can perform different sets of accounting operations. They can be applied for ledger posting and preparation of statements simultaneously or they can be used for posting different entries in one operation and automotically for tabulating and dating. As each item is posted, a record is made on a separate audit sheet which facilitates cross-checking.

Accounting Models. Forms of simulation of a business situation in financial terms. Other forms of model of business situations include computer models and mathematical models.

Accounting Rate of Return (ARR). A method of capital investment appraisal based on the net profit a project brings expressed as a percentage of the Book Value. Projects can then be selected on the basis of the highest ARR; the main weakness of this method is that it ignores the time value of Money, although it does allow for depreciation which other methods sometimes exclude.

Accounting Records. These are records which are maintained according to the needs of the business concern.

Account Payable

1. Sums (perhaps represented by promising notes) due from the company for supplies purchased by the corporation and not yet paid for.
2. A term used in double-entry book-keeping to indicate the records of the amounts credited to others for goods and services purchased, and the amounts paid for those purchased.

Account Payee. These words, or their equivalent, such a 'a/c' are frequently added to the crossing of a cheque with the idea of safeguarding it in transmission.

Account Receivable. The amount owed to a business by its customers, who are customarily granted anywhere from 10 to 90 days to pay for merchandise already shipped.

Account Receivable Insurance. Refers to a fire insurance policy that provides coverage against losses due to the inability to collect outstanding accounts receivable because of destruction records.

Account Rendered. A statement sent by a seller to his customer of the amount that the customer owes, details of which may have been previously sent.

Account, Sales (A/s). An account sent by one agent to the consignor showing the total quantity and the amount to be realized after deducting freight, commission, etc.

Accretion. In finance, refers to an addition of principal or income to a fund as a result of a plan of accumulation.

In real estate, the acquisition of title to additional land when an owner's land is built up by gradual deposits made by the natural action of water.

Accrual

1. An accrued expense or an accrued revenue.
2. Amount calculated as being owning for goods an services prior to their appearance in the balance sheet.

Accrual Basis in Accounting. In accounting, a system of charging income and expenses to the period in which they are earned or incurred rather than to the period in which they are actually received or paid. Corporation almost always keep their books on an accrual basis to avoid a misleading income statement. Individuals or very small firms on the other hand, usually keep their books (and tax returns) on a cash basis because it gratly simplifies book keeping.

Accrual Costing. In accounting, the expensing of goods and services as they are consumed.

Accrued Asset. In accounting, it refers to the interest, commission, or revenue earned but neither received nor past due.

Accrued Depreciation. In accounting, it refers to the difference between the cost of replacement of equipment or real property as of the date of the appraisal at the time of acquisition and the appraised value at the present time.

Accrued Dividend. Unpaid and undeclared dividend on preferred stock.

Accrued Expense (or Accrued Liability). The amount incurred up to a specified data of a liability that accumulates continually but is customarily payable at fixed times. For example, if a firm pays for electricity once a quarter then the cost of one month consumption of electricity is an accrued expense at the end of that month.

Accrued Income. The cumulative running of interest, usually on a day-to-day basis on a capital asset.

Accrued Revenue. The amount accumulated, upto a specified date, of a continually increasing debt, due to one, which is customarily payable at fixed times.

Accumulated Dividend. A dividend which has not been paid when due and which has become a liability of the corporation to be paid, presembly, at some future time.

Accumulated Income. Net income which is retained and not paid out in dividends or dissipated by subsequent losses.

Also referred to as accumulated earning and accumulated profit.

Accumulation Bin. Refers to the place where a product is assembled; usually a physical location intended for the accumulation of all components that comprise an assembly before the order to perform the assembly is sent to the production flour.

Accumulation Plan. Refers to an arrangement under which the purchaser of shares in a mutual fund (open-end investment company) agrees to acquire more shares over a given period of time.

Accumulation Schedule. Refers to a table in which computations are provided for the periodic write-up until maturity of the discount relating to an investment or obligation.

Accumulator. Means the register and associated equipment in the arithmetic unit of a computer in which arithmetic and logic operations are performed.

Accumulator Register. Synonymores with accumulator.

ACER Speed and Accuracy Test. Clerical aptitude test in which pairs of numbers and names are checked against each other within a time limit. The test takes 10 to 15 minutes.

Achievement Analysis. Examination of stages in the progress of a project, perhaps at project milestones.

Achievement Motivation. A form of Motivation theory developed by David McClelland which suggests that individuals are driven by varying degrees of a need for achievement (nAch). Individuals with a high nAch constantly require proof of their having made their mark—for example, financial regards.

Achievement Motivation Test. One of several Psychological Tests developed of achievement. The most widely-used is the Thematic Appreciation Test (TAT).

Achievement Test. Or attainment test. General term used in psychological testing, particularly in the USA, for a test that measures achievement in a particular occupation (*e.g.* job knowledge test rather than potential or aptitude or intelligence.

Acid-test Ratio. Refers to the ratio of a firm's liquid assets to its current liabilities. The ratio indicates the firm's ability to pay its debts. (Also known as the 'quick ratio.')

Acquisition. The purchase of a firm or of its assets.

Acquisition Cost. The funds which are required to acquire goods or services.

Acquisitive Need. Refers to a motivational factor; the desire to possess or hoard material possessions such as money, property, fancy automobiles and clothing. The objects of the acquisitive need are often those that are esteemed by the individual's societal affiliations.

Across-the-board. Applying to everyone, or all cases, or everything. As in 'across-the-board increase': increase in wages of the same extent for every employee in an organization.

Across-the-board Settlement. Agreed pay increase that gives of the employees concerned an equal proportional increase in pay.

AC Test of Creative Ability. Psychological test of US origin devised particularly for engineers and engineering workers.

Action Ex Contractu. Legal action to recover damages for the breach of a duty arising out of a contract.

Action Ex Deliction. Legal action to recover damages for the branch of a duty existing by reason of a general law.

Action Learning. A managment-development activity in which a manager is required to solve an actual problem of an existing organization.

Action of the Sun. In real estate, it refers to a consideration in the selection of a retail store. the shadier side of the street is usually more desirable.

Action Research. A form of research into organizations which differs from controlled experiment in that it explicitly recognizes that the act of doing research will have an influence on the organizations being studied. Action research projects aim to contribute both to the development of the organization under study and the theoretical body of knowledge. This approach is described by Peter Clark in Action Research and Organizational Change (London: Harper & Row, 1970).

Action Skill. Refers to the ability to carry out skillfully the behaviour required by a situation—*e.g.*, in some forms to T-goup trainig or sensitivity training.

Action to Quite the Title. Refers to an action to clarify one's title to property by removing any interests or claims of others.

Action Training. Training with a strong reliance on activity learning and such participative techniques as case studies, role playing, games and simulations.

Active Crops of Executives. An organization of executives who are still employed and who have volunteered to offer expertise in many operational aspects of business.

Activities Analysis. One of three techniques identified by drucker to be used in deciding the organization structure appropriate for a company, the other techniques being decision analysis and relations analysis. Activities analysis is used to establish what are the key activities in the company, as distinct from generalized assumptions.

Activity. A term used in Project Network Techniques to describe the work required to complete a specified Event.

Activity Chart. Diagram showing the break-down and composition of a series of operations or a process-plotted against a time scale.

Activity on Arrow. Commonly used method of representing a series of associated activities in critical path scheduling or network analysis. Each activity is denoted by an arrow, as in the diagram. This method of representation, though simple in concept, is often more complicated to use than the activity on node system.

Activity-on-arrow Network. A network in which the arrows represent activities.

Activity on Node. Method of representing a series of associated activities in critical path scheduling or network analysis. Each activity is by a circle or node' instead of an arrow, which is conventionally used. The inter-relationships between each activity are shown by lines known as dependencies, as in the diagram to form precedence diagrams.

Activity Rate (for Working Age Population). Proportion of the population of a given age likely to being employment or seeking employment.

Activity Ratio. In production, it refers to the ratio of a number of actively used records in a file to the total number of records in the file. May also be used with reference to electronic data processing. In finance, any one of a set of financial ratios that deals primarily with the utilization asset entrusted to corporate management. These are especially useful in tracking the performance of operating managers responsible for specific functions such as inventory management, cash management, and credit policy.

Activity Sampling

1. As work sampling.
2. Recording instantaneous observations of the work or other activity that is being performed by an employee or a machine at specific points in time.

Activity Vector Analysis (AVA). Psychological test developed in the USA for use in temperament and personality testing. It has had mixed fortunes and reactions as a personnel selection test.

Act of Bankruptcy. An action committed by a debtor that a court will recognize as a ground for making a receiving order (the first stage of making the debtor bankrupt).

Act of God. Refer to an act of nature that is not reasonable foreseeable. In insurance, a natural event, such as flood, lightning, earthquake, or hurricane, that leads to a property loss and could not have been prevented by reasonable care or foresight.

Actual Cost. Cost data which is based on transactions that have been completed, is contrasted with costs that have been estimated.

Actual Marketing Data Analysis. Method of exception reporting introduced by German firm, Coordinated Management System GmbH. This analytical tool automatically calculates deviations in market share and market development from the average level in any particular market breakdown. Available through Nielseh.

Actual Market Volume. Sum total of suppliers' sales made at a given price or in a given price range to a specific market segment.

Actuary. An actuary is defined in a Oxford English Dictionary as an expert in statistics, especially one who calculates insurance risks and premiums.

Ad ***(colloquial).*** Advertisement Advertising.

A/D. See Analog-to-digital Converter.

Adaptability Test. Mental ability or intelligence test used particularly in US industry for personnel placement purposes. It is used to predict performance in wide range of occupations.

Adaptation. Advertisement adapted from basic layout and copy to fit different space, shape and size.

Adaptive Control ***(Self-optimizing centrol).*** A type to control in which the set points/control targets alter in response to changing conditions so as to achieve optimum performance under varying conditions.

Added Hours. In cases where employees work overtime, the amount paid is calculated by adding hours to the normal working week for which the employee is paid. For example, two hours worked at double time would add four hours' payment at the standard rate.

Adaptive Control System

1. A control system in which automatic means are used to adjust the system being controlled in a way that is

intended to achieve optimum performance by the system at all times rather than a predetermined value of the controlled condition. (Also called a self-optimizing control system).

2. A control system continuously monitoring its own behaviour and, by adjusting its parameters it is able to suit itself to changing environment.

Added Value. An attempt to 'measure' productivity by calculating the additional value given to a product or job by people or machines doing work on it (now used as a basis for some bonus 'incentive' schemes).

Addendum

1. Addition or explanatory note at the end of a written report, survey, etc.

2. Addition to a motion at a formal meeting. The procedure for handling an addendum is the same as that for an amendment though, unlike the latter, it does not seek to alter part or parts of the motion, but only to add to it.

Addressing Machines. Addressing machines are used to print addresses on envelopes, wrappers or labels, to be sent frequently to regular customers. They are also used for putting the names and addresses of customers on the monthly statements of accounts.

Adequate Distribution. Distribution of retail products in advance of advertising campaign so that response can be satisfied.

Adequate Price. Price which is just enough to make the employer decide to employ a worker to make the product.

Ad Hoc. Latin, "for this." Refers to a limited or particular situation. An ad hoc committee is one limited to a specific purpose and may be dismissed on completion of its task. An ad hoc decision means "for this purpose only." An ad hoc attorney is one appointed to perform a special task in a particular case. Often refers to occasional market surveys.

Adjournment. Temporary stopping of negotiation, usually to allow time to consult or think. It can be a device to 'postpone' depression of a problem indefinitely.

Adjournment, Motion for. Motion at a formal meeting to the effect:

(a) that the meeting be adjourned either for a stated period or sinc die (*i.e.*, indefinitely), or

(b) that discussion of a particular item of business be adjourned, usually unit a stated future time.

Adjustable Peg. A system that permits changes in the par rate of foreign exchange after a nation has had long-run disequilibrium in its balance of payments.

Adjusted Basis. In income taxes, the basis used to compute depreciation or gain or loss on sales of fixed or noninventory assets.

Adjusted Cost Basis. For accounting purposes refers to the value of property equal to the original cost plus improvements less depreciation.

Adjusted Earned Income. Taxable income that is earned income.

Adjusted Gross Income. For income taxes, the gross income of an individual less business expenses where applicable, dedication allowable for income producing property certain losses from sales or exchanges or property, self-employment expenses, and moving expenses.

Adjuster. In the insurance industry, an employee of an insurance company authorised to study, and make recommendations to his employer relative to, the cause of an event that has resulted in a claim, the amount of the loss, and the extent of the insurance company's liability.

Adjusting Entry. In accounting, an entry which is made to correct or offset an error, accrual, write off, determent, etc.

Ad Litem. (Latin: For the suit.) Used to describe an appointment of a person to manage the affairs of an incapacitated person for the purpose of bringing or defending legal proceedings.

Administration Costs. Indirect cost charged to a department or factory, etc., as its share of general administration costs for the organization as a whole over and above indirect costs attributable solely to the department or factory.

Administrative Accounting. Refers to that part of the accounting process generally associated with management.

Administrative Expense. Expense incurred in the general direction and management of an enterprise; contrasted with expenses incurred by spcific functions such as selling or manufacturing.

Administrative Law. The law relating to the discharge of functions of a public nature in government and administration.

Administrative Management Theory. An approach to management theory, particularly associated with Henr Fayol. Many Parker Follet and Lyndal Urwick and popular in the 1930s. It followed the Scientific Management tradition of Frederick Winslow Taylor and was in turn followed by the Human Relations School or Management Training. The main emphasis in this theory is on formal organizational structures and hierarchies, and the particular defined responsibilities and accountabilities associated with them. Good overviews of the work of these theorist can be found in D. Pugh (ed.), Organization Theory: Selected readings (Harmondsworth: Penguin, 1976) and J. Child, Organizations: A guide to theory and Practice (2nd edn., London: Harper & Row, 1982).

Administrator. In business, a person who directs, co ordinates, or controls the activities of subordinates.

Administrator Ad Litem. An administrator of a deceased person's estate appointed for the purpose of litigation only.

Adoption Theory. The body of knowledge concerned with the responses individuals and organizations make to innovations. In the diffusion of innovations—whether new products or processes—adoption over time tends to follow a normal distribution across the population. Everett Rogers identifies five groups of adopters: the innovators, early adopters, early majority, late majority and laggards, (E. Rogers. The Diffusion of Innovations (2nd Eden. London: Macmillan and New York: Free Press, 1982). If the adoption data is plotted on a cumulative basis over time it gives rise to the characteristics S. shaped curve for adoption of innovations.

ADR. European Agreement on the International Carriage of Dangerous Goods.

Ad Referendum. When applied to a contract, this terms means that although the contract has been signed, certain matters have been left over of consideration when they actually arise.

Adulteration. The act of debasing a commercial commodity or substituting an inferior article for a superior one in order to gain an illegitimate profit. The term is usually applied to the debasement of foods, drugs or conmitics.

Ad Val. Abbreviations of ad valorem.

Ad Valorem (ad val.). According to value. Especially a tax that is proportional to the value of the goods or transaction, on which it is levied.

Ad Valorem Subsidy. Refers to a fixed-percentage subsidy granted to producers of commodities as a form of financial aid or relief from hardships resulting from economic conditions beyond the control of the producers.

Advance. Any payment made before it falls due, thus representing a loan.

Advance Against Securities. A Central Bank's assistance to the banking system in a country is made available, in the main, through the alternative facilities of advances from the central Bank.

Advance Bill. An invoice submitted before the goods or services itemized therein have actually been delivered or performed. It is usually requested by buyers for tax purposes or some similar reason.

Advance Factory. Built by the Government in regions in need of development, the factory then being rented at attractive rates to an industrial firm setting up in the region.

Advancement. A payment made by a trustee out of the capital of trust funds to a beneficiary for the purpose of establishing him in life.

Advantage. The ability of one nation, region, or supplier to produce a good or service at a lower cost (with less, labor, or less land, or less machinery) than others. A producer who makes a single item more cheaply than practically any other is said to have an absolute advantage.

Adverse Selection. The insuring of a group of risks that represents an above-average expectation of loss. also the tendency of poor risks to seek insurance.

Advertise

1. To act as an advertiser.
2. To put out advertisements.

Advertised Bidding. The practice of publicly obtaining bids for contracts for goods or services advertised bidding requires highly detailed specifications, which cannot be restrictive (as for a brand name or patented item) and which must be published.

Advertisement. A form of public announcement intended to promote the sale of a commodity or service, to advance an idea or to bring about some other effect desired by the advertiser.

Advertisement Department. Part of a publishing or other organization in the communications business concerned with selling advertising space or time, either to an agency or direct to a client.

Avertisement Manager. Executive responsible for selling space, airtime, sites and other media facilities to advertisers, as distinct from advertising manager who is responsible for a company's advertising.

Advertisement Representative. Firm dealing in space for local and foreign newspapers, and for magazines sub-contracting their space—selling operation.

Advertiser. Organization or person on whose behalf an advertisement appears, and who ultimately pays the bill.

Advertising. Placing paid public presentations or announcements about products, services, or activities, with the objective of persuading the public to buy particular goods or services or to accept a given point of view or concept. The person or institution paying for such announcements is called the advertiser or sponsor, and the means of presenting it are collectively known as the media.

Advertising Agency. An individual or organization that is concerned with marketing. It is an expert body which prepares and places advertising for others.

Advertising Agency Remuneration. There are many ways by which advertising agencies obtain their income, including:

1. Traditional media commission only, plus charges (cost and commission) for work and materials such as artwork, production of TV commercials, blocks, typesetting, print and point-of sale material.
2. Fee plus commission, basic service fee paid by client and agency accepting usual commissions from media.
3. Flat fee only. Chiefly applies to agencies whose accounts produce negligible commissions, or where there is practically no above-the-line (*i.e.*, media) advertising.
4. Cost plus free. client pays for cost of work done together with fee for agency facilities, overheads and profits.
5. Cost plus. Sometimes similar to fourth method, percentage being added the cost of work done, this percentage covering overheads and profits. Again, the work itself, *i.e.*, artwork, is chared at cost.
6. Commission credited. Increasingly popular way of overcoming dilemma of inadequate commissions. Consists of a client's fee from which is deducted the commission received from media. Thus client pays a fee over and above the gross media rates, and agency loses nothing by rebating part of the commission.

Advertising Allowance. A deduction permitted by a producer of distributor to a wholesaler or retailer in exchange for advertising a product or service locally. The practice whereby recipients are asked to share the cost of local advertising is called cooperative advertising.

Advertising Budget. Sum of money set aside for spending on an advertising campaign. Sometimes represents total sum available to cover all advertising expenditure including overheads. Alteratively referred to as 'Advertising appropriation.'

Advertising Coverage. The extent of market or segments which is covered in an advertising campaign.

Advertising Executive. An idividual responsible for advertising work within a department or agency. This often involves taking responsibility for particular customer accounts and planning overall advertising strategy and campaigns.

Advertising Information Group. Informal international group monitoring treats to advertising freedom and promoting self-regulation.

Advertising Management. An employee of a firm who supervises the production of the firm's advertisements and decides which media will carry them.

Advertising Medium. Vehicle of communication which provides for some form of advertising, *e.g.*, the press, television, ratio and transport services.

Advertising Messages. Advertising includes the following forms of messages: the messages carried in newspapers and magazines; on outdoor boards, on street cars and posters, on radio and T.V. broadcasts, and in circulars of all kinds, whether distributed by mail, by person, through tradesmen, or by insertions in packages; dealer-help materials, window display and counter-display materials and efforts; neo signs; house organs when directed to dealers and consumers; motion pictures usd for advertising; and novelties bearing advertising messages or signature of the advertiser. Labels, tags and other literature accompanying marchandise are deemed advertising because they reasonably may be said to fall within the definition of advertising media given above.

Advertising Objectives (advertising goals). The targets towards which an advertising campaign is directed—for example, increased customer awareness, increased market share, increased sales etc.

Advertising Property. A special value built into a product at the outset so that the brand is exploitable. This may be in the shape of the product or a package which is an integral part of the product and not merely a container.

Advertising Rates. This rates charged by various media for disseminating advertisements.

Advertising Regulations. Conditions imposed upon advertising by media owners, trade associations, or government.

Advertising Schedule. Programme of planned advertisement insertions, showing detailed cost, timing, nature of media and the bookings to be reserved.

Advertising Scheme. Scheme advertising.

Advertising Specialty. A useful article which is given away by an advertiser and which is imprinted with the advertiser's name and address and/or a sales message. The most common types of advertising specialty are calendars, writing instruments and matchbooks. (Also known as an 'advertising novely).

Advertising Strategy. The overall plan of an advertising campaign.

Advertising Theme. Theme advertising.

Advice. When a banker issues draft, he sends an advice, called a letter of advice, to the banker upon whom the draft has been drawn, giving him particulars of the amount, number, date and payee, so that, when the instrument is presented for payment, the drawer banker may be able to satisfy himself that the draft is in order. In the absence of an advice, a banker would hesitate to pay a draft: at least, this would be so when the practice has been followed previously.

Advice Note. A document sent by a sellers to a buyer stating the descriptions quantity of goods that have been despatched, to him.

Aerial Advertising. Various ingenious methods of advertising in the sky have been used in different countries, must common being sky writing with smoke Persil famous pre-war user of this technique) and trailing of bannel.

Affidavit. A declaration in writing made an oath before a person entitled to administer oaths—a commissioner for oaths, normally a solicitor. It is a criminal offence deliberately to make a false statement in an affidavit.

Affiliate. Refers to a corporation or other organization related to another by owning or being owned, by common management, by a long-term lease of its properties, or by other control devices.

Affiliated Company. One under the same ownership.

Affiliated Manager. Manager who places greater emphasis on being liked and staying on good term with every body than on exercising leadership and control.

Affiliation. Refers to a connection which is existing between a holding or parent company and its subsidiary, or between two corporations or other organization owned or controlled by a third.

Affiliation Need. A motivational factor, the desire to be associated with, or to be in the presence of, another person or persons. The need to "belong" to a group.

Affirmative Action. Us term for the hiring, employment and promotion of people previously discriminated against.

Affirmative Warranty. See Warranty.

'Affordable' Method. One of a variety of ways of arriving at an advertising budget, on the basis of what a company can afford, rather than what task has to be achieved.

Affreighment. A contract for transporting goods by sea. Also known as charter party or ocean bill of lading.

After-look Journalizing. In a system in which extensive recovery facilities are required to safeguard against system failure, a journal is made of amendments to files. This term indicates that an entry is made to the journal after each change made to the file concerned.

Afternoon Shift. A shift that is worked mainly during the afternoon—*e.g.* :

1. The later shift during a day in a double day-shift system;
2. A shift worked mainly in the afternoon in a three shift system, typically worked from 1400 to 2200;
3. A part-time shift worked, for example, from 1400 to 1800.

After-sales Services. Depending on product or services, after-sales service embraces everything that enables customer to enjoy full benefits of product and to be satisfied in event of complaint. May include spares and parts, repairs, inspection, instructions, advice or guarantee.

Against all Risks. Term used in marine insurance meaning insured against all generally accepted risks.

Age Life Depreciation. Refers to a method which is used by real-estate appraisers in estimating depreciation of building, based on expected life.

Agency

1. The relationship of trust in which one person (the agent) is authorized by another (the principal) to represent him in dealing with third parties.
2. The powers or functions of an agent.
3. A firm that acts as an agent for others.
4. An administrative division of a government.

Agency Bills. Bills of exchange drawn on and accepted by the branches of foreign banks.

Agency Shop. A place of employment where all employees doing particular types of work must pay subscriptions to particular trade unions although they may refuse actually to join a union.

Agency Shop Agreement. An agreement made between one or more employers and a trade union or joint negotiating panel unions, under which the individual worker belonged to a trade union or paid a regular contribution to it in lieu of trade union dues, unless he was a conscientious objector and made a contribution to charity instead.

Agenda. Details of business to be transacted at a meeting, made out by the person calling the meeting or the secretary appointed to do so. The agenda is sent out to those invited to attend. It is generally accompanied by an invitation to appoint a proxy if a member cannot attend personally.

Agent

1. Someone who transacts business on behalf of other. In law, a person who has the power and authority to put another person (who is called the 'principal' of the agent) into binding legal relationships.
2. Insurance agent. A person appointed by an insurance company to sell insurance policies for the company. some firms insist on exclusive representation; others deal with agents who represent more than one firm. In either cash they usually are paid on a commission basis.

Age of Debt. Management accountancy term meaning extent of customer credit.

Agency Catalogue. Mail order catalogue distributed to agents who sell to friends and neighbours on credit terms, as with mail order clubs.

Aggregate Demand Price. Aggregate demand price at any level of employment may be defined as the amount of money which all the entrepreneurs in the economy taken together really do expect that they will get if they sell the output produced by this given number of men. It represents the expected receipts if a given volume of employment is given to workers.

Aggregate Income. An amount which is lying being between the value of the gross product and net national product. It is another name for national income.

Aggregate Supply. Refers to the amount of gods and services produced by all firms in the economy during a given time period in response to demand expectations. In the short run, aggregate supply is a relatively fixed quantity of output, which can, however. be increased over the long-term, as population grows and resources are expanded.

Aging. An analysis of individual accounts receivable according to three time elapsed after the due or billing dates.

Agreed Procedure. Negotiated between management and trade union(s) as the procedure to be followed in attempting to solve any grievances before resorting to strike action. Where a strike is called without first going through the agreed procedure, it is known as an unconstitutional strike or a wildcat strike.

Agribusiness. Refers to the sector of the economy which is concerned with the production processing, and distribution of agricultural products, including farm supplies (machinery, fertilizers, pesticides, herbicides) needed for production, various agricultural services (animal husbandry, milling, etc.), and also the economic agencies that serve agricultural producers (credit institutions, marketing associations, etc.).

Agricultural Co-operation. Broadly speaking, it means the application of the co-operative principles to the requirements of the farm-population.

AH4 Test. Both a verbal and non-berval general intelligence test (and also an element of mumerical optitude test), taking about an hour to conduct and used with different norms according to the level being tested.

AH5 Test. Higher level version of the AH4 Test.

Aided Recall. A technique used in psychological testing in which individuals in interviews are prompted to talk about something by reminding them of associated thing. It is particularly used in Market Research.

AIG. Advertising Information Group.

AIMA. All India Management Association.

Aiming. Type of psychomotor skill. An individual's ability to perform swiftly and accurately a sequence of movements demanding eye-hand co-ordination.

Airway Bill

1. A term used to describe the document made out on behalf of the consignor of goods by air as evidence of the contract of carriage. It, or a copy thereof, accompanies the goods throughout their journey.
2. A way bill covering carriage by air.
3. It may also known as air consignment not. It is used as a contract of carriage by air.

AITUC. All India trade Union Congress.

AJF. Adjusting Journal Entry.

All India Service. The All India service ACT, 1951 provided for the constitution of two service, *viz.* the Indian administrative Service and the Indian Police Service. The act was amended in 1963 to provide for theconstitutionof three more all India service, viz. the Indian Service of Engineers, the Indian Forest Service and the Indian Medical and Health Service. The Indian Forest service was constituted on 1 July 1966. The Indian Administrative Services is controlled by the Department of Personnel and training while the Indian Police Service is controlled by the Ministry of Home affairs. The Indian Forest Service is controlled by the Department of Forests and Wild life.

Alcohol Advertising. An advertising practice which sets out rules to which any advertiser of alcohol must adhere. 'Advertisements should not be directed at young people or in any way encourage them to start drinking.

Alienation. The condition of a worker who becomes a more cog in the production process, spending all day on an assembly lime doing the same simple task over and over.

Alienation Clause. A special type of acceleration clause that requires payment of an entire loan balance upon sale or other transfer or title to real property.

All India Management Association. It was founded in 1951. It is an apex body which is committed to the proud development of the practice of modern scientific management in India.

It acts as an examining body of AIMA diploma in management. Individual memberships consists of Fellow, Member and Associate Member. It represents India at the CIOS-World Cuncil of Management in Geneva. He is also the member of the Asian Association of Management Organization of CIOS (AAMOCIOS). Address: Management House, 14, Institutional Area, Lodhi Road, New Delhi-110003.

All India Organisation of Employees (AIOE). It was established in 1933. It has been the central organisation of employees to protect and promote their interest. It is the associative body of Federation of Indian Chambers of Commerce and Industry. Address: Federation House, Tansen Marg, New Delhi-110001.

All India Trade Union Congress (AITUC). This labour organization was founded in 1920 for representing the interests of the workers and to co-ordinate the activities of all workers organizations in the country.

All-in Rate. Wage rate that incorporates various eatras, such as bonus payments in addition to the basic time—related payment scheme.

Allocate. To spread a cost systematically over two or more time periods, objects, activities, processes, operations, or products. In government accounting, to transfer an appropriation, or a part thereof, from one agency to another.

Allocation of Overheads. Apportioning indirect costs and expenses (*e.g.* cleaning materials, lighting heating and depreciation) which cannot be directly indentified with particular cost centres (centres).

Allocation Problem. A problem concerning the distribution of limited resources among competing alternatives insuch a way as to minimize total cost or maximize total income. Also called a 'programming problem'.

Allonge. Refers to an attachment to a document that provides for endorsements when no space for the purpose remains on the document proper.

All-or-none Embargo. Where the employees of a company insist that privileges such as payment-by-results work or overtime should be granted equally all or none of the without favoritism.

Allowed Time. The time, which, for the purposes of wage payment, is taken to be the normal time for performance of measured work. It consists of the standard time for the job plus a bonus increment and/or a policy allowance.

Alternate. A person who is appointed to act as a substitute for another person in performing specified duties whenever the other person is unavailable.

Alternate Directors. If the articles of association of a company permit, a director can nominate, an alternate or substitute director, who can act when his principal is absent, and his acts done within the scope of his authority are binding on the company. The appointment of an alternate director should be in writing and notice given.

Alternate Standard. Work study term for the alternative Standard time when a specified different or alternative method or work is used.

Alternating Day and Night. A two-shift System in which one group of workers work for a period (*e.g*, a week, fortnight, or month) on a day shift then for the same period on a night shift.

Alternate Standard (Alternative standard). A work study term. If there are different ways a carrying out a task, then, when setting Standard Times, an alternative standard is also set for each different way.

Alternating Shift. Where shift workers change periodically to a different shift (often weekly or monthly).

Alternative Marketing. Unconventional marketing strategies, or marketing or unconventional goods or products-outside mainstream marketing. Could be opening up new markets like Sinclair. Research and home computers, or Barratt Developments and their original ways of marketing houses.

AMA/International. Formerly International Management Association (IMA). Set up in 1956 as an affiliate of the American Management Associations, with centers in Argentina, Belgium, Brazil. Canada, Mexico, and Venezuela; headquartered in New York City.

Amalgamation. A merger by agreement of two or more concerns with or into a major organization. Two or more companies working as a group or otherwise may liquidate themselves under law and sell their assets and liabilities to a new company which issues its new shares in exchange for the net worth of property received from the amalgamating companies. Under amalgamation, therefore, the existing companies cease to retain their entity or existence.

Amendment. At a formal meeting, an amendment may be moved as what the mover of it believes to be an improvement in the action proposed in the motion before the meeting. An amendment should not be a direct negative or merely destructive in intent, and a chairman may also refuse to have it put to the meeting if he judges it to be either irrelevant or frivolous.

Amongst Matter. Position of an advertisement, where it is situated amongst editorial material.

Amortization. It is the writing off of assets—the lives of which are determined not by deterioration or obsolescence but by the expiry of the tenure of ownership. The principal instance would be a leasehold property.

Amortized Cost. In accounting, the cost of an asset minus the portions written off or depreciated.

ANA. Initials of Article Number Associations.

Annuity Fund. The fund that is created as a result of an annuity agreement.

Annuity Method. Refers to a method of depreciating an asset.

Ante-dated. Ante-dating is the placing of a date on a document prior to that on which it is actually signed. A bill of exchange is not invalid by reason only that it is ante-dated.

Anthropometry. In work study, the study of human body measurements.

Anticipated Cost. An addition to operating cost that results from the use of LIFO inventory evaluaton during a period of rising prices. also known as inventory profit.

Anticipation Stock. Raw materials, parts or finished goods purchased or manufactured in advance of expected demand or in anticipation of rising costs and prices.

Anticipatory Repudiation. A breach of contract occurring when a buyer of real estate informs the seller before closing escrow that he does not plan to fulfil the transaction.

Antitrust Law. Law relating to, legislation or action (especially in the USA) to curb monopolies and restrictive trade practices.

Apparent Effectiveness. Factors of managerial behaviour which, although considered to be admirable, may not be related to or appropriate to the output requirements of the job. Examples include characteristics such as always maintaining a tidy desk, being good at public relations, making decisions quickly, and arriving promptly for meeting or work.

A Posteriori Reasoning. Also known as analytical or inductive reasoning, it is a type of reasoning which is directly based on observation and inducting generalization. It is the opposite of a prior reasoning.

Appliance Credibility. Customer acceptance that company is good at making its product. If company is well-known for making, say lawn mowers, appliance credibility is likely to apply if company produces a lawn raker, but less likely if it diversifies into making, say, a foot-pump for motor-car tyres.

Aptitude. Fitness, natural ability, readiness to learn—usually used to describe potential ability—to learn specific skills, for example, mechanical skills.

Aptitude Test. A test of a person's ability to learn a task or of potential abilityto perform a task.

APU Occupational Interest Guide. Interst test or inventory used in personnel selection, career guidance, etc. to build up a picture of the personal interests of a candiate or employee. The test consits of 112 choices between pairs of activities, resulting in a profile of eight interest categories, namely, outdoor; mechnical; computational and clerical; scientific; persuasive; artistic and musical; literary and social service.

Arithmetic Ability (Ar). Personnel selection and vocational guidance test devised as part of the engineering apprentice test-battery of the National Institute of Industrial Psychology in the U.K.

Arm's-Length Bargain. A bargain between person on terms that have not been affected by any connection between the persons.

Arm's Length Market Price. Stated price before any detailed negotiation.

Arrangement. Debtor's plan for the serttlement of unsecured debts or the extension of time over which repayments will be made.

Articles of Association. It contains the regulations concerning the constitution and management of joint-stock companies registered under the companies acts. It includes the by-laws governing the interal working of a joint-stock company, such as elections, functions, powers, salary etc.

Articles of Incorporation. Synonym for certificate of incorporation.

Artificial Person. An enterpirse, business firm, or organization that has powers, either granted by law or by custom, that resemble those of a natural person.

Artisan's Lien. A legal claim against another's property as security by a personwho has invested labor upon, or added value to such property and who has not been reimbursed for the value of the labour and materials.

Artists' Medium. Material used by artist for his particular visual expression, *e.g.*, pencil, ink, paint photography.

'A' Shares. Ordinary shares of a joint-stock company, carrying no votes, or simply non-voting shares.

As is. A term for secondhand or damaged without either an express or implied warranty by the seller, the term in effect warns the buyer to inspect the tiems carefully, since the burden of determining their condition falls on him or her.

As is Goods. conditionof sale that a buyer will accept delivery of goods ordered 'as they come' and without warranty.

Asking Price. The price at which a good or a security is offered for sale. In some circumstances, such as in local retailing, asking price is takento indicate willingness on the part of the seller to negotiate the final selling price to some level below the asking price.

Aspirational Groups. Type of reference group brought together for the purpose of examining consumer buying motives. In an aspirational group, the individual is brought into contact with a group to which he aspires to belong, so that his buying behaviour is influenced by how he thinks the group behaves or purchases. Thus, aspirational groups reveals snob motivations in buying. Other forms of reference group include membership dissociative groups, face-to-face groups, and family groups.

Assembly Kit List. In manufacturing, a bill of material, assigned an order number, that contains the quantityand total number of parts needed to complete a specific job order.

Assignment. The transfer from one party to another of the right or interst in real property, or of the title to and interest in an item of personal property; for example, ownership of a patent or receivable may be assigned or transferred.

Assignment Analysis. A method of job evaluation developed for professional and technical jobs in which the assignments that the job holder carries out are graded according to complexity, experience required and so on.

Associate Broker. A licensed natural or legal person who acts for another in a real estate or related transaction.

Associated Company. A company X is said to be an associated company of a second company Y if X is not a subsidiary of Y but Y participates in X's commerical and financial policy decisions (*e.g.* by representation on X's board of directors) and either Y holds a substantial block of X's voting shares or X and Y are essentially partners in a joint venture or consortium.

Association. A group of individuals united voluntarily for achieving a determinate purpose/s and held together by mutually determined code of procedure and rules.

Associative Socialist. All those who believe that voluntary association on the basis of some pre-conveived plan is sufficient for the solution of all social questions.

Assumed Liability. the assumption of the payment of an obligation incurred by another.

Assurance. Tends to be used interchangeably with insurance in practice but, technically, an assurance policy covers what is bound to happen but at an unknown time, while an insurance policy is taken out against what might happen.

Assured. A beneficiary of an insurance policy; a person who whould be indemnified by another against a risk of loss.

Asynchronous Working. Refers to a mode of operation for a machine in which the completion of one operation is able to initiate another.

ATM. Automatic Teller Machine.

Atmosphere. Qualitative or subjective value of a medium or publication for advertising, purposes.

Attachment of Earnings. The court order made on an employer to deduct money payable to the court at specified periods direct from the employee's (debitor's) wages or salary.

Attainment Test. Or achievement test. Type of psychological test that measures knowledge in a particular area or attainment in a particular kind of skil rather than potential or aptitude.

Attendance Bonus. An addition to normal wages which an employer promises to give to any of his employees who achieve a certain stadard of time keeping or lack of absence from work.

Attendance Pay. A bonus paid for good attendance or time keeping.

Attendance Time. The total time spent by an employee either working or available for work, for which payment is made over a period.

Authoritarian Management (Autocratic Management). A style of management which emphasizes non-consultation and acceptance without challenge of directives issued by a manager. Ofted associated with such a style is the belief that people require an element of strong discipline and control.

Attention Value. Extent to which an advertisement can secure the initial attention of a reader, sometimes expressed in quantitative form in Starch or other page-traffic studies.

Attention Value. Extent to which advertisement has been noticed and remembered by respondents.

Audit Trail. A notation accompanying a transaction entry or posting that refers to its source records or documents.

Audit Year. The year covered in an annual or balance-sheet audit; usually the fiscal year.

Auditor's Report. A written declaration prepared by an auditor following an audit conducted by him. Using standard language, it is addressed to the management of the firm whose financial records have been audited, and it contains details of the scope of the audit, comments on operating results and financial condition, a funds-flow statement, causes of changes as compared with preceding years, and procedural suggestions.

Autarky or, Autarchy. Derived from the Greek word autarchia meaning self rule; in economic parlance it refers to national economic self-sufficiency.

Authoritarian leadership. A style of management in which the leader plays a strong, directive role in setting group goals and in planning and directing the activities of the members of the group. The authoritarian leader delegates few of the functions of leadership to the members of the group.

Authoritarian Theory. Assumes that human relations considerations are irrelevant in business, and that most people are naturally dependent, indolent, selfish and uncooperative. They therefore require strong direction and control to maintain discipline and achieve the appropriate goals.

Authority. A person who makes decisions, gives opinions, judgement or information or takes action that affects other people is said to have authority if the people affected believe that, if asked, he could justify his actions in terms that they are willing to affect.

Autocracy. A type of power structure in which one individual -an autocrate has power over all others.

Autocrat. A basic style of management characterized by inappropriate emphasis on task orientation at the cost of relationships orientation. The autocrat is perceived as having no confidence in others, as unpleasant, and as interested only in the immediate task.

Autocratic Control. Tight personal control of a company of department by the chairman or a manager. Also known as Caesar management.

Autocratic Management. Synonym for Authoritarian management.

Auto-elucidatory and Auto-instructional Methods. Presentation of questions so that a traniee/student is passed to further material appropriate to the answers he/she gives. This happens, for example, when using branching programmes with teaching machines or progammed texts.

Automatic Cancellation. System under which any outstanding items at a particular point in time are deleted from an order and cancelled. Thus, clerical systems are not impeded by balances and the purchaser is free to buy elsewhere or re order at a later date. The term is sometimes used if the contract has a specified or implied completion date. After that date, no further deliveries will be accepted. An example of this may be when goods have been ordered specifically for a seasonal trade.

Automatic Check. Any facility, software or hardware, for automatically carrying out a check for the absence of specific errors.

Automatic Saving. If a person's net income is too large to spend, the unspent income is called automatic saving.

Automatic Selling. From of distribution outlet in which goods are retailed through some automatic device such as a vending machine. Also in use by banks for dispensing money and garages for pertrol.

Automatic Stabilizer. A device to check business fluctuations. It is one that works against the cycle of its own accord, without requiring deliberate action on the part of public authorities. One device of this kind is the federal progressive income tax. This postulates increasing or decreasing taxes.

Automatic Teller Machine (ATM). It is a robot which dispenses cash and, income cases, delas with certain other basic banking transactions of a kind which traditionally would have been handled by a cashier to teller over bank counter.

Automatic Test Equipment (ATE). Automatic Test Equipment). Equipment, usually computer-based, which carries out testing of components and products automatically. It is extensively used in the electronics industries.

Automatic Guided Vehicle (AGV). Autonomous Guided Vehicle). A driverless or robot cart which travels around a factory floor carrying components, materials and finished products. It has the advantage that the route which it follows is determined by computer and is not fixed like a conventional conveyor.

Automation. The replacement of human labour by more or less automatically-run machinery, particularly electronically controlled equipment.

Automatization. Replacement and/or extension of human control by machine.

Autonomous Bargaining. Where, in workplace bargaining, trade unions and employers' associations have very little control over proceedings. Autonomous bargaining is where local bargainings has been set up as a matter of policy rather than where it happens through erosion of the power of trade unions and/or employers' associations.

Autonomous Work Groups. A pattern of work organization which gives a group of workers considerable scope and responsibility for planning and carrying out production. It is an important element in Socio-Technical Systems.

Autonomy. The property of self-determination in individuals or in an organization. It can refer specifically to the degree to which an individuals or group is free to make decision without having to refer to others.

Auxiliary Activities. In institutional accounting, the business operations carried for the service of employees and patrons but not necessarily directly related to the primary functions and purposes of the institution. Examples are found in a university that maintains dormitories, a bookstore, cafeterias, and so on.

Auxiliary Capital. Alternatively it can be called instrumental capital. Goods that aid labour in production such as tools, machines, railways, docks, ships etc., and raw materials of all kinds.

Available to Promise. The uncommitted portion of a company's inventory or planned production, usually calculated from the Master Production Schedule.

Availability. In indisutrial psychology, availability reflects the perceived limitations of the environment. It is determined by the accessibility of goals that can satisfy a given need, as perceived by the individual.

Available Quantity. In materials requirements planning (MRP), the available quantity of a given part is equal to the sum of the onhand quantities in all stock locations.

AVCO. (Acronym from Average Cost.) A method of estimating the change in value, over a period, of a stock of some good. It is used in the same circumstances as FIFO but valuation consists of calculating the average unit cost of the stock and multiplying by the number of units remaining at the end of the period.

Average Salary. Alternative term for pensionabe salary in calculations for an average salary pension scheme.

Average Salary Pension Scheme. Calculates pension in relation to the average or total income throughout working life; an agreed percentage of pensionable salary in each year being earned as the pension for that year's service.

Avoidable Costs. A class of costs which are the consequence of a particular decision made by management—such as entry into a new market or the developemnt of a new product. They differ from unavoidable costs in that different decisions might avoid such costs wereas some costs-like salaries and buildings and equipment—are unavoidable.

Award. The documentation, or the content, of a decision made by an external court, commission or trinal; also of a committee jointly established by trade unions and employers to examine conditions of employment; a pay increase.

Awareness Survey. Similar to attitude survey and opinion poll, and awareness survey studies respondents' familiarity with the subject. Pericdic surveys measure the shift in awareness over time Methods or evaluating PR programme aimed at improving awareness.

B

Back Cover. In advertising, the back cover of a magazine usually available at premium rates for advertising. Special rates apply to both inside and outside back covers.

Backed Note. An authority, endorsed by broker, the master of ship arranging the loading of goods for shipment.

Backhual. In rail and truck transportation, the practice of carrying a shipment beyond its destinations and then returning it, partly over the same route.

Backlog. The total of a business's unfilled orders at any one time.

Back Order. The portion of a customer's order that has not been shipped against an accepted order that is in backlog.

Back Pay. Wage/salary for work already done but for which proper payment has not been received. This differs from retrospective payment, which arises from an agreement to back date a new system or level of payment.

Back Selling. Promotional efforts of secondary suppliers who supply components, ingredients and other materials which are incorporated in the production of products but may not be known to or be identifiable by the final buyer.

Backward Integration. Acquisition or take-over of a main supplier or manufacture by a distributor or retailer of a product or service in order to be certain of suppliers, oil take-over of a raw material supplier by a manufacturer for the same reason. The opposite process, usually intended to give control over markets, is forward integration.

Backward Pass. In project network techniques the calculation of latest event times, or of latest start times of activities and earliest start times of activities.

Backward Scheduling. A production-scheduling technique wherein the schedule is calculated by starting with the due date for completion and working backward to determine the date at which the job must be started.

Backwash Effect. An unfavourable situation which arises in less developed countries as a consequence of the overemphasis on expert trade (generally raw materials (at the cost of the growth of domestic production industrialization of rural areas.

Bad Debts. Accounts going out of business and still owing money to suppliers. Also an item in financial accounts referring to actual amount of monies so lost, or written off.

Bad Title. A defective legal document used as evidence of lawful ownership of land.

Bag. Open ended container for wrapping goods usually at the point of sale. Made from paper or plastic, and sometimes including paperboard for added protection. Often bearing distinctive printing, indicating origin, and advertising goods or services.

Bailee. A person who is entrusted with the possession of goods and, by a warehouse receipt, bill of lading, or other document of title, acknowledges such possession and contracts to deliver those goods.

Bailment. A transfer of possession of goods without the passing of title, as on consignment for safekeeping, repair, or sale.

Bailer. A person who gives possession over some of his property to another person during bailment.

Balance-due. The quantity of material or parts ordered on a purchase order or requisitioned on a work order but not yet received.

Balance Economy. An economy which aims at stabilization of employment at a high level.

Band Chart. A chart in which the difference between two curves is emphasized by shading in or colouring the space between them.

Band Curve Chart. Or cumulative band chart. Where the component parts of a whole are plotted on a graph, one above the other. The areas between the curves may then be shaded to show the composition of the whole. A band curve chart may be used to show the breakdown of production, sales, etc.

Banded Pack. A form of sales promotion in which consumers are offered two or more packages of a product, or a package of a product plus another product from the same manufacturer, attached together (usually by a band of tape printed with details of the offer), at a reduced price.

Banding. The rationalizing of pay structures and the substitution of a defined number of pay brackets or bands for a wide variety of separate rates. Job evaluation techniques are often used to establish which jobs should be placed within each band. The term 'broad banding' is sometimes used where a large range of jobs is placed within each band.

Bandwidth

1. In telecommunications, the limits in frequency terms which define a particular communications band.
2. In Flexible Working Hours, the total working day, composed of core time and flexible hours.

Bank Draft. An order issued by a seller's bank against a purchaser's bank directing payment of money, usually through an intermediary bank. Bank drafts generally are negotiable and are similar to the cheques drawn against standard checking accounts except that they are drawn by one bank on its account in another bank.

Banker s Reference. A process of ascertaining the past financial stability of a prospective borrower on the basis of records of his dealings with his commercial bank and other trade channels.

Bank Holiday. Any legal holiday or other special occasion when banks remain closed, usually but not always along with most other businesses.

Bank Note. A kind of paper currency that is, in effect, the promissory note of a bank. Such notes promise to pay the bearer on demand the amount stated on the face of the note.

Bank notes are now issued by the central banks. In the 19th century, almost all banks issued notes (even now in some countries, e.g. France and Scotland).

Bankrupt (Adjective). Having a special status imposed by a court because of involving. In England and Wales a bankrupt person's property is vested in a trustee who must use it to any off creditors as failles possible. Creditors may not take any action against a bankrupt person; they must deal with the trustee.

Bankrupt (noun). A person who is bankrupt.

Bankruptcy. The word, 'bankruptcy" may be traced to the Latin banks meaning "table", and ruptus, referring to "broken" and may be associated with the custom of merchants in the Middle Ages who declared themselves bankrupt by breaking their counters. Bankruptcy a declaration by court of law or other authority that an individual or company is insolvent, that is it is unable to meet its debts on due dates. It is also known as insolvency.

Bankruptcy Notice. A notice requiring a judgment debtor to pay his debt within a certain period or given a satisfactory guarantee that the debt will be paid. Failure by a debtor to comply with such a notice is an act of bankruptcy.

Banner. Relating to an advertisement headline stretching across open space. Also large board or piece of fabric held or towed aloft bearing some slogan or symbol.

Banque d' Affaires (Universal Bank). A type of bank which handles the business of both a Merchant Bank and a Clearing Bank, often taking an Equity State and an active role in managing the businesses to which it lends.

Bar Chart. A way of representing information in graphical form, using rectangles or bars to illustrate different magnitudes- for example relative proportions or percentages.

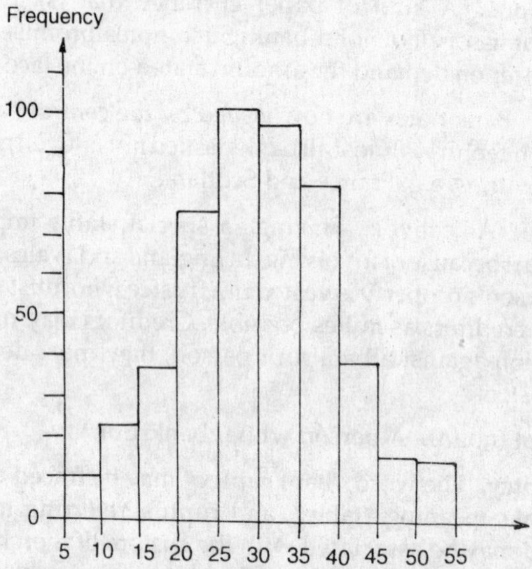

Bar chart

Bargain (noun)

1. Any transaction on the Stock Exchange.
2. An advantageous purchase.
3. An agreement between two persons on the terms of a contract between them.

Bargain (Verb)

1. To negotiate the terms and conditions of a contract.
2. To engage in collective bargaining.

Bargaining Scope. Range of items, procedural and/or substantive, to be covered by collective bargaining between management and trade unions; *e.g.*, might extend beyond wages and hours of work to such matters as discipline, redundancy and scale of manning.

Bargaining Structure. Ground rules established in a company to facilitate bargaining between management and trade unions.

Barth System. A system of payment by results in which :

1. A standard time is set for a unit of output;
2. An hourly rate of pay is set;
3. A work's output for a period is counted and he is paid:

(Number of units X standard time per unit X number of hours actually worked) X hourly rate.

Named after an American industrial engineer, Carl George Lange Barth (1960-1939).

Base Stock Method. A method of inventory valuation in which a minimum amount of goods (the so-called base stock), carried at all times, is valued at its long-term normal price; while the goods carried in excess of this minimum are valued according to some other method.

Basic Producer. A manufacture who uses natural resources to produce materials for other manufacturers. Examples include glass, rubber, and wood pulp producers and steel companies that process iron ore and produce steel ingots.

Basic Product. Or industrial product, Product marketed not to the pubic or consumer, but to industry as a component or constituent part in other products.

Basing Point System. A system of delivered pricing in which the price quoted by the seller is the factory price plus the cost of shipping from one or more places called basing points, from which the goods may or may not be actually shipped.

Batch. Refers to a collection of transactions, in the form, for example, of source documents, punched cards or a group of records on some magnetic storage device, any group of records are preocessed as a single unit, *e. g.*, a block.

Batch Costing. Process or activity of allocating costs to a batch of identical items of production, treated as a single unit.

Batch Mode

1. A mode of producing goods in groups with similar characteristics—batches—rather than continuously. Batch processing is used when the production process is interrupted—for example, by the need to move to different machines for different operations, or by the need to wait for such machines to be reset to make different batches.
2. In computing, batch mode or batch processing refers to operations which are not carried out sequentially in real time but are stored up and then executed as a batch—for example, when the computer is not busy processing other work.

Batch Production. Productive activity, of which the output, over a period of time, consists of numerous small batches of different products and in which any production facility is involved, at different times, in work connected with various products, the production facilities (*e.g.*, machine tools) used for batch production are usually capable of performing a wide range or work. (Also known as 'intermittent production' or 'lot production').

Battery. A collection of test which have a similar purpose or are to be administered one after another at a single session.

Bayesian Analysis. Statistical techniques which use and establish probability curves to help in decision-making by exploring potential outcomes of different options.

Banyan Statistics. A type of statistical analysis for management decision making, developed for translating subjective forecasts into mathematical probability curves. In many typical business situations there are no normal statistical probabilities because alternatives are unknown or have not been tried before. Bayesian statistics use the best estimate of a given circumstance as if it were a firm probability.

Bayes Theorem (Bayesian Theorem). Recently acquired sample information combined with prior personal probabilities, so producing revised probabilities in order to embark on new courses of action which may then, repeatedly, be subjected to further inputs of information and revised. It is close to the process of elimination with the use of probability theory.

Bazaar. Although associated with markets and oriental bazaars, the term has Western usage meaning a variety store like Wool-worth. Also applied to groupings of traders under one roof, *e.g.*, coin, stamp, antique dealers.

Beam-right Agreement. An agreement between the owner of an existing building and the builder of a new, adjoining structure to permit use of an existing wall as support for the new structure.

Beanstalk. A stack of trays or shelves used for displaying products at the point-of-sale.

Bearer. The person in physical possession of a negotiable instrument payable to the bearer. In such a case, title (legal ownership) is defined by physical possession.

Bed and Breakfast Deal. Sale of an asset followed by an immediate repurchase of the same asset, order to establish that its capital value has changed at a time when it is most advantageous to report the change for the purposes of capital gains tax.

Behavioural Theory of the Firm. A theory originally developed by Richard Cyert and James March and expounded in their book. A Behavioral Theory of the Firm (Engle-wood Cliffs: Prentice-Hall, 1963), which argues that organizations are coalitions of different interest groups and have multiple goals representing their different views. This influences the pattern and outcome of decision making in a way which introduces considerable uncertainty and challenges the assumptions about rational behaviour which are often found in classical management theory or in economic modals of the firm.

Behavioural Research. Research into human behaviour, single or in groups, particularly in connection, with consuming or buying habits but also concerned with wider aspects of social and organizational conduct.

Behaviour Study. Market research statistical technique for assessing the behaviour pattern and the opportunities existing in a particular market.

Below-the-line Advertising. Above-the-line. All other kinds of advertising not in traditional five media. Sales promotion, merchandising, point-of-sale, direct mail, exhibitions, sponsorship, print. Not PR. Thus, budget may be divided into two sections. Above-the-line expenditure usually the responsibility of the agency, below-the-line handled internally by company advertising manager or brand manager, who may use specialized agencies.

Below-the-line Promotion. Marketing term for sales promotion in such forms as reduced price special offers, premiums and point-of-sale displays. The term above-the-line promotion, on the other hand, is used of sales promotion in the form of expenditure on advertising in the Press, on television or in other media.

Benefits in Kind. The term is usually used in relation to those emolument of an office or employment which are paid other than in money. Thus, benefits in kind might include a motor car, petrol for private motoring, private living accommodation, interest-free or low-interest loans, medical insurance, free suits of clothes and other so-called 'prequisities' of a particular employment. In some cases, the benefits attach to particular types of employment. In some cases, the benefits attach to particular types of employment, *e.g.,* free coal enjoyed by miners and free travel enjoyed by Rail employees.

Beravement Pay. Pay given to an employee while he is given leave because a close relative of his has died.

Bernreuter Personality Inventory. Psychological inventory developed in the USA of use in temperament and personality tests.

Best Brand Rating. Based on consumer opinions of the best product for particular purposes, cunterpart for brand share as revealed by retail audit research. Given high brand recall, the two results should be similar.

Better Conditions Clause. Sometimes included in a collective agreement to the effect that any practices (practises) more favourable to employees than those spelt out in the agreement shall continue in force.

Bilateral Trade. A relationship of balancing trade between two countries. Under bilateral trade, the trade between two countries, strictly speaking must eventually balance.

Bilateral Trade Agreement. Agreement between two countries to extend to each other specific privileges in their international trade which are not extended to other countries.

Bill. As used in commerce and finance, a generic term identifying a variety of documents having to do with currency, the shipment of goods and the collection of debts. The term is used as an abbreviation of a bill of exchange or as synonymous with a draft often in association with one of a number of qualifying or descriptive objectives.

Bill Broker. Bill brokers are merchants whose traditional business is the buying and selling of bills. They are more usually referred to nowadays as discount houses.

Billing

1. In business and trade, the submission of invoices for goods or services.
2. In advertising, the total of all advertising placed by an agency for its clients during a given time, used as a yardstick of the agency's standing.

Bill of Entry. A bill of entry is a document prepared by the importer for the purpose of paying the custom duties. It is prepared in triplicate and contains full information regarding the goods due to arrive.

Bill of Exchange. A bill of exchange is an unconditional order, drawn by one person against a second person, ordering the second person to pay a specified some of money to the first person, or to a third person named in the bill, or to the bearer, such payment to the made their on the presentation of the bill or after a specified period of time named in the bill has elapsed.

Bill of Sale (Conditional). Document indicating transfer of title but where transferer reserves the right to retake title upon fulfilment of specific condition.

Bin Card. A record of usage of a stock-keeping unit that is kept near the place of storage. It normally records the quantity and date of each movement of stock in or out of the store.

Bingo Card. Enquiry card bound into a magazine and containing matrix of numbers or letters which correlate with similar keys in advertisements or editorial items. Facilitates reader enquiries and is usually prepaid for return to publisher, May also be referred to as readers' enquiry card.

Biological Drive. Modern American psychologists version of what were once called instincts except that they are more closely related to bodily functions than to innate tendencies provoking emotions. Four groups, classified, being associated with learned drives:

1. In born drives on which survival which of the individual depends. Basic drives to breathe,. drink, eat, eliminate waste Products, rest and avoid pain.
2. Partially inborn drives on which survival of the species depends. Drives to mate and care for young.
3. Inborn and learned drives concerning survival of the individual and the species. Drives to escape or attach.
4. Another set of inborn and learned drives, of similar significance, are those to explore and seek sensory stimulation.

Bionics. Refers to the studio the functions and characteristics of living systems in relation to the development of hardware designed to operate in a similar manner.

Black. To declare that one will not handle certain goods-especially as part of a trade-union campign against a firm that used, manufactured, processed or transported the goods.

Black Box. Any system in which the inputs and outputs are known but the internal workings are not. For example, automatic controllers could be described as black box for most people: the inputs-control instructions-and outputs-control of the process-are known, but how the system actually operates is unknown.

Black Capitalism. An effort begun in the late 1960s to increase the ownership and control of business by black people. Its objective is to improve the job market, the ghetto economy, and condition and status of the black community.

Black Economy. The informal sector of the economy where work is done but no record of its is officially available and on which on tax is paid

Blacking. Action of employees who during industrial action refuse to handle or work on goods, or components that they consider are being processed or supplied by employers in a way which evades the industrial action. May take form of sympathetic action by workers in other organizations, or even indorses, and may also continue after the end of the industrial action in which it began.

Blackleg. A worker who does not support union action: for example by working when others are on striker, by refusing to join a union by accepting employment in place of a union members who is on strike or by working for less than union rates. (Also called a scab'.)

Blacklist (Noun). List (especially one circulated among a group people or firms) of people who are not to be employed or of people or firms who are not to be given credit.

Black Market. A market consisting of illict buying and selling of goods in violation of legal price control, rationing, etc. the process of buying and selling of goods at prices above those fixed statutorily; in many countries, because of import restrictions, several commodities of necessity to consumers and basic intermediate goods are supplied by a process of rationing and price regulation, thus giving rise to such dealings.

Blanket Agreement. Collective agreement resulting from industry wide bargaining or national bargaining.

Blanket Coverage. Satuation advertising of a particular area. In TV advertising method generally replaced by showing of commercial to achieve calculated audience rating, after which it is rested and shown again after an interval. This avoids both waste and monotony of saturation advertising.

Blanket Mailing. Indiscriminate, mass mailing of a news release, an abuse of press relations to be discouraged, Examples: mailing of managerial appointment story to all national newspapers when perhaps only two or three print such announcements, or mailing of agricultural story to entire farming press when it is relevant to only a section.

Blanket Order. Also standing order. A purchase order for the long-term requirements of a particular item-usually one year's worth—to be shipped "as released." When stocks of such items run low, the buyer asks the supplier for shipment of another part of the outstanding blanket order. Blanket orders on small, regularly used items save paper work, time, and inventory costs, and often result in a price reduction (because the supplier knows a certain quantity will be sold over the year).

Blind Advertisement. And advertisement which is anonymous, *i.e.*, it omits the name of the sponsor as in 'situations vacant' where the company does not wish to disclose its identity and uses a box number or similar device instead.

Blind Test. A form of Market Researching which consumers are asked to test in product which has all-identifying markings removed—often in comparison with other similar competing products which are also disguised.

Blink-meter. Used in advertising research to measure the frequency of a person's blinking, so giving indications of interest or arousal.

Block Design

1. Form of intelligence test in which the person being tested has to assemble coloured cubes to make up a given design.

2. Markeresearch them for concentrating or clustering the sample used in a survey instead of using random sampling. The resulting cluster sample may be used as a sampling point and may be covered by, for example, a canvass or a random walk.

Blocked Accounts. Non-resident funds which cannot be transferred freely.

Blocked Currency. A currency of a country is said to be blocked when the government of that country creates categories of its currency that can be used only for purchases within the country.

Blocked Needs Satisfaction. When the satisfaction of a need its blocked, a reduction in the strength of the need may result.

Block Release. An arrangement under which employers give their employees a period off work in one or more continuous 'blocks' without loss of paying order that the employees can attend a course of further education.

Block Vote. A form of voting at large meetings or conferences where delegates representing the interests and views of large groups not at the meeting indicate as they vote the size of the block of votes which they represent.

Body Copy. Main copy in advertisement, as opposed to headlines or illustration.

Bolt-on Promotion. Ready made promotion (*e.g.*, scratch-card games, which can be linked to a product in a sales promotion exercise.

Bonded Block Loading. An effective and secure method of loading freight; the items are stacked in the manner of overlapping "bricks."

Bonded Goods. Imported goods on which duty has not been paid. They are held in a bonded warehouse, e.g., supervised by a Customs and Excise official, awaiting payment of duty or for re-export or for use in goods due to be re-exported. Sold only to those going aboard at duty-free shops.

Bonded Warehouse. A warehouse in which goods may be stored without customs duty or excise duty being paid until they are withdrawn from the warehouse. The proprietors of the warehouse enter into a bond to guarantee that duty will be paid when necessary on the goods they store.

Bonding of Salesmen. Buying indemnity against possible loss arising from negligence of dishonesty through employment of salesmen.

Bonus. Any payment in addition to regular or base wages. It may be in the form of a Christmas bonus or other annual allotment, or it may consist in higher rates paid for night-work, overtime, hazardous work etc. Also used in connection with incentive wage systems to designate amounts earned in excess of base or guaranteed rates.

Bonus Account. A savings account that pays a higher than normal rate of interest.

Bonus Earnings. Earnings over and above herely paid rate or basic salary.

Bonus/Extra Sized Packs. Larger pack, or pack with an additional smaller package of the same product but sold at the price usual for a standard pack.

Bonus Formula. The formal provisions in an incentive bonus plan that determine the total funds available for bonus purposes in a given year. Individual bonus awards are made from this total pool.

Blue Sky Research. Long-term high-risk reasearch which involves a high level of speculation (both financial and intllectual) but which might yield significant gains by opening up totally new fields support unity.

Bonus Increment. In payment systems, an addition to standard time which is used as an incentive.)

Bonus Payment. An incentive payment to salesmen for above-the-norm achievement; often ex-gratia rather than contractual.

Bonus Schemes. Arrangements for relating bonus earnings to performance measured in terms of output, profits, sales or some individual target. The scheme will contain some formula for relating the reward, to performance.

Bonus Stock. Common stock offered as a bonus, either to the underwriter of the issue as additional incentive, or to buyers of bonds or preferred stock in the same company.

Book Inventory. A statement of inventory that is not the result of a physical count. It is accomplished by adding the unit and cost of incoming goods to previous inventory figures and deducting the units and cost of outgoing goods.

Book-keeping. Keeping the financial records (books) of a business or other economic unit, recording all the transactions in which it engages. Book-keeping is a branch of accounting.

Book of Account. The records of a firm's financial records.

Boom or Bust Cycle. A business Cycle which involves alternating periods of rapid growth follwed by severe slumps.

Born Salesman. Sales or other personnel attributed with natural quanlities that tresult in superior selling achievement.

Borrowing Allocation. The level which a board of directors sets as the upper limit on borrowing to finance capital investment in a firm.

Borrowing Requirement. The amount an organization needs to borrow in order to finance all its commitments during a financial year. In the national sense the government has a public sector borrowing requirement (PBSR) which indicates the amount of borrowing necessary to finance public spending.

Borrowing Time. Where under a payment-by-results scheme a worker uses time allocated for one task to push ahead with or complete another task.

Boston Ledger. A type of ledger in which the record on each account moves horizontally in columner sections assigned to consecutive accounting periods. Several accounts may be kept on a single page. This form of ledger may eliminate the need to prepare a separate trial balance.

Boston Box. A matrix diagram which was developed by the Boston Constulting Group in the USA in the 1960s to help explain their theories about business strategy. The principle has been that companies can break their product range down into four categories—stars, cows, dogs and question marks—and develop a strategy accordingly. The breakdown is carried out by plotting the position of products on two axes-one for market share and one for market growth; this gives a matrix or 'Boston box'.

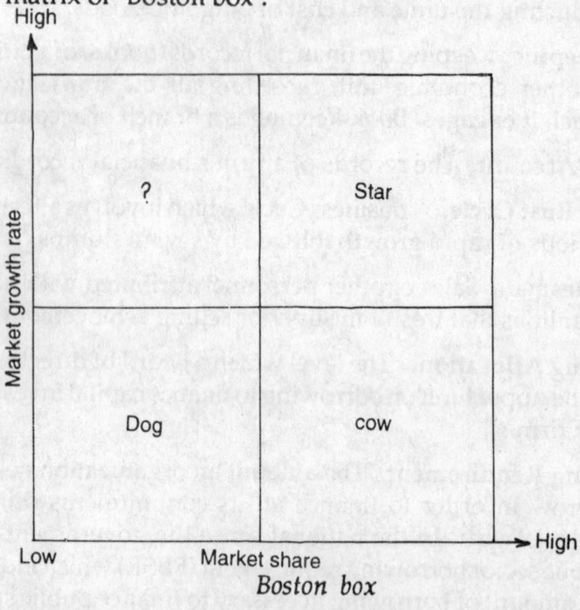

Boston box

Dogs have been poorly performing, old products swhich should be disposed of from the range; cows are mature products which continue to earn regular revenue; stars are new, high-performing products which require considerable strategic effort to exploit while they are still stars in the market; and question marks are newer products about which the market pattern is not yet clear.

In recent years this approach has come under attack from alternative views of strategy, notably that offered by Michael Porter and his team at the Harvard Business School.

Bottom-up Approach. An approach to planning or decision-making which is based upon consultation with those at thebottom of an organzational hierarchy—as opposed to top-down approaches in which instructions and decisions come down from the top.

Botton up Management. Term coined by William B Givern Jr in the USA for the responsibility and relationship down the chain of command as distinct from the more commonly recognized upwad relationship.

Boulwarism. In industrial relations, a position in which an employer makes an analysis of what it considers reasonable—in terms of wages, conditions etc—and themn refuses to negotiate beyond this positions in Collective Bargaining. The term takes its name from a former vice-president of the General Electric Company in the USA.

Bond in Insert. An insert that is attached publication.

Bounty. The payment by the state of a specific sum per unit of an artical—so much per unit produced or per unit imported per unit exported. It differs from subsidy in that a subsidy is paid as a lump-sum or upon some other basis than that of commodity unit.

Bourgeoisie. By the term bourgeoise is meant the class of modern capitalists who are the owners of social production and employ wages labour. (The proletariat constitues the class of modern wage-earners who sell their labour power in order to live).

Boutique. Organization providing a specialized advertising sevice rather than a full range of facilities. Usually associated with creative services.

Boycott. A refusal to participate in something on grounds of principle. For example, refusing to use a particular service or buy a product because the firm involved in its supply is in breach of an agreement, or practises some form of discrimination.

Box-jenkins Techniques. Type of exponential smoothing techniques which, with computer aid, are used to improve forecasting and to take into account variations from earlier forecasts.

Brainstorming. It is a technique far encouraging creative thinking. A problem is presented to a small group of people who spend a few minutes formulating alternative statements of it and then some time stating their ideas as rapidly as possible (the ideas may be tape-recorded but are commonly written, often on flip charts so that the group can see them). During the production of ideas, four principles are observed:

1. Quantity is important—the more ideas that are produced the more likely it sis that they will include a good one;
2. Cross-fertilizsation should take place—people should try to build onthe ideas produced by others;
3. There must be no criticism of others' ideas—this would dampen their enthusiasm;
4. Individuals must also suspend judgement and not evaluate their own ideas-an idea may seem extra ordinary to one person but may, through the principle of cross-fertilization, get the groupto generate useful ideas.

Branching Network. In project networks a condition in which the network branches to a series of optional routes. The choice of which route to take depends on information obtained when that point is reahed inthe project and cannot be planned in advance: it is feft upto the discretion of the project manage ras to which course will be most suitable.

Brand. A name, term, symbol or design (or a combination of these) that serves to identify goods or services of one seller or group of sellers and to distinguish them from those of competitors. A brand name is a word, letter,or group of words or letters so used; it differs from a trademark in that the latter is basically alegal term and must meet critteia established by law. Thus, a Ford automobile signifies a brand identifying the Ford Motor Company; its brand name is Ford, whether spoken or princted; "Ford" written in a special script or other distinctive form is a tademark. Both brand names and trademarks are protected by law, their ownership and used having been established by continued usage.

Broad-line Strategy. (full-line strategy). In strategic management, a srategy based on having a hih variety within a product line.

Broadsheet

1. Printed promotional material usually with one or two folds, but opening up into a relatively large sheet.
2. Term referring to newspapers other than to-bloids.

Broken Lot. Goods offered for sale in smaller than normal quantity. Includer damaged packaged goods where some contents have been lost or removed.

Brown-spearman Formula. Method of validating an intelligence test. Particularly when its length has been increased and the validity of the extended test needs to be checked.

Budget. The term is derived from the old English word Bougette the sack or pouch from which the Chancellor of the Exchequer extracted his papers presenting to parliament the government's financial programme for the ensuring fiscal year. It has been defined as the "document containing a preliminary approved plan or public revenues and expenditures."

The term budget refers to anticipated revenue and proposed expenditure by a government in the budget (i.e, next financial year).

The central budget is presented by the Union finance Minister to the parliament a few daysbefore the commencement of new fiscal year.

Budgetary Control. Budgetary control is a system which is used by management in which targets are (budgets) set and actual performance compared with them. The purpose is to as certain where, how and why actual results get diverged from the budget and what action is essential to achieve the budget. Computers are used for recording and reporting the information needed in a budgetary control system (for example, on spreadsheets on personal computer).

Budget Determination. Consideration and decision-making on the size of a subject.

Budgeting

1. The process of activity of preparing budgets.
2. In computing, it refers to the process of allocating resources to a particular development activity so as to constrain the resources which are utilized for the project.

Budget Preparation of. The process of preparing a firm's budget is much the same in all businesses.

Buffer Inventory. A buffer stock is maintained as a safeguard against delays in delieveries of materials on order, strikes, or slowdowns for any unpredictable reason, or to cover sudden and unforecast increases in demand. The level of this inventory may be determined on the basis of scientific models or pure judgement growing out of past experience. Also known as safety stock, reserve stock, or protective inventory.

Buffer Stock. Stock maintained as cushion against unfroeseen fluctuations in the demand or scarcity of any commodity specially with regard to foodgrains, cotton, sugar, tea etc.

Building Lease. A lease of land, typically for a term of 99 years, at a rent known as a 'gound rent' under which the lessee covenants to erect specified buildings on the land, and to keep the buildings in repair and insure them during the term fo the lease. At the end of the term the buildings become the property of the lessor, but now generally a lessee has a statutory right to buy out the lessor's interest.

Build Schedule. Statement and record of the modifications made to a project as it progresses, listing all drawings and other documentation. May be based on the original product drawing list.

Build-up Method. Variation on target method of determining advertising appropriation. Allocations made to different media, and totalled to arrive at the budget. Or, allocations made for departments of a store, divisions in a company, or brands in a range.

Built-in Obsolescence. Planned improvements, modifications or new models, permitting promotion of new features and maintaining sales and encouraging replacement of order models. Mainly to accelerate replacement rate of consumer durables, and so maintain optimum production.

Bumper Strike. Now largely outdated type of industrial action in which strikers are directly supported financially by similar workers in other factories.

Bumping. Also backtracking. The desplacement of one worker by another with more seniority, common in industries where labour contracts include rigid seniority rues. The term " backtracking" comes from the fact that a senior employee may move to a lower level job causing the layoff of a junior employee.

Burden Cosk. As indirect cost.

Burden. The cost of manufacture or production that are not readily identifiable with specific products; examples are factory over-head, indirect costs and employee fringe benefits.

Bureaucracy. The term is usually applied to a system of government the control of which is so comletely in the hands of officials that their power jeopardises the liberties of ordinary citizens.

Bureaucrat. In organizational behaviour, a manager whose style is to use a low task orientation and a low relationships orientation in a situation where such behaviour is approapriate, and who is therefore, more effective than other types of managers.

Bureaucratic Concept of Organization. The traditional model of an organization, which emphasizes superior-subordinate relationships. Orders flow from the top down through a chain of command, and individuals carry out the orders.

Bureaucratic Management. A style of management based on the principles of bureaucracy, emphasizing rules, procedures and hierarchical authority.

Bureau De Change. This is a shop or sometimes merely a counter where one type of currency may be exchanged for another. It is primarily a service for tourists.

Burglary Insurance. Basic protection against loss due to crimes committed by outsiders rather than by employees of an organization or authorized visitors. It applies only when there is physical evidence of forced entry. Coverage is provided for specific goods or property and damage incurred in the course of the burglary.

Burn in. A form of test, used particularly in the electronics industry, which allows a component or system to run for a sustained period in order to ensure its reliability and adherence to required performance specifications.

Business. That part of organised individual activities which are concerned with the attainment of requisites of living or well being of a man or bnusiness activities. They involve work or efforts connected with the production of wealth.

Business Administration. The science and art of conducting an enterprise with a maximum efficiency and minimum cost.

Business Agent. In labour relations, the highest official in a union or labour organization operating on a local baisis. The business agent is usually salaries and is either elected or appointed to perform the principal work of the local union, such as negotiating contracts, settling, grievances, and building membership rolls.

Business Care Advertisements. Small advertisements resembling business cards in directories of services published in newspapers and magazines.

Business Corporation. Joint-stock company.

Business Costs. A firm's business costs are its total money expenses as computed by ordinary accounting methods. These expenses include all payments and contractual obligations made by the firm together with the book cost of depreciation on plant and equipment.

Business Criterion. As commercial criterion (management technique in public administration).

Business Game. Enactment by students or trainees of business situations based on presentaiton of skilfully selected information followed by progressive decision making leading to assessment of profitability and other crucial factors. Sometimes involves use of a computer. Often played competitively by teams, particularly in managtement training. Ajudication can be human or computerised. Sometimes known as management game.

Business Name. Name under which a person or organization trades and, under most legal systems, has to register. May be related to a trade mark.

Butty System. Early form of labour-only subcontracting in which the 'butty' was the gang leader who was paid by the emplyer/contractor and who in turn paid wages to the members of the gang. The butty system was sometimes operated on a family basis which the head of the family as the butty.

Buyer. A manager withresponsibility for Purchasing within a firm.

Buyer Behaviour. (consumer behaviour). A branch of marketing involving the study of why consumers purchse particular items and what influence their choices.

Buyers' Panic. A market in which buyers suddenly greatly outnumbers sellers at a particular price-level. The oppsite of a sellers' panic, it is most visible in the stock market but can occur in any financial or commodity market.

Buying Behaviour. Way in which a buyer behaves when deciding whether or not to buy a product or srvice and the factors that detrmine the behaviour. These include rational and emotional factors, the life style of the purchaser and the particular product life cycle.

Buyers' Market. Market situation in which excess manufacturing capacity and over-supply of a commodity puts buyers in strong negotiating position as the result of an imbalance between supply and demand. Particularly affects movement of prices for seasonal goods.

Buying Group. Group of associated buyers, *e.g.*, farmers, retailers, horticultural societies, buying in bulk and selling at low price to members.

Buying Motives. All those factors within a person of organization which combine to create a desire to purchase. Such factors are usually complex and comprise logical criteria like price, quality, delivery; but also highly subjective considerations, often difficult to locate, let alone measure, such as prestige, brand image colour, shape, and packaging.

Buying Office. A centralized purchasing office that serves a number of retail stores. Chain stores are commonly served by a central buying office; independent store sometimes jointly hire a central buyer to improve their bargaining power.

Buying Point. Manufacturer's outlets such as central buyer of groups and chains, wholesalers and hypermarkets.

Buying Singnals. Indirect indications of a prospect's growing interest in the product being presented.

Buying Syndicate. Collective negotiating and buying group.

Buyout. The takeover of a company by its employees, generally by purchase at a very low price or, sometimes, as an outright gift from the owners. It tends to occur when wage rates have become so high that the business can no longer be operated profitably. The employees who become the new owners generally take a wage cut, which they hope will be offset by their sharing in the company's future profits.

Buzz Group. A form of Brainstorming group used in management problem-solving.

Buzz Word. Pejorative way of describing the frequent use of fashionable management terms by those who do not necessarily understand their full meaning.

Bye-turnman. Person employed in casual labour.

Bylaws. The rules adopted by the members or the board of directors of a corporation or other organization for its government.

These rules must not be contrary to the law of the land, and they affect only the rights and duties of its members who are officially affiliated with the corporation or organization. They are not applicable to outsiders.

By Product. Any product resulting from manufacturing or processing a firm's primary product.

C

C. A high level programming language which was developed at Bell Laboratories,for writing systems software.

C & F. Cost in freight to port of destination.

Cable Transfer. In foreign trade, a Bank Draft, transmitted by cable or telegraph instead of mail. The correspondent bank then notifies the payee of the remittance's arrival.

Cafeteria Syatem. Applied to remuneration implies a choice for the individual employee in the make up of his personal salary and fringe benefits package. A small but increasing number of employers give their more senior executives a degree of choice in straight salary or deferred benefits.

Calendars. A below-the-line medium which serves as a permanent advertisement in a prominent place, and also promotes good-will. The advertiser may use his own pictures and print his own calendars.

Call Analysis. A technique used in marketing to measure the performance of different salesmen by examining the frequency and effectiveness (*e.g.* conversion of enquries to orders) of calls made to customers.

Callback. Market research term for a visit to an interviewee or informant who has already been interviewed once or who was not available for interview at the time of the first visit. If the informant has already been interviewed once, a product may have been left for a product placement test between the two visits.

Call-back Pay. Extra pay given to workers who are asked to return to work (called back) outside regular hours, to make repairs to perform other emergency services.

Call Frequency. Frequency with which salesmen visit or contact customers. Distinguished from conventional journal cycle by customer categorizing into groups of varying priority.

Call Frequency Schedule. Salesman's journey pla`n.

Calling Cycle. Average period of time between salesmen's or maintenance engineer's calls on customers.

Call-in Pay. A guaranteed minimum payment for being specially called in to work. (Also known as 'call-back pay').

Call-off. A form of materials purchase in which a supplier is given a schedule of goods likely to be required over a future period-say one year. The actual number of goods are called off against that schedule in batches, as and when needed by the producer.

Call Offs. Items of copy describing aspects of an illustration in an advertisement, usually surrounding the illustration and connected to it by lines.

Call-off System. Arrangement for buying manufactured parts for use in assemblies by which the purchaser places a firm order fr a specific quantity of the parts to be manufactured over, say, the next year on the basis that required quantities will be delivered as and when the manufacturer needs them.

Call Report. Summary, usually in writing, of visit by salesman to a customer, account executive to client, or similar business meeting.

Campaign. Organized course of action, planned carefully to achieve predefined objectives. Can relate to advertising, sales, public relations, or any part of the promotional mix.

Cancel Order. A market or limited-price order given to a securities broker, to be executed in whole or in part as soon as it is represented in the trading arena. The portion not so executed is to be treated as cancelled.

C & F. Cost and Freight.

Canvass

1. To interview a selected group either for research purposes or within a selling procedure.
2. Used in research to indicate coverage of an entire population rather than just a sample. Synonymous in this sense to polling or conducting a census.
3. In form of 'cold' canvass, reference is made to salesman calls on prospects not previously.

Canvasser. Sales represntative or selling agent calling direct on users or consumers. Cold canvassing is the term used to describe a salesman's uninvited (often the first) call on a prospect.

Capacity. In business and industry, the potential output of a business with existing plant, workers, and equipment. A firm or factory actually producing a this level is said to be working at full capacity. Excess capacity or overcapacity, on the other hand, means the same as overproduction (by a firm or entire industry) relative to demand for a product.

Capacity Cost. The cost of operating a plant or unit at full capacity.

Capacity of Firms. The amount of land, buildings, plant and machinery and other fixed capital of a firm.

Capacity Planning. A part of the planning process in manufacturing which seeks to balance the forecast demand against the available capacity for performing various operations.

Capital Accumulation. An increase in man made equipment such as machine tools, buildings and other structures and stocks of goods used for or capable of being used for the goods and services.

Capital Asset Pricing Model (CAPM). In Portfolio analysis the CAPM provides a mathematical model of the various different kinds of risk involved in the market and thus a means of identifying suitable avenues for diversification.

Capital Commitments. Specifically capital expenditure contracted for but not yet paid.

Capital Consumption Allowance. In national income accounting, the equivalent of what is called depreciation in private business accounting.

Capital Credit. The present acquisition of long-term productive facility such as land, buildings, and machinery against promises of enterprisers to pay in the future.

Capital Deepening. An increase in capital relative to other resources, especially labour; usually applied to a nation, but can apply to a region or to a business firm.

Capital Equipment. An umbrella name for the several different kinds of equipment used to produce products or services, such as machinary, office equipment, test equipment etc.

Capital Flight. A situation where capital seeks investment outlets outside the country; a phenomenon generally observed in most developing countries for a variety of reasons, *e.g.*, uncertainties associated with new national philophies, nationalization of industries, repariation restrictions, lack of incentives, policies tending to resrict profit levels, high levels of taxation, etc.

Capital-intensive. Describing an industry, economic sector, or economy that requires a large proportion of capital input relative to labour or land.

Capitalization Ratio. The total of fixed assets (after depreciation) divided by net worth; one of many ratios that are sometimes used in measuring quantitatively the effectiveness of an entrepreneurial effort.

Capitalized Expense. An expense item usually charged to profit and loss that is added to the capital-asset acount because it is related to a period of construction.

Capitalized Value. The capital equivalent of an annual payment. Capital values are determined by the rate of interest and the rent produced.

Capital Productivity. The ratio of value added to capital employed—a measure of how efficiently capital is used when making investments.

Capital Reconciliation Statement. Statement of Sources and Application of Funds.

Capitalist Industry. An industry in which the material instruments of production are owned or hired by private persons and are operated at their orders with a view to selling at a profit, the goods or services that they help to produce.

Captive Audience. Meaning that the audience for the advertisement is unlikely to go away or divert its attention to other interests. A cinema audience is considered more captive than a domestic TV audience which is surrounded by distractions.

Card-stacking Method. Merit rating technique in which the names of each of a group of employees is written on a card for a manager or supervisor to stack in order of merit bearing in mind such factors as general productivity, quality of work, job knowledge, safety consciousness, cooperativeness, etc. Once stacked in order, the cards are usually divided between the poorest ten per cent; the next 20 per cent; the middle 40 per cent; the next 20 per cent; and the best ten per cent.

Card Steward. Trade union official or shop steward having responsibility for collecting trade union dues.

Card Vote. A form of Block Vote in which the number of votes for which a Delegate has a Mandate are indicated on a card.

Carrying Costs. Cost of holding items in stock including interest on funds invested in stock warehouse space, depreciation, obsolescence, insurance, etc.

Carry Over. Carry over transaction. In Indian termionology it is called Budla. It is also called contango, carrying over, give-on and continuation.

Carry-through Rate. Charging the higher time segment rate when a broadcast programme spans two segments.

Cartel. An association, often international, of firms in the same industry, established to limit competition by allocating markets among its members, regulating prices, and other means.

Catogram. Or map-graph. May shaded or marked to provide management with certain required information. For example, it might be shaded to indicate density of sales, etc., or it might be marked, possibly with flags, to indicate the positions of factories, distribution points, etc.

Cascade Network. A form of Project Network diagram related to Critical Path Analysis.

Cascaded Systems. In production, multiple operations in which the input of each stage is the output of a preceding stage.

Cash Drain. By cash drain, **R.G.**Hawtrey meant the flow of currency into the hands of individuals, for their daily needs. This definition approximated Keynes's later transactions motive for holding cash balances.

Cash flow Statement. A statement of a firm's actual or projected cash inflows and outflows measured at suitable intervals (weekly, monthly, etc.) over a period.

Cash Forecast. Schedule of the estimated cash flow through a business for a period of time. It takes account of money required for wages and salaries and the approximate dates for major items such as capital expenditure.

Cash Premium Coupons or Vouohers. Cut from press advertisements or packs, or received as maildrops they represent so much off the price of a product when a purchase is made.

Cash Sale. In business law, a transaction in which title to goods passes when the buyer pays the seller, as opposed to a conditional sale, in which the seller retains title.

Cash with Order. (C.W.O.). A requirement by a seller that any order for his goods must be accompanied by payment for them.

Casting Vote. May be made by the chairman of a meeting when there is a tie in voting. The chairman may use his casting vote irrespective of whether he has earlier used his ordinary,'deliberative' vote.

Casual. Describing an employee or a job that is irregular in some way, in that it is occassional, temporary, or part-time. Casual workers usually do not accrue seniority, and often they do not share in benefits such as pension plans.

Casual Labour. Workers not employed on a regular basis, but only as and when work is available. The casual labour system has been operated in certain industries where the availability and throughput of work have been uncertain.

Casual Work. Work, or opportunity for employment, that occurs intermittently. (Also known as 'daywork.')

Casual Worker. Someone who is employed temporarily to perform, casual work. (Also known as a 'casual' or a 'dayworker')

Catalogue Buying. Purchasing of goods from catalogue by direct mail, by telephone or thorugh salesmen rather than through retail outlets.

Catalogue Marketing. Selling direct from a mail order catalogue.

Catalogue Store. (US spelling, catalog store). A retail establishment in which few goods are displayed to the public who choose what they want from printed catalogues and tell assistants who get the goods from storerooms.

Category Analysis. Market research technique for checking whether market conditions and opportunities are propitious for the development of a product.

Caveat Emptor (Lat.: 'let the buyer beware'). An established principle in Common Law which puts the onus on the purchaser of something to ensure that it is good quality, value for money etc.

Ceiling Price. The highest price obtainable or permissible in the sale of particular goods or services. It is the price to change above which is an offence.

Ceiling Reserves. A proposal to put additional reserve requirements on all deposits in excess of some specified amount.

Cell Organization. A form of organization based on gouping activities and workers together into a cell concerned with one particular product or sub-assembly.

Cellular Radio. A form of mobile communications in which radio telephones are linked to a computer system which constantly changes frequency so that the signal remains strong despite moving around of the equipment.

Census. Account of a given portion of the population or some other charateristic in a given area (housing, industry, etc.) and the statistical information derived from it.

Census of Production. A method of calculating national income. According to it, an attempt is made to find out the total net value of all goods and services produced in a given year.

Its another name is Inventory method.

Census Survey. Market research or other kind of survey which involves an examination of the total prospective market, or, in statistician's terms, the universe of total population. A survey based on part of the market or population only is a sample survey.

Central Area Shopping. Buying in shopping areas or centres with large thresholds of customers.

Centralized (Of an organization) consisting of a number of distinct units (e.g., units that are geographically dispersed) that are all directed and controlled by one small group of managers from headquarters.

Central Place Theory. Shopping place theory based on Christaller's study in 1993, translated into English 1938, of a model of urban centre that services a surrounding area. Central place located at a point requiring least amount of travel and having equal accessibility. Subsequently modified by Losch (1954), Berry and Garrison (1958), Backman (1958) and others, with criticisms of its notion of demand, Daly & Brown (1964), Szumeluk (1966) and others.

Certificate of Value. A statement in a transfer or conveynce that the consideration being received is less than a certain amount so that conveyance duty is either not payable or is payable at a reduced rate.

CFR. Trade terms under which the seller is responsible for bringing the goods to a named port of destination but the buyer is left to arrange insurance of the goods for the journey.

Chain Discount. A series of trade discounts, usually related to quantity purchases and indicated as a progression of percentages. For example, a series of 30+5+5 would be calculated from the published list price or the suggested end-user purchase price, taking first a 30 per cent discount, then an additional 5 per cent discount from the result, and once more a 5 per cent discount from that result to arrive at a net purchase price.

Chain of Command

1. Synonym for line of command.
2. Line of command. Formal line of communication in a company or organization through which instructions and information are passed downwards and information passed upwards and laterally. Also line management and staff management. Adherence to the chain of command and its implied recognition of clear management authority is maintaining unit of command.

Channel of Distribution. Specific means of channelling goods from their point of origin to their point of sale or consumption, *e.g.* wholesale to retail distribution or manufacturer to mail order concern.

Channel Strategy. Choice of channels of distribution. Whether a company should sell direct to consumer or retailer, through wholesales or factors back own brands, export through agents, or manufacture and sell abroad.

Charge Account. Also open account credit. A system of allowing retail purchases on credit widely used by deepartment stores, hotels, airlines and other transportation companies, oil companies, and others, as well as by banks that offer central charge plants.

Chargehand. An employee who to some extent, does the same work as others in a group of workers but is given some supervisory duties as well.

Charging What the Traffic Will Bear. A form of pricing based on what a seller thinks customers are willing to pay. When this involves charging different prices for the same goods, it constitutes a form of price discrimination.

Charisma. Capability, of a person to influence a wide range of the behaviour of other people (or to persuade the people to accept a wide range of his views), especially when the capability seems to be an innate capacity.

Charismatic Management (charismatic authority; charismatic style). A Management Style based on the authority accepted by members of an organization due to personal qualities—charisma—of the manager.

Charity Promotions. Sales promotion schemes in which contributions to a charity are offered instead of consumer benefits. Should have right appeal, be easy to understand, and support a worthwhile cause.

Charm Price. The price affixed to merchandise, and ending in a "9" or any number other than "0" for the purpose of attracting the consumer. Retailers claim that price tags of Rs. 59.95 or Rs. 42.95, are more appealing to customers than the relatively similar Rs. 40.00 or 50.00.

Charter. A document issued by a legislature or other government authority granting certain rights and privileges to a bank or corporation, and also imposing certain restrictions on it.

Chartist. In investment, an analyst who forecasts securities prices from charts of past prices and price movements.

Cheap. Low price relatively to other prices for similar goods. Usually avoided in business, because it tends to be associated in the minds of consumers with inferior goods; alternatives used may be inexpensive, competitive, or covered by the use of the expression 'Sale price', or 'bargain'.

Checking Copy. Copy of a publication sent to an advertiser or an advertising agency to show that an advertisement appeared as specified. (Also known as a 'voucher copy').

Check List. Comprehensive categorization of actions to be taken in order to achieve a given effect with maximum efficiency.

Check-off. A procedure by which an employer, with written permission of a worker, withholds union dues and other assessments from his or her paychecks and transfers the collected funds to the union. This provides security for the union from the standpoint of prompt collections from its members.

Check-off Agreement. An agreement between employers and trade unions that the former will deduct union dues directly from employees' wages on behalf of the latter.

Chief Executive. A member of an organization who has authority over all other members in determining the conduct of the organization.

Child Resistant Containers. Ones which are difficult for a child to open easy for any adult, such as press down and turn caps on pill bottles.

Child Labour. The employment of children under a particular legal age.

Christmas Tree. In manufacturing, a bill of material in graphic form that displays the structure of a product and how its assemblies and subassemblies are related.

Chronic Unemployment. Long-term unemployment, that is, lasting six months or longer. It is caused by a variety of factors, among them structural changes in the economy (Structural Unemployment), techonologic changes (Technological Unemployment), or a slowdown in the economy as whole (cyclical Unemployment).

Chronocyclegraph. A composite photograph of how a worker performs a job. Light bulbs which produce a pear-shaped flash of light at regular intervals are attached to each of the worker's hands. A long—exposure photograph is taken which shows the path of the hands (and also the direction-from the shape of the flashes—and speed—from the distance between successive flashes). This is superimposed on a conventional photograph of the worker so as to show the path of movement in relation to the layout of the workplace.

Cinema Advertising. An advertising medium which has seen many changes since the advent of television with the closure (or conversion into bingo halls) of big cinemas, introduction of smaller cinema, and more selective audiences with greater emphasis on young cinemagoers.

Circulating Capital Goods. A capital good that is destroyed in the course of use by a single use. Coal and similarly expendable fuels are examples.

Circulation. In publishing, the number of copies of a single issue of a periodical (newspaper, magazine, journal, etc.) that are sold or distributed. This figure is particularly important to advertisers, who want to know the size of the audience they can reach through a particular publication.

Circulation Manager. Publisher's executive responsible for promoting sales of copies to wholesale and retail trade.

Circulation Representatives. Circulation manager's field staff who sell copies of journals to wholesalers and retailers, and organize promotional activities such as posters outside newsagent's shops (small double crown billboards, or posters and banners at football matches, motor races and exhibitions).

Civilian Labour Force. The total working population of a nation. It consists of all non-monetary personnel 14 years of age or more, who are either gainfully employed or are unemployed but seeking a job.

Class. A group of members of a registered company whose interests in the company are in some way different from those of other members.

Class Conflict. The conflict between the working class interest in high wages, and the employing class, interested in low wages.

Classical Liberalism. Sometimes referred to as Nineteenth century liberalism, it is a philosophy having strong faith in free and competitive markets unalloyed with government restraints and controls.

Classical Management School. The name given to a group of early researchers and writers in the field of organizational behaviour and management. This group includes Chester Barnard, Mary Parker Follett, Frederick Winslow Taylor and Lyndall Urwick.

Classification Method. A method of job evaluation in which descriptions of a small number of classes of jobs are established and the classes ranked in order of value. The jobs to be evaluated are then assigned to a class by comparing their job discriptions with the descriptions of the classes. (Also known as the 'grade method' or 'grading method').

Classified Advertisement. An advertisement in a section of a news paper or magazine that contains many advertisements, all set of the same simple style, grouped according to a classification scheme devised by the publisher.

Clerical Aptitude Test. Used in personnel selection, etc. to test ability to check and classify words, figures, symbols, etc. quickly and acurately. These are qualities needed in some non-clerical as well as in clerical work.

Clerical Work Improvement Programme. A technique for work measurement in offices based on Predetermined Motion-Time Systems.

Clerical Work Measurement. Systematic analysis of clerical work in order to determine the amount of time it should take to perform the work assigned to an individual, a group of clerical staff or an office.

Client. Person or organization, for whom a service is performed, such as advertising, market research or public relations. Some-times used to refer to customer.

Clock Card. A card on which a particular employee's starting and finishing times are stamped by a device connected to a clock, each day or each shift. (Also known as a 'time card').

Clocking-in (or on). The recording by employees of the times at which they start and leave work, usually by punching a card in a time clock.

Close Company. Company controlled by five or fewer shareholders and in which the public holds less than 35 per cent of the equity.

Closed Ended Question. In a questionnaire, a question which seeks a specific answer, such as yes or no, as distinct from an open-ended one which invites free flow of thought which can be taped, reported verbatim or summarized.

Closed Mortgage. A mortgage that cannot be paid off before maturity.

Closed Shop. A firm or part of a firm that agrees to hire only union members. A means of providing security for the union, the closed shop traditionally existed chiefly industries where a high level a skill or short-term employment was involved.

Closed Union. A labour union that restricts its membership through high initiation fees, long apprenticeship requirements, or similar means. By so doing, it may seek to create a scarcity of skilled workers to keep wages high, but often religious and/or racial prejudice and nepotism also are operative.

Closing the Sale. Salesman technique in requesting his order from a buyer (and securing it).

Closure. Method of terminating discussion on an item at a meeting or conference, usually at the chairman's discretion or according to the rules of procedure or standing orders of the organization concerned.

Cluster Analysis. A statistical technique used to sort large quantities of information into clusters having some similar elements which have been identified in Factor Analysis. It often makes use of complex computer—based techniques to search for clusters in multiple dimensions.

Cluster Sampling. A sampling procedure used when the population is widely dispersed geographically but where representative groups ('clusters') can be identified. A random sampie is taken from each cluster.

Codes of Practice. Laid down conditions under which business should be conducted in a particular area of activity.

Codetermination. The policy of giving labour unions representation on a company's board of directors to an extent equal to that of the stockholders.

Coding Frame. Pattern of likely answers which can be coded on questionnaire (or afterwards from open-ended answers) so that individual answers may be aggregated into limited number of categories.

Cognitive Dissonance. A theory put forth by Leon Festinger, a behavioral scientist, dealing primarily with the relationships that exist between perceptions about oneself and one's environment. Dissonance is created when two perceptions that are relevant to each other are in conflict. This creates tension and causes the individual to try to modify one of the incompatible elements to reduce the tension or dissonance.

Coincidental Method. Interviewing technique to question listeners or viewers. Used in USA to measure audience figures by making telephone checks on what programme people are watching or listening to. Not as effective in Britain where domestic telephones are less common.

Coincident Technique. Technique in market research interviewing in which a consumer or user is asked about somethings that is happening or something that he is doing at the time of the interview.

Cold Call. A visit or telephone call be a salesman to a previosuly unapproached (cold) potential customer.

Cold Storage Warehouse. A refrigerated warehouse that provides controlled, low temperatures for the storage and preservation of perishable foods such as fruits and vegetables.

Collective Agreement. A collective bargaining contract agreed upon by management and a union, describing wages, working conditions, and other matters of mutual interest.

Collective Bargain. Resulting from collective bargaining a collective agreement between, on the one hand, an employee's organization, trade union of bargaining unit and, on the other hand, an employer or employers' association concerning the employment or non-employment of people and other factors such as wages and conditions of employment.

Collective Contract. Type of worker's control stemming from guild socialism and based on the notion that a group of workers should be responsible for organizing and supervising their own factory or shop in return for producing an agreed output. Has points of similarity with autonomous bargaining.

Colophon. Inscription a front to publication giving author's publisher's printer's names and other details regarding copyright, ISBN number.

Colour Coding. Identification of subject by colours. Can be applied to packaging so that associated products can be linked by a common colour as with certain razors and their particular blades.

Colours. Most popular colours said to be blue, red, green, magenta, organge, yellow, respectively. (Burnham, Hanes and Bartleson).

Colour Vision Test. A test to check for the existence of and the extent of colour blineness.

Column Inches. Measurement of area derived from the width of a column of type in a publication, multiplied by its depth. Column centimetres now applies under metrication and is replacing colmn inehes in practice.

Commando or Pioneer Salling. Intensive selling into new markets, often with an entirely new product and sometimes by a specially employed sales force instead of or augmenting existing personnel.

Commando Sales man. Auxiliary salesman, usually hired for occasion, operating in team, and probably supplied by specialist organization, who shortens the journey cycle of the regular sales force, or enables a concentrated sales effort or comb-canvass to be made.

Commando Sales Team. Sales force introduced over and above normal staffing for the purposes of a particular sales promotion campaign.

Commercial Apprentice. Young man or woman indentured or otherwise contracted to an employer to learn commercial skills usually in conjunction with appropriate further eduction.

Commercial Axis. Stem of a shopping centre from which other shopping streets—string streets—radiate. Main Street or High street.

Commercial Credit. The debt or promises to pay of enterprisers or businessmen incurred or given in the present acquisition of goods to be used in productive operations.

Commercial Crops. Also called cash crops, they consist of cotton, jute, oil seeds, sugarcane, tobacco, fruits etc. They are to be distinguished from food crops.

Commercial Radio/TV. System of broadcasting radio or TV programmes independently of advertising, commercials occurring only in natural breaks when they are limited to a specified number of minutes per day.

Commercial Ribbon. Linear developed shopping areas which occupy main roads, or discrete shopping streets.

Commission. A form of payment made to someone who obtains business for a firm-often a percentage of the value of that business.

Commission Agent. Agent paid on a commission basis for the business be obtains, the principal then dealing with the customer.

Commodity Deflation. Defects in the cost of investment over the volume of saving.

Commodity Exchange. Also, board of trade, produce exchange. An organized market where traders buy and sell contracts for immediate or future delivery of certain commodities.

Commodity Market. The market in which commodities are bought and sold. The other types of market based on the subject of transaction are factor market, money market, capital market, bullion market, stock exchange etc.

Commodity Warehouse. A warehouse specializing in storing and handing commodities such as wool, cotton, potatoes, or tobacco. Commodity warehouses deliberately restrict their service to sspecific types of commodities.

Common Carrier. Carrier prepared to transport goods of any description for anyone willing to hire its services.

Common Cost. Cost incurred generally and not readily attributable to particular activities or departments.

Common Market. Where two or more countries agree to form a customs union between themselves and a common external tariff against goods and commodities imported from other countries.

Common Ownership. Principle that everyone who works permanently for an enterprise should have a proprietary share in it.

Communication Blockage. Point at which information ceases to flow, especially in internal communications as when message from management fails to travel through channels of communication to reach everyone, probably due to an individual who does not communicate.

Community Integration. Theory that workers are less strike prone where they are more completely integrated with other worker in the community as a whole but more strike prone where-as with coal miners and seamen, for example, their work leads them to live in their own isolated communities where they tend to develop and sharpen a sub culture and industrial grievances peculiar to those communities.

Company. Broadly, any group of people voluntarily united for performing jointly any activity, business, or commercial enterprise. Synonymous with firm. Partnerships and corporations are also considered to be companies.

Company Agreement. An agreement reached between management and unions after Collective Bargaining at the level of an individual company (including companies with more than one plant).

Company Bargaining. Collective bargaining in quest of a company agreement.

Company Director. The member of the board of directors appointed to run a company by its shareholders. A director may or may not be a shareholder himself.

Company Model. Computerized model of the overall operation and activities of a company or organization.

Company Profile. Description of an organization in terms sufficient to make direct comparison with other organizations, such as number of employees, product range, sales turnover, market penetration, or promotional expenditure.

Competitive Market. A competitive market is easily defined only for a perfect market or perfectly competitive market; it is then a market in which the individual buyer or seller does not influence the price by his purchases or sales. Alternatively stated, the elasticity of supply facing any buyer is infinite, and the elasticity of demand facing any seller is infinite.

Competitor's Advertising Method. Basing advertising appropriation on what rival firms are spening. May be used when a firm is uncertain of the likely cost of promoting its product, and judges by expenditures of other firms or when it desires to match another firm's competitive activity.

Component Bar Chart. Or, sometimes, compound bar chart. A bar chart on which the bars are divided into component parts, as in the illustration, to indicate how the totals represented by the bars are made up.

For example, the performance of four companies per year for the past five years, or as in the diagram, the number of different types of employee in a firm.

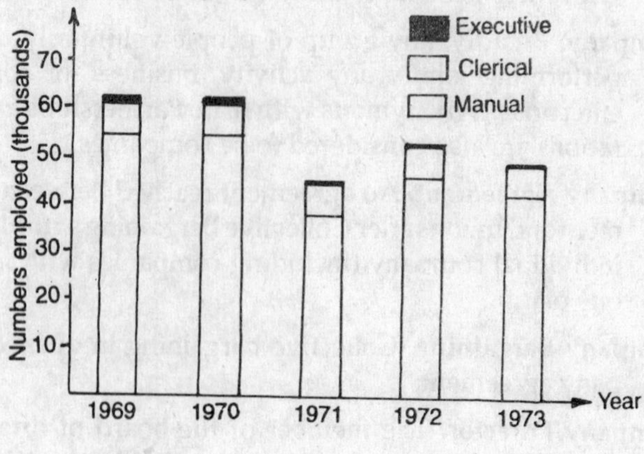

Composite Demand. The total demand for a given good or service from all sources, even though it involves a variety of uses. For example, low-carbon steel sheets are used in a wide range of manufactured products, including automobiles, refrigerators, office furniture, etc.

Composite Method. Arriving at advertising appropriation by a combination of methods. For seventeen methods appropriation. This electric method may also consider many other factors and inflouences such as production capacity, market conditions, selling problems, efficiency of distribution methods, and seasonal fluctuations.

Compound Trading. Retailing which aims at widening range of merchandise carried, either of related or unrelated goods, plus extension of customer services, *e.g.*, garden centres, petrol stations.

Compromiser. In organizational behaviour, a manager whose style is to use a high task orientation and a high relationships orientation in a situation that requires a high orientation to only one or to neither. This manager is perceived as being a poor decision maker, as one who allows various pressures to influence him too much, and as avoiding or minimizing immediate pressures and problems rather than maximizing long-term production.

Compulsory Winding up. A winding up of a company ordered by a court. (Also called 'compulsory liquidation'. Compare voluntary winding up).

Concealed Surplus (of Labour). Manpower surplus concealed by labour hoarding.

Concentration Analysis. Concentrating on those areas which are of major significance, *e.g.*, major customers, key products, stock levels of expensive items, etc. A development of the Pareto concept.

Concentration Market. Geographical, industrial and purchasing market concentrations. Important factor in industrial market research which may be required to record changes within market, and a chief difference between industrial and consumer market research.

Concept Testing. Means by which a new product idea is tested for its acceptability in the market before a prototype in made. Used as a first stage in screeening a new product coocept. The potential benefits are put to prospective buyers and users to test their reactions to an idea. May also be used for pretesting advertisement.

Conditional Sale Agreement. An agreement for the sale of goods or land under which the purchase price or part of it is payable by instalments and the property in the goods or lands is to stay with the seller until conditions specified in agreement are satisfied.

Conditional Sale Contract. A legally enforceable agreement for the purchase of property on an instalment payment basis. The buyer does not receive clear title to the property until all payments have been completed. Also known as instalment sale contract.

Conditions of Employment. Issues such as wages, benefits, hours of work *etc.*, usually covered in an employee's Contract of Employment.

Consequences Analysis. Project evaluation technique in which the effects of various alternative outcomes that might results from a major management decision are compared with the scale of company operations. The object is to assess the extent to which a shortfall or failure might affect the business.

Consignment Account. Special accounts must be kept by both a seller (or principal) and his agent to record the rule ownership. When goods are distributed through agents, the ownership remaining vested in the seller, the transaction is said to be on consignment.

Consignment Distributor. Distributor who pays for the goods he has bought only as he re-sells them.

Consignment Note. Document listing the goods that are supplied (by the consignor to the consignee) with a particular order.

Consignment Selling. Goods sent to distributors who take possession by title remains with manufacturer until consignment is paid for.

Consortium. A group of individuals and/or companies which join together to undertake a specific project.

Constituent Company. Subsidiary company which belongs to a parent or group of companies. The accounts aree normally consolidated with the other organizations which make up the whole company.

Constraint. A prior limit on the solution that will be acceptable to a problem.

Constructive Dismissal. Legal term for situation where an employee leaves his employment on the face of it of his own accord, but in reality because the employer has made the employment intolerable. Under most legal systems this constitutes unfair dismissal.

Consultative Management. A managerial style which is characterized by consulting subordinates about decisions that will affect them while making it clear that their views are for information only and will not necessarily influence the decision. Often forms part of the paternalistic management style.

Consumer Acceptance Test. Market research term for making a product or service available under controlled conditions in order to discover how far it is acceptable to consumers.

Consumr Advertising. Loosly relating to all advertising of goods or services to the mass market of individuals or families. Used in contrast to industrial or capital goods advertising.

Consumer Cooperative. A retail business (and sometimes also a wholesale business) that is ownd and may be operated by some or all of its customers in order to reduce the costs of marketing. The members of a cooperative ordinarily save through a patronage divided, a portion of the net earnings that is distributed periodically to each member in proportion to the value of his or her pruchases from the cooperative during the period since the last dividend.

Consumer Durable. Consumer goods designed for long-term use, such as washing machines, refrigerators or hi-fi systems-as opposed to consumer disposable, designed for one time or short-term use, such as food-stuffs.

Consumer Promotion. Sales promotion aimed directly at the consumer or ultimate customer through cut-price offers, trading stamps etc. Promotions aimed at distribution are known as trade promotions.

Consumer Research. Branch of market research concerned particularly with markets for consumer goods and services intended for the individual's own use or consumption (*e.g.* anything from toothpaste to motor cars).

Consumer Satisfaction. Satisfaction of a consumer want is an essential part of the marketing operation. Fundamentally, a person buys (acquires) a product or service for the satisfaction it will provide.

Consumption. The purchase and use of goods and service to satisfy needs and desires. The purchaser/user and individual or an institution.

Contact. Market research term for a person met in an interview though not necessarily providing enough information to be classified as an informant.

Container. Large metal box in which goods are packed in bulk for shipment by road or rail to continer port. Also means of containing or packing goods; *e.g.* bottle, jar, tube, carton, box, aerosol, etc.

Containerization. An approach to the stoage, handling and transport of goods using standard-sized containers which can be manipulated by special-purpose machinery and transported on specially-designed vessles, rail trucks or lorries. Its advantages include the systematization of freight movement to permit easy flow between different transport media.

Contingency Allowance. When calculating the standard time for a job in work study, it is usual to add to the basic time a small allowance (typically, no more than 5% of the basic time) to represent time that the worker has to spend while working on the job being measured, on matters other than that job (such as adjusting tools, answering the telephone, or consulting with a superior).

Continuous Process. A method of production that enable the uninterrupted flow of materials and parts into a processing operation and of completed end products cut of the operation.

Continuous Production. A production system in which the production units are organized and sequenced according to the essential steps of a manufacturing process. The routing of the job is fixed, and changes in setups are seldom required.

Contract Guarantee. General term covering performance, repayment and tender guarantees.

Contract of Employment. A contract by which one party agrees to be an employee of the other party. A contract of employment may be oral or in writing.

Contract Research. Research (especially scientific or technolgical) carried out by an organization, the results of which are to be used by another organization which commissioned the research.

Contributory Pension Scheme. A form of Pension scheme which involves employees paying a fixed proportion of the income into a scheme to which their employer also contributes.

Contribution Analysis. Estimating the difference between product selling prices and their variable costs per unit, so calculating the extent to which each unit contributes to fixed costs and profits.

Contribution Margin Ratio. The ratio of contribution from selling a given quantity of a product to the sales revenue made by selling that quantity.

Control Chart. Synonym for quantity control chart.

Control Group. Identical sample to one which is exposed to experimental stimuli but to which no such stimuli is given. Thus, its reactions, or lack of them, can be compared with those of the experimental group giving a base point from which to make measurements.

Controlled-circulation Journal Magazine. A periodical publication that is sent free of charge to individuals selected because of their job title, business or profession and which consists largely of advertisement.

Controlled Funding (Pensions). Techniques used in the annual premium costing of pension schemes such as final salary pension schemes where the eventual pension will be related to an unknown future salary. Controlled funding techniques are used to forecast likely future salaries, and therefore, realistic present premiums, the forecast being made statistically refer by applying them to large group of employees. Controlled funding, techniques include adaptable funding, flexible funding and planned funding. Forecasting of future salaries and pensions is particularly critical in a self-administered fund.

Controlled Report. In performance appraisal procedure etc. a type of report in which a senior manager works to a prescribed check-list in assessing the performance and ability of a more junior executive. Other management appraisal techniques include free report, task-based appraisal, ranking, factor rating, forced choice approach and critical incident technique.

Control Question. In a questionnaire, that which seeks to check consistency of answers given and efficiency, even honesty, of interview. Control questions generally have known answers, or the likely proportion of certain answers is known. Validity of all other answers in checked. Alternative forms of control may be postcard checks to verify answers or to seek additional information.

Conversion Training. Retaining for occupation that is slightly rather than radically different from previous occupation. Cf booster training, refresher training, retraining, updating training, upgaraded training.

Conveyance. The transfer of title to land from one person to another: the instrument that effects and records the transfer.

Cooling-off Period. A period during which a trade union is forbidden to call a strike or an employer is forbidden to enforce a lockout.

Cooperative. A form of organization whose purpose is to gain for producers or consumers, depending on the type of member organization, the profits or savings that would otherwise accrue to middlemen. Its capital is contributed by the members, who are the stockholders.

Differences between Cooperative and Condominium.

Condominium	*Cooperative*
Individual takes title to unit.	Individual owns stock in the co-operative and right of occupancy to a specific unit.
Individual owners vote on proportionate basis.	Each individual has one vote, regardless of unit's size.
Individuals are taxed separately on their units.	Cooperative as a whole is taxed, and individuals pay their share through monthly rent or maintenance charges.
Individuals are liable only for morrtgage and taxes on their own unit.	Each individual is dependent on solvency of the whole cooperative.

Co-opt. To invite someone to join an established group of people (*e.g.*, a committee) in order, for example, for the group to benefit from his special experience or to atteempt to silence his criticism of the group.

Co-ownership. Shared ownership and usually control of an enterprise by employees.

Copartnership. An arrangement by which all those who work in a firm share to some extent in the profits, capital and control of the firm. The share of profits or capital is in addition to the normal wages paid in the firm's industry.

Copy Platform. Main copy theme of an advertisement.

Copy-rotation. Using a systematic rota of different advertisements in order to enhance attention and impact.

Copy Test. Test of advertising copy, either before or after publication aiming to discover readers' comprehension, interest, brand preference, company image, etc.

Copywriter. Persons who writes copy for advertisements or other promotional material. Usually employed by an advertising agency, but in technical areas, will more frequently be employed by the firm manufacturing and/or distributing the producers concerned.

Core Group. A central group of workers in an organization operating some form of Flexible Manning who have long-term security of employment and constitute the permanent core, as opposed to peripheral workers who are taken on and laid off as and when required.

Core Time. Particular periods in Flexible Working Hours during which all employees must be in attendance. Outside this core time employees are free to choose their working hours.

Cornering the Market. Person or organization contriving to take advantage of a monopoly situation, during which prices and terms can be unilaterally controlled.

Corporate or Prestige Advertising. Any form of advertising which as its objective the building up of a company's reputation. Has a closer affinity to public relations activity than to advertising or sales promotional activity.

Corrective Advertising. Correction of a false or misleading calim in earlier advertising. Corrective advertising can be a major item in advertising budgets.

Cosmopolitan Wealth. The things which belong to the whole word are termed as cosmopolitan wealth. It also includes oceans, inventions and scientific skill. (The other types of wealth are:

(a) individual wealth,

(b) national or social wealth, and

(c) representative wealth.)

Cost-effectiveness. A technique adopted by management in the public sector for analyzing specific expenditures to determine whether the same expenditure could be used more effectively in another direction, or to ascertain whether the expenditure can be reduced without negatively affecting the expected benefit.

Cost Reduction Plan. A form of Payment-by-results scheme where cost savings are agreed by employers and employees. Any extra savings achieved are translated into a bonus for employees.

Cost Ledger. A subsidiary ledger for the accumulation of accounts used in computing of summarizing the cost of goods manufactured or of services produced.

Cost of Advertising. Selling costs, costs incurred on advertisement and salesmanship in order to pursuade the consumers to consume a particular commodity and not that of rival producers.

Cost-reduction Plan. Type of incentive or payment-by-results scheme in which cost savings above an agreed level are shared between the employer and the employee in agreed proportions.

Cost-volume-profit Analysis. Analysis of the relationships between actual or potential sales revenue from a product and the costs of producing and selling it for different volumes of production and different selling prices.

Count and Re-count Offers. Salesmen count stocks of their product held by wholesale retail customers, then recount on next call, and pay bonus on stocks sold in meantime.

Counterconformity. A form of non conformity in which a person's judgement and action are impelled by group pressure to deviate even more widely from the group norm than if the pressure had been omitted or relaxed. The counterconformist tends to activity oppose the group and compulsively dissent from it.

Cover. Outer faces of a magazine usually available for advertising purposes, *i.e.* front, back, inside front and inside back cover.

Coverdale Training. A form of group training in which groups are given taks to perform and analyse their performance. The technique is intended to develop people's ability to work in teams and to form teams in order to plan projects or carry out plans made by others. Name after an English behavioural scientist, Ralph Coverdale (1918-75).

Covered Time. Time spent on work for which a bonus or piece work scheme exists but where it is not used. Instead of payment by result, payment is on a daywork or other time related payment scheme.

Cover Price

1. Normal retail selling price of newspaper or magazine,. usually shown on front cover page.
2. Retail selling price of a publication. High cover prices compensate for lack of advertisement revenue which subsidizes price of mass circulation newspapers and magazine. However, today's production costs often mean that even popular journals are not wholly subsidized by advertisement revenue.

Cow. Expression used to describe products whose performance is past their best but which remain profitable. They are 'milked' *i.e.* provide a source of funds for new product development.

Coworker. Someone that a person works with who is neither his superior nor a subordinate.

Craft Training. Training which, in conjuction with appropriate further eduction, and usually under terms of an apprenticeship, leads to status of craftsman, or, a little more archaically, journeyman.

Craft Union. A labour union whose membership is limited to people who work at the same craft.

Crawford Small Parts Dexterity Test. Pegboard test of psychomotor skills, orignating in the U.S. The first part involves the use of tweezer-type instruments to place small pins in holes and then to place collars over the pins. The second part of the test involves screwing down small screws at speed.

Creative Conflict. Concept developed by Mary Parker Follett that if opposing views can be integrated rather than simply resolved by compromise, conflict can be used as a means of achieving progress. Virtually as constructive conflict.

Creative Group. Collection of individuals specializing in the development of creative ideas, particularly for the origination of advertising campaigns.

Credit Interchange. Exchange of information about a particular customer by firms mutually concerned, sometimes by personal contact, by letter to telephone.

Credit Manager. Executive responsible for determining customers credit ratings as part of the credit control function.

Credit Reporting Agency. An organization that will supply information about the financial standing of individuals or firms. (Also known as a 'credit agency' or 'credit bureau').

Credit Sales. Sale made on credit over a short term, where the ownership of the goods passes with possession. In the case of hire-purchase extending over a longer period, the creditor retains ownership, until a statutorily fixed portion of the debt has been paid.

Credit Screening Criteria. In mail order or direct response marketing, adoption of some charge such as enrolment fee to help test customer reliability.

Credit Union. An organization financed by member's subscriptions, of which the principle objectives are to make loans (often at favourable interest rates) to members and to pay individends (out of the interest received) to subscribers. Membership of a credit union is open to people in a category defined in the union's rules usually employees of a particular company).

Crippled Leap-frog Test. A variation of leap-frog testing in which the test arithmetic is casried out in only one part of store, not on different locations.

Criterion Behaviour. Term used particularly in programmed learning, but also in some other areas of training, for a detailed specification of what is expected of a trainee/student after training or a defined part of it.

Criterion Group. Specially selected group of employees to whom psychological tests etc., are adminishered, to assist in making an evaluation of the tests.

Criterion Test. Test to measure terminal behaviour of a trainee/ student after training and thus to establish extent to which he/she has achieved criterion behaviour and objectives of training. Can also be a test before training to *identity* individual's training needs.

Critical Incident Technique

1. Group training method beginning with participants describing incidents in a given period which presented them with difficulties.

2. Management technique devised by J.C. Flanagan which involves analyzsing critical incidents of successful or unsuccessful job behaviour which are used to produce a check list for assessing performance.

Cross-booking. Where employees on piece work, or on a combination of piece work and day work, do not book the actual time taken on each job but, instead, book shorter than actual time on some jobs and complementary longer than actual time on other jobs in order to benefit or smooth out piece work earnings. Cross booking may be associated with a work group informally restricting output under a fiddle or quota restriction.

Cross-branding Promotion. Form of sales promotion when one manufacturers pack refers to a brand from another manufacturer, usually as some kind of premium or money off offer. Such packaing often handled by a contract packer.

Cross-frontier Company. Company which operates outside national boundaries, as distinct from multi-national company which has separate companies registered in each country.

Crosswalk. A diagram showing the relationship between items in proramme budgets and those in budgets that have been prepared for departments or other budget centres of an oranization.

Cumulative Audience. Agregate of persons or home reached by successive issues or broadcasts; synonym for cumulative reach.

Cumulative Reach. Number of people in a targget audience reached without duplication by a given promotional schedule over a particular period of time.

Cumulative Timing. A method of timing a job using a stop watch in time study in which the hands of the stopwatch are allowed to continue to move without returning them to zero at the end of each element of the job. The time for each element is obtained subsequently by subtraction.

Cumulative Voting. A system of voting for the directors of a corporation that enables a shareholder to multiply the number of his or her shares by the number of directorates being voted on and cast the total for one director or a selected group of directors.

Current Demand. Present willingness in the market to pay the ruling price for goods.

Current Maturity. The portion of a long-term obligation that is to be retired during the next twelve months; usually classified as a current liability.

Current Ratio. Also, working capital ratio. In analyzing a balance sheet, the proportion of current assets to current liabilities. Most analysts hold that for a manufacturing company the minimum current ratio should be 2 to 1, that is, current assets should be at least twice as great as current liabilities.

Curriculum Vitae. A summary of a person's life given by him when applying for a job. It usually contains date of birth, eduction, qualifications and previous jobs.

Customer. Person or organization actually making the purchasing decision not necessarily the 'consumer' or 'user'. Legally, a party to a contract for the sale of goods.

Customer Classification. See Functional discount; price discrimination.

Customer Group. Classification in some form, *e.g.*, demographic, of members of the population likely to be customers.

Customer Loyalty. Pattern of repeated purchasing—by a person, household or firm—from one supplier, or of repeated purchasing of the goods of one producer (brand loyalty, or institutional brand preference).

Customer Orientation

1. Preoccupation with customer needs within an effort to build a sound enterprise with prospects of growth.
2. Sales philosophy, represented in packaging and retailing especially, of serving customer needs rather than traditional ways of distributing and serving. Marketer has to regard the customer as the target of his operations.

Customer Profile. Total list or estimate of all customers divided into pertinent categories, *e.g.*, age-groups, with each group expressed in percentages of the total.

Customs Quotas. The practice of allowing a certain amount of commodity (being imported) at a favourable duty and after that point charging normal duty.

Custom Union. A trading alliance of two or more member countries that have no trading or customs barriers between them. Member countries of a customs union may operate a customs barriers or common external tariff applicable to non-member nations.

Cut-price Merchandise. Goods subjected to cut prices. May or may not refer to goods of inferior quality.

Cut-throat Competition. Prices in the market reduced to the point where no supplier is likely to make a profit. Usually means all suppliers selling at prices below cost in order to minimize possible losses, particularly of perishable or depreciation goods. Normally a result of supplies temporarily exceeding demand.

Cycle of Advertising Development. Four stages; moving strategy definition (what to say and to whom); creative development (how to say it); communication assessment (have we said it); and campaign evaluation (what was the effect of what we said?).

Cyclical Unemployment. Unemployment caused by a downturn in the business cycle, specifically by lack of demand for labor.

D

DAF. Trade terms under which the seller will make the goods available at the frontier of the buyer's country.

Damages. A sum of money claimed or awarded as compensation for loss or harm suffered by a person or by his property or reputation.

Dangerous Occupations. All those that present hazards to the health or life of workers.

Dangle. An arrow in an activity-on-arrow network, that has no preceding or succeeding event or activity at one end.

Data Dredging. In statistical analysis, the process of examining data that have been collected for specific purposes but that contain much more information than has been used for the original investigation.

Data Flow Chart. A diagram of the sequence of operations, both manual and automatic, involved in processing data. A data flow chart identifies the particular items of data at each stage and is normally used to describe a complete data processing system.

Data Logging. The collection of data about various performance characteristics in a production system or item of equipment—for example, production rate, machine utilization, time lost for breakdown etc. It is used as an input to production management.

Data Reduction. Refers to the selection and editing of operands to derive facts from large volumes or raw data.

Dated Earned Surplus. The earned surplus or retained earnings of a corporation accumulated from the date of a reorganization or quasi-reorganization.

Date of Deed. A deed takes effect from the date of its delivery and not necessarily from the date on which it is stated to have been executed.

Day Rate (or Daywork). Basic time related payment scheme (*e.g.*, and most commonly, so much an 'hour'). May be used on its own or topped up with payment-by-results, an incentive payment scheme or some other form of premium payment.

Day Release. Arrangement under which employers give their employees a period off work (typically one day a week) without loss of pay in order that they can attened a course of further eduction.

Day Shift. 1. A shift that is worked mainly during the hours of daylight. 2. The morning shift in a three shift system.

Daywork. 1. Synonym for time work. 2. Work that is performed mainly during the hours of daylight. 3. Synonym for casual work.

Dayworker. 1. Synonym for time worker. 2. An employee who always work on a day shift or who works mainly during the hours of daylight. 3. Synonym for casual worker.

Debt Limitation. A plan designed to restrict curreent expenditures of governments to a limited amount in excess of current revenue collection by establishing the maximum amount of debt which may be incurred.

Debt Management. The process of managing the national debt, *i.e.*, arranging for the payment of interest and the refinancing of maturing bonds.

Debt-to-equity Ratio. A ratio that measures a company's financialo Leverage. It is calculated by dividing all debt (both short and long term) by all equity capital, including preferred and common stocks, earned and unearned surplus, and surplus reserves.

Debtors to Sales Ratio. Debtors expressed as a percentage of sales.

Decasualization. Process by which the workers in an industry are switched from a casual labour system to regular employment.

Decentralization. Assignment of accountability from central unit of control to individual units within an orgganization, involving transfer of decision-making authority and responsibility.

Decentralisation of Indistry. The opposite of localisation of industry which is also called territorial division of labour. The term refers to dispersal of industries throughout the length and breadth of the country.

Deception. To provoke spontaneous and revealing responses under motivational depth interviewing research, respondents may be diliberately deceived by given information. Challenges them to refute statements and so expose attitudes.

Decision Analysis. One of three techniques identified by Drucker to be used in deciding the organization structure appropriate for a company, the other techniques being activities analysis and relations analysis. Decision analysis is used to establish what are the key decisions in the company, as distinct from generalized assumptions.

Decision Dynamics Training. Management development technique developed by Strathclyde University using videotapes and simulation exercise with the emphasis on examining the overall operations of the decision making group rather than a detailed examination of self or others.

Decision Making. Process of being made aware of a course of action, idea, product or service, gathering information about it is interested, undertaking a test or trial and finally adopting it. Can be applied to introduction of a new product, or to buying in general and is not unlike AIDA in advertising.

Decision Making Unit (DMU). The DMU consists of all those people who are involved, at various stages, in the decision to buy. They play different roles such as advising specifying and actually ordering. Important that marketing, sales, advertising and PR efforts are directed at the right people, possibly at people additional to the final buyer. Wives influence purchase of cars, husbands not only influence purchase but may make payment for domestic appliances. The operator of technical products can influence purchasing decisions. In particular, PR may need to be addressed to publics other than the sales and advertising target group.

Decision Rule. Any rule set-up to help make decisions in the face of upcertainty.

Decision Theory. Various mathematical techniques—such as game theory risk analysis and sensitivity analysis—which are used in Forecasting to explore the likely outcomes of different decision options.

Declining Balance. A method of calculating depreciation of a fixed asset in which the amount of depreciation is a fixed percentage of the previous year's depreciated value. (Also known as 'diminishing balance').

Declining Balance Method. A method of depreciation in which the annual charge for depreciation is arrived at by applying a fixed percentage to the remaining value of the life of an asset. One of several methods other than the straight line method for calculating the cost of the lost usefulness or the used-up life on an asset. Usually modified by a quantifier-for example, 'double' or 'triple' declining balance method.

Decreasing Variation. In statistical analysis, the principlee that the reliability of a smaples increases as the square root of the number(n) in the sample increases. A sample of n=100 is twice as reliable as a sample of n=25 because the square root of the former is twice the square root of the latter.

Deduction.

1. In general, any cost or expense set off against revenue.
2. *Payroll deduction*. Funds withheld from wages prior to their being paid, for purposes such as employee savinggs plan contributions, insurance premiums of various kinds, repayment of employer loans, payment for goods purchased from the company, donations to charities, etc.

Deduction Theory of Wages. It states that wages are what is left to the workers out of the product after rent profit, and interest have claimed their share.

It is another name for F.A. Walker's Residual claimans theory of wages.

Deed, Warranty. A deed containing a covenant of guarantee, in which the grantor assures that the title is free from defects, that the property is free of encumbrances other than those listed, and that the grantor agrees to protect the grantee against any loss by reason of the existence of any other title or interest in the property at the time the deed is executed.

Defective. A unit of production which is some way does not conform with specified requirements.

Defensive Investment. Any investment, domestic or foreign, undertaken principally to insure against loss rather than to make a profit.

Deflationary Gap. The amount by which the theoretical volume of spending necesssary to maintain full employment or to absorb all available goods and services at prevailing prices exceeds actual private spending and government expenses.

Deflationary Policy. Policy promoting a contraction in spending.

Deflationary Unemployment. The unemployment which results from a general insufficiency of jobs. It is often called 'involuntary' unemployment.

Deflator. Present price level divided by price level at some past date is termed as deflator.

Defraud. To cheat another or to withhold wrongfully that which belongs to another; to deprive one of some right by deceitful means.

Delayed Response. Reaction to marketing initiative at a later time but often within the expected period of time.

Delayed Updating. Refers to a method of updating a record or set of records in which fields in the records are not amended unless all alternations related to a specific transaction (or set of transactions) have been processed.

Demand Elasticity. Responsiveness of sales or demand to relatively small changes in price. A product is said to be 'elastic' when a small change in price greatly affects demand.

Demand Forecasting. Undertaking a series of value forecasts at different selling prices to establish the optimum profit opportunity. It is based on the principle of elasticity, whereby demand increases at lower prices and decreases at higher prices.

Demand Function. Relationship between demand and the determinants of demand such as price, substitute products, income, or credit facilities.

Demand Inflation. Inflation caused by an increase in demand that cannot be met, with the result that prices rise. Cost push inflation is caused by an increase in costs.

Demand Information. Reversal of traditional supply of information, such as news, with individual demanding what he wants from. View data, teletext, electronic newspapers. Active participants replacing passive participants.

Demand Pull. Resultant of demand stimulants applied in marketing; works in conjunction, for example, with sales push.

Demand-pull Inflation. Inflation caused by an excess of demand for goods in an economy over the economy's ability to supply the goods. The prices of goods tend to go up because of unsatisfied demand by consumers. Manufacturers wish to increase output and so have a high demand for labour, which becomes scarce so wage rates go up. Increased wages give people more money to spend and this increases demand for goods again. Governments usually try to cure demand-pull inflation by reducing consumers' ability to spend (by increasing taxes, reducing the rate of growth of the money stock, or reducing government expenditure).

Demand Schedule

1. A table showing the number of units of a commodity that buyers would be willing and able to purchase at various possible prices during a given period of time, all other factors remaining the same.
2. A list of the demands for something when it is offered for sale at various prices.

Demarcation Dispute. A dispute between trade unions over which union's members should perform a job.

Democratic Leadership. A style of management in which the leader plays a permissive role, sharing the functions of leadership with the members of the group by encouraging their participation in goal setting and in planning and directing the activities of the group.

Democratic Management (Democratic Leadership). A style of management which is based upon consultation and participation in the decision-making process—as opposed to Authoritarian Management in which a single manager takes all decisions.

Democratic Planning. When planning is adopted under a democratic type of government, it is called democratic planning.

Demographic Market Profile. Age, sex, social grade, geographical distribution and other characterisitics. *e.g.* 18 to 24-year-old females., C1—C2, UK'.

Demographic Targeting. Aiming messages at specific sections of the public, and ability of de-massified TV to reach numerous delivery systems.

Demographics. Categorization of people according to age, sex, income. occupation, geographical distribution, so that; in marketing, market segments may be determined.

Demonstration. Showing the product or service in action. Sometimes used to refer to an artificial situation where audiovisual equipment is used instead of the actual product/service itself.

Demonstration Effect. The stimulation of consumer demand through advertising, displays of greater varieties of goods, and similar means. Such actions may increase consumer purchases even when consumer income has remained stable propensity to consume), both on an individual or family level and on an international level.

Demonstration Stoppage (or strike). Strike rising, usually spontaneously, as a demonstration of workers' feelings on a particular issue rather than one mounted in the expectancy of a protracted struggle. A demonstration strike is also known as aspontaneous strike.

Demotion Payment. Made to an employee to compensate for being demoted.

Denigration. Advertisements should not unfairly attack or discredit other products, advertisers or advertisements directly or by implication.

Department Head. The manager of a department of an organization.

Department Store. Large store selling a wide range of commodities, particularly clothing, `where merchandise is segregated into different departments, each having a specialist manager, usually wholly responsible for own buying and selling but subject to central control.

Dependency Arrow. Synonym for sequence arrow.

Dependent Variable. Statistical term describing a factor which changes as a result of some other directly linked factor—another variable—which is independent, e.g., sales, which may increase as a result of advertising. Advertising is then the indepdendent variable and sales the dependent variable.

Deposition. Testimony in a law case given under oath, particularly as a written statement by a witness for use in court.

Depression. Period during which a nation's productive resources are persistently underemployed; often manifests itself through a long period of high unemployment among a community's labour force.

Deprivation Question. Technique used in group depth interviewing, respondents asked which product they would miss most if it were no longer on sale.

Depth Interview. Informal conversation between interviewerand respondent but with underlying crossexamination following clearcut objectives. Intended to descover facts which might not emerge from direct questioning.

Depth Interview of Focussed Interview. Interviewing technique without a questionnaire, respondent being asked open-ended questions. Unstructured or non—directive interview.

Design. In marketing,used as a generic term embracing all types of visual work, *e.g.*, roughs, typography, graphics, finished art, for all kinds of application—advertising, exhibitions, print work, house styling.

Design Advisory Scheme. A scheme operated by the Department of Trade and Industry to provide advice, consultancy and some financial support via grants and loans to firms wishing to improve their design management and performance.

Disigned Decay. Managacture and marketing of disposables, e.g. nappies, handkerchiefs, bottles.

Design Factor. Term used particularly in market research to indicate the level of efficiency and reliability of a sample used for a survey.

De-skilling. Modifying methods of performing a job to reduce the level of skill or skills demnded.

Desk Training. On-the-job commercial and clearical training.

Devaluation. Reduction of value of home currency in favour of foreign currencies, so that exports compete more favourably in overseas markets. Opposite to revaluation.

Developer, In organizational behavior, a manager who uses a high relationaships orientation and a low task orientation in a situation where such behaviour is appropriate. He is perceived as having implicit faith and trust in people and as being primarily concerned with developing them as individuals.

Development Area. Area of unemployument and depression towards which Government attempts to attract industry, using devices such as investment grants and tax concessions.

Development Corporation. Body set up to develop an area or New Town by attracting industry, this being done by means of grants and trading estate facilities, Commercial directors and PROs engage in programmes of advertising and PR to attract enquiries and create awareness of opportunities.

Dexterity. Manipulative ability achieved through good coordination of motor and perceptual skills.

D-group. Type of T-group used in management training and devleopment. The trainer attempts to relate group behaviour to the participants' own work experience.

Diadic. Paired comparison test involving informants reporting on two products or advertisements, one against the other.

Diadic Product Test. In market research, a product test based on consumer reaction to two products submitted simultaneously for comparison and reaction.

Diagonal Intergration. In this, auxiliary goods or services required for the main process or production in an industrial concern are provided inside that organisation.

Diary Method. Research technique in which respondents keep a regular written record of events such as reading a publication, viewing television or purchasing certain goods.

Differential. A difference between wage rates to total remuneration of different individuals or groups of employees, which is part of a planned or negotiated pay structure.

Differential Sampling. Or use of a weighted sample. Where the sample chosen for a survey or study is deliberately weighted or biased to give special attention to a particular element in the population.

Dilutee. Term, often pejorative, for a worker who has undergone shortened training and often experiences difficulty in gaining trade union acceptance as a semi skilled worker on the grounds that this would 'dilute the level of skill in the work place.

Dimension. Measurable quantity, used in marketing research to compared responses at different levels or in regard to platforms.

Direct Advertising. Advertisement that are distributed to their audience as individual items and not as part of a publication containing other material. The most common examples are leaflets, brochures and catalogues distributed by retailers by post (directmail advertising) or by door-to-door distribution. Also the use of such advertisements.

Direct Cost. A business cost that is directly related to producing a product or service.

Direct Distribution. Depends on number of stages in channel of distribution. Own shops have direct from maker distribution compaed with, say, ironmongery or stationery items, or fruit and vegetables where it is indirect.

Direct Expenses. All costs directly attributable to a product, a project, or an accounting centre.

Direct Investment. That which involves participation in management. setting up of firms or acquisition of assets as distinct from owning shares.

Directive Interview (structured interview). An interview which involves asking the respondent a series of prepared questions, often in a prepared sequence, with the aim of directing the interviewee towards particular subjects.

Direct Labour. Those members of the workforce directly enganged in producing goods or services, as opposed to those carrying out supporting activities such as maintenance or staff function.

Direct Labour Cost. A labour cost that relates to payment of a direct worker. Also the total of such labour costs associated with a particular activity, product or cost centre, or over a particular period. (Also known as 'direct wages').

Direct Mail. Selective advertising medium using mailing lists and the postal services.

Direct Mail Advertising. A form of advertising through letters, cards, and other literature sent by mail to potential customers. It is used either to solicit mail-order purchases or to direct customers to particular products or retail stores.

Direct Mail Selling. Sending specially prepared sales literature through the mail to specially selected prospective purchasers of a product or service, inviting them to place orders directly instead of through shops.

Direct Marketing. Also known as direct response marketing. Selling direct to customers, using media such as direct mail, catalogues, shopping magazines, off the page press advertisements, telephone, viewdata or teletext.

Direct Negative. Amendment to a motion proposing the direct opposite of the intention of the motion. The meeting or conference chairman should not accept a direct negative. The obvious course for anyone seeking to propose a direct negative is to vote against the motion itself.

Direct Sale. A sale made by a manufacturer direct to a consumer and not through a retailer or other intermediary.

Direct Selling. Selling without the use of a retail outlet, distributor broker or wholesaler or any other form of middleman.

Direct Worker. An employee whose work is directly concerned with the production of his employer's products. (Also known as a 'direct').

Disaggregated Data. To discover effect of advertising on puchases it is possible to identify behaviour of individuals, especially with returns from panelists using diaries.

Disbursement List. A printed list containing the identity and quantity of parts and assemblies to be withdrawn from stock and dispatched to the starting point of manufacture or assembly on a given day.

Discounter. A retailer who specializes in selling goods (especially consumer durables) at low prices.

Discounted House. Large store or branch of chain, offering mainly durable consumables at heavily discounted prices but providing little or no handling, delivery or credit services to customers.

Discovery Method. Method of teaching in which work is arranged and topics chosen so that trainee/pupil learns for himself rather than learning directly from the instructor/teacher. Sometimes known as heuristic method.

Discretion. Competence of a person to make a specified decision according to his own judgment alone.

Discretionary Content. The discretionary content of a task that has been assigned to someone consists of the aspects of the task that are expected to be carried out according to plans or decisions made by that person using his own judgment.

Discretionary Time. Free time. After work and family/social commitments, what do people do? Important to advertisers of do-it-yourself, hobby, cultural and pleasure products.

Discriminating Monopoly. A market situation in which the monopolist divides his sales among a different number of 'market' and charges different price in each market.

Discriminating Protection. The policy of protecting the goods produced by a few select domestic infant industries from the 'invasion' of foreign goods, through either banning of such importations or levying prohibitive protective tariffs.

Discrimination. In employment, different treatment of workers based on race, sex, age, religion, ethnic or national background, or union membership (or nonmembership), concerning hiring, wages, promotions, training programs, or any other terms and conditions of employment.

Discrimination Test. Market research term for a test in which people—the informants—are confronted with a number of products or packagings etc., and asked to discern the difference between them. Such a test often takes the form of a triadic product test, which has the attraction of being statistically checkable.

Discussion Group. Motivational research technique in which assembled group of respondents answers questions put by psychologist. Motivational research.

Dismiss. To carry out the dismissal of an employee.

Dismissal. Action by an employer to end an employee's contract of employment.

Dismissal Wage. A type of wage guarantees.

Dispersion. In opposition to theories of clustering, *e.g.*, Hotelling; other theorists claim that when there are separate markets or an uneven distribution of potential customers it is better for competitors to choose dispersed locations for their stores. Moves back towards Christaller's central place theory. Hoowever, depends on trade.

Dispute. Traditionally, industrial relations disputes in general have been known as trade disputes, with the term industrial dispute becoming more common in modern items. Disputes involving inter-union rivalry may be demarcation disputes, jurisdictional disputes or recognition disputes.

Dispute Benefit. Or strike pay. Paid by trade unions to workers on strike to compensate for loss of their normal wages.

Disputes Procedures. Procedure agreed between employers, or employers' associations, and trade unions for resolving industrial disputes.

Dissatisfiers. Factors describing the relationship of the employee to the context or environment in which he does his work. These factors which may, for example, include company policy, salary, interpersonal relationship and poor working conditions, being about job dissatisfaction known also as hygiene or mainntenance factors.

Dissociative Groups. Type of reference group brought together for the purpose of examining consumer buying motives.

Dissolution of Company. A company is dissolved when winding-up proceedings have come to an end (Winding Up), or when the Register of Companies has struck the company's name off the Register as defunct.

Dissolution of Partnership. The death, bankruptcy, or retirement of a partner dissolves the firm, and if the remaining partners continue in business a new partnership is created.

Distance Learning. The range of techniques and technology to enable students to learn at a distance from their techers rather than face-to-face. Examples include video, television, radio, written material, audio-visual etc., and such materials may sometimes be augmented by some form of tutorial support.

Distress Merchandise. Merchandise that has been reduced in price to increase the probability of sale.

Distribution Check. Survey taken at retail outlets to measure levels of distrubtion being achieved.

Distribution Cost Analysis. After Charles Sevin, technique for market-oriented profitability studies when reveal what different market segments contribute to plant and overheads and return on capital.

Distribution Mix

1. The channels of distribution used by a firm.
2. Combination of sales chains used by a company or other organization.

Distribution Planning. Determining the optimum methods of distribution and preparing and implementing programmes to put these methods into effect. This will involve a selecting the best channels of distribution.

Distribution Research. Study of movement of goods between place of production and time of consumption, and attitudes and behaviour of various kinds of distributor to manufacturer or producer.

Distributor. Firm which buys and sells on its own account but which deals in the goods of certain specified manufacturers. Common in trades where special representation, stocking and service facilities are required, *e.g.*, motor transport.

Diversification. Introduction of new products into existing markets or of existing products into new market to extend life cycles and offset decline.

Divestment. Action or process, undertaken by a firm, of transferring ownership and control of part of its activities to another firm.

Division of Labour. The principle of dividing a job into all of its component operations and having each operation (or a small number of operations) performed separately by one worker. Each worker thus becomes a specialist in one or a few operations, presumably achieving maximum efficiency in his or her specialty and eliminating the time needed to shift from one kind of work to another.

Document. Any form or voucher containing details of some transaction.

Dogs. Products liked by management but probably uneconomic and should be dropped.

Dollar Gap. Adverse balance of payments in a country with a dollar currency.

Domestic. In business, any transaction within a state or a nation, as opposed to one involving two or more states or countries.

Domestic Exports. Exports of goods or commodities produced with in the country of origin.

Domestic Gold Standard. The modern gold standard serves two functions. In the first place it is a method of controlling the volume of the currency. The second function of the gold standard is it to preserve the stability of exchange rates.

Door-to-door Selling. Also, house-to house selling. A method of retail distribution in which individual sales-persons call on customers in their homes, either by prior appointment or by ringing the doorbell.

Dormant Parner. A partner who plays an inactive role in the management of a business and who is not known to the public as having an interest in the enterprise.

Dotting Test. Sometimes used in psychological testing of fatigue and concentration. The person being tested has to mark with a dot the centres of circles passed in front of him her at a regular rate but in irrgular positions.

Double Barrelled Question. Single question actually posing two questions simultaneously. When answered there is doubt as to completeness of the answer.

Double-day Shift System (or double-day system). A system of shift-work in which two shifts are worked each day, typically 06.00-14.00 and 14.00-22.00.

Double Daywork. A type of payment by results in which a standard level of output is set and two time rate are set. Workers who do not achieve the standard are paid the lower time rate, workers who reach or exceed the standard receive the higher rate.

Double Decker. Two outdoor advertising panels sited one above the other.

Double Employment. Holding of two jobs by one person. This happens, for example, in moonlighting.

Double Factoral Terms of Trade. Net barter terms of trade devided by the relative change in productivity in the exports of a given country and in the foreign industries producing its imports.

Double Front. Twin poster sites arranged to utilize both sides of the front of a bus or other commercial vehicle. Usually each a 'single sheet' or smaller.

Double Page Spread. Two facing pages in a magazine or newspaper, used in advertising as if they were one single sheet, *i.e.*, the design carries right across the gutter in the centre.

Double Placement. Product testing technique (used by Home Testing Panels, subsidiary of William Schlackman Ltd.) in which products A is tested against new product B. Combination of panel and interview methods used, 200 interviews being conducted by field worker, 200 panel members completing a postal questionnaire.

Double Pricing. Where a product carries two prices, either actually or by implication, offering to sell to consumers (the technique is used mostly consumer goods) at the lower of the two prices.

Double Tariff. Tariff that distinguishes either between autonomous and conventional duties, or between maximum and minimum duties.

Double Taxation. Where tax on the same income, profits, etc falls due in two or more countries according to the individual laws and regulations of those countries. There are double taxation agreements between most countries to arrive at a compromise so that the individual corporation etc. involved does not have to pay the full taxes of both countries.

Double Time. Payment of wages at twice day rate or time rate, most usually for certain overtime or working special hours.

Downer. Short strike or stoppage intended to draw attention to a particular grievance. It usually involes workers in 'downing tools' but not leaving the factory premises. A 'downer' is a form of demonstration strike.

Downgrading. Movement of an employee to a job that has fewer responsibilities and/or involves less skill and/or lower status and/or, especially, has a lower rate of pay.

Down Payment. A partial payment of the total purchase price rendered by a buyer to a seller at the time of purchase, with the understanding that the rest will be paid later, according to the terms of their agreement.

Downstairs Merger. A merger in which a parent corporation becomes a subsidiary.

Down Time. Period during which a machine is not operative due to mechanical failure, machine adjustment, nonavailability of materials, labout of maintenance work.

Down turn. A contraction of economic activity leading to the period of deprssion or slump.

Drawing Accounts. Credit male available to salesmen in anticipation of future earnings most usually operative whre a substantial part of remuneration derives from a commision on sales.

Drum. Large sylindrical metal container mainly used for bulk packaging of liquids.

Dual Membership Agreement. Agreement between two trade unions for one of them to represent certain of the other's members in particular situations.

Dual Prices. A system in which a goods is simultaneously sold at two different prices within a given area.

Dual Unionism. Where two or more trade union represent similar types of workers in the same bargaining unit.

Due Date. In purchasing, the expected date or receipt for a part; in manufacturing, the expected completion date of a part.

Due-date Rule. In manufacturing, the sequencing of jobs to be rurn on the basis of the due dates, taking the earliest due date as the first job to be run.

Dummy

1. An arrow in an activity-on-arrow network that is inserted only to show that two events must takes place simultaneously. Also known as a 'zero-time activity'.
2. Simplified represeentation of a proposed publication, package or other promotional item.

Dummy Activity. Used in critical path planning and network analysis to indicate events not connected in the network by one activity but nevertheless having an essential relationship in time. A dummy activity is shown as a dotted arrow.

Dumping. Sale of the same product in different markets at different prices.

Duopoly. A market situation in which two sellers control the market. It may be either a perfect duopoly or an imperfect one, depending, on whether or not there is product differentiation.

Duopsony. The condition that exists when two buyers control the demand for goods and services offered by many producers.

Duplication (in Advertising). Extent to which the audience of one medium or vehicle overlaps that of another.

Duplication Analysis. The degree of interpurchasing between brands, sizes or varieties. The analysis can be used to evaluate the structure of a market, brand loyalty, size loyalty, range loyalty or segmentation.

DuPont/Pyramid. Evolved as an expression of the management ratios pioneered by the DuPont Company of America, a tree chart of ratios leading up to the key ratio

$$\frac{\text{net profit x 100}}{\text{capital employed}}$$

Below the key ratio are two main branches of the tree, one being

$$\frac{\text{net profit x 100}}{\text{sales}}$$

with its breakdowns, and the second branch of the tree, capital employed, with its branches.

Durable Consumer Goods. Non-perishable consumer goods like residential house, furniture etc. Which can be used over a fairly long period of time. Such goods are to be distinguished from semi-durable goods.

Dynamic Analysis (Dynamics). The study of the behaviour of systems, single market or whole economies in disequilibrium situations.

Dynamic Determination Certain forces engendered by a process of expansion which determine the limits to which it will proceed.

Dynamic Equilibrium. An economic system might be said to be in dynamic equilibrium if its total stock, including both things and people, change at a constant rate (per cent per annum) and if the rates of production and consumption of all five items of the stock increased at the same rate.

Dynamics. The analysis of economic change over time and the processes of adjustment to change. Necessarily such study involves analyzing changes that have occurred in the past.

Dynamic Theory. Different from other theories about the development of personality, and concerned with contemporay manifestations of personality in interaction with the environment.

E

EAM. Abbreviation of electrical accounting machines.

Ear, Ear Space or Title Corner. Advertisement at the top of the front page of a newspaper, on either side of the title or masthead.

Earliest Event Time. In Network Analysis, the earliest time at which an event in a network can take place.

Earliest Finish Time of an Activity. (or earliest finish date of an activity or earliest finish). The earliest possible time at which an activity in an activity-on-node network can be completed.

Earliest Start Time of an Activity (or earliest start date of an activity or earliest start). The earliest possible time at which an activity in an activity-on-node network can be started.

Early Shift

1. The earlier shift during a day in a double day-shift system.
2. The morning shift in a three-shift system.

Earnings

1. Money received by a person from being employed.
2. Net profit of a firm measured either with or without deducting payments of corporate income tax interest on debt capital and preference dividends.

Earnings Drifts. Extent to which wages or earnings rise above national rates through the influence of such factors as local rates, overtime, workplace bargaining, payment by-results schemes bargaining creep, etc. Also known as wage drift.

Earnings of Undertaking or Management. What remains of a businessman's profit after deducing interest on his capital at the current rate (allowing where necessary for insurance) is generally called his earnings of undertaking or management.

Earnings Relationships. Relationships between the levels of earnings of the different work or groups occupations in a factory or plant.

Earnings Report. A statement issued by a company showing its earnings or losses over a given period, usually one fiscal year.

Economic Activity. The production and distribution of goods and services. Also, the contribution of persons to the production and distribution of useful goods and services.

Economic and Monetary Union. One of the basic elements necessary in setting up a Common Market.

Economic Batch Quantity (EBQ). The quantity of a manufactured item made in batches that should be produced in one batch in order to meet a particular regular demand with minimum production and stockholding costs.

Economic Dynamics. Analysis of economic systems, through time, and particularly in relation to behaviour of markets, firms and the national economy in general.

Economic (or Productive) **Employment.** Employment which brings about a net addition to total product produced by the country.

Economic Environment. The conditions under which man conducts struggle to satisfy his wants.

Economic Indicators. Treasury figures and charts published monthly and quarterly, covering national output and investment, incomes, consumptions and prices, external position, maney and credit, enemployment. These form important appraisal aids as also the basis for management decisions and hence serve to reduce entrepreeneurial risks. These include market research series, price indices, production indices income and expenditure series, import and export statistics.

Economic Man. In economic theory, an ideal human being who behaves in a totally rational fashion, who is perfectly informed and whose economic motivation when making decisions is towards maximizing utility.

Economic Model. An abstract framework representing the relationships between the elements of an economic system. Seeks to explain the bahaviour of persons and institutions in the economy.

Economic Organization. The way in which an economy is organized, that is, who owns or controls the means of production and distribution of goods and services.

Economic Planning. A totality of arrangements decided upon in order to carry out a project concerned with economic activity.

Economic of Waste. An economic analysis in which there can be many unemployed resources—men and machines—which could be usefully employed.

Editing. In market research, checking that questionnaires are complete and ready for coding and analysis. Also, checking returns from respondents or panel members for inconsistencies, and referring queries to interviewers. Before reports are processed, computer edit runs are made to check data against standard criteria.

Editorial Avertisement. Advertisement designed in the form of a piece of editorial matter. Such advertisements must, however, be clearly labelled 'advertisement'.

Editorial Publicity. Space in a journal or newspaper in which a product, service, or company is discussed or publicized at the discretion of the editor.

Edridg-green Lantern Tests. Form of colbur vision test in which the subject is presented with a number of lights of different coloures and different degrees of brightness.

Educational Technology. Organized design and implementation of learning systems taking advantage of modern visual aids and communications and teaching methods. A systems approach to the teacher-learning process.

Efficient Market Hypothesis. The theory that in a Market with numerous investors who prefer the highest possible yields with the lowest possible risk for their investment—a market like the stock market, for example—no amount of information will influence the outcome, for the investor can achieve no more (and no less) than a fair return relative to risk.

Effort Bargain. Agreement between management and trade unions which lays down the amount of work to be done for the agreed wage, not just the hours to be worked. An effort bargain hinges not only on the level of pay but also on the payment-system (*e.g.* day rate, payment-by-results etc.).

Egoistic Needs. Industrial paychologist's term for the personal sources of job satisfaction other than remuneration. These include self-respect, the respect, of others, sense of achievement, status, prestige, etc.

Eighty-twenty Rule. In marketing, and empirical rule reflecting the common experience that a relatively small proportion (20 per cent) of items in a company's catalog generate a large proportion (80 per cent) of the company's total activity in sales.

Election Polls. Opinion polls, using either quota or random surveys, to predict likely results of an election. Accuracy of finding may depend on size and kind of sample, questions asked and closeness to the event.

Electronic Funds Transfer System (EFTS). A techinique using computers to transfer funds between banks.

Electronic Mail. Communication based on computer networks which allows users to send and receive, store and forward messages sent between terminals and to obtain Hard Copy for their records if necessary.

Electronic Media. Advertisements making use of neon signs or lights, and capable of movement by electric impulses.

Electronic Time Study Systems. Work Study tools enabling data collection and record storage and analysis by computer. Such systems are replacing the traditional stopwatch and enable observers to concentrate their attentions more fully on analysis rather than measurement.

Element (of Work). Originated with work study practice of breaking, work down into very small elements for method study and work measurement. Larger elements are appropriate in training except, for example, in skills analysis training of operatives.

Embezzle. The act of stealing money or property entrusted to him or her by that employee.

Emerson System. The system which lays down a certain "task" but the task is usually not so severe being designed for the average worker and the bonus is equivalently smaller and is graduated according to the nearness which the worker gets to the task.

Emolument. The return from personal labour received or accrued in the form of compensation, such as a salary, wage, fee, commission, award, price concession, or other personal benefit.

Emotional Appeal. Product advertising appealing to emotional desires rather than logic, economy or utility.

Employed Person (or employee). One who works for an employer, as opposed to a self-employed person working on his own account, or an unemployed person seeking employment, or a non-employed person neither in employment nor seeking it.

Employee. Person who enters into a contract with another (the employer) to perform work-(1) under the control of the employer or another of that employer's employees and as part of the organization run by the employer- in return for wages or salary or some other valuble consideration.

Employee Benefit. Something of value, apart from agreed regular monetary payments of salary or wage, given by an employer to an employee—*e.g.*, sick pay or subsidized meals.

Employee Contribution. The money individual employees pay to participate in company benefit plans, especially common in the areas of insurance, pension, and saving plans.

Employee Handbook. A book, given by an employer to all his employees, that gives information on employer-employees, relations.

Employee Participation. Participation by the employees of a firm in the process of taking decisions concerning the firm's activities.

Terms with similar meanings include: 'co—determination','co-partnership', co-ownership', 'democratic management', 'industrial democracy', 'joint consultation', 'participative management' and 'workers' control'.

Participative management and 'democratic management' are used only to refer to the managerial style of an individual manager the other terms refers to methods of influencing the running of a whole firm.

Employee participation' and 'industrial democracy' have the most general meaning; both refer to any arrangement by which the opinions of the employees of a firm are automatically considered during decision-making.

Copartnership and 'co-ownership' are used to describe schemes in which employees acquire a significant proportion of the ownership of the firms they work in. However, their influence on the running of the firms is often as limited as that of non-employed shareholders.

Joint consultation and 'co-determination' usually do not involve any ownership of the firm by its employees: 'codetermination' implies that certain decisions can be taken only by a joint committee of workers and management; joint consultation implies only that there is a formal system by which management can obtain the opinions of workers.

Workers control may or may not involve actual ownership of the firm by its workers but does imply that employees must approve all managerial decisions.

Employee Relations. Relations between an employer and his employees regarded as individuals rather than as members of unions.

Employee Relations Index. Assessment of the quality of employee and personnal relations by noting trends in such factors as labour turnover, absenteeism, sefety, medical needs, use made of suggetion schemes, grievances.

Employee's Contributory Negligence. If, in a case for industrial injury compensation, it can be shown that the employee in question acted in a negligent fashion which contributed to his accident or to the seriousness of his injuries—for example, by failing to wear a safety helmet-the damages may be reduced.

Employers' Federation. An association of employers within a sector or country. Typical activities include negotations with trade unions, lobbying government, providing advice and assistance to members and generally representing their interests.

Employees' Provident Fund. Retirement benefits in the form of provident fund, family, persion and deposit linked insurance are available to the employees under the Employees Provident Fund.

Employer

(1) Person or organization that enters into a contract with someone who thereby becomes an employee.

(2) Person or organization that has employees.

Employer Reference. Where an employer seeks to use a disputes procedure or a grievance procedure. Such a step by the trade union side is known as a union reference.

Employers' Association. A body whose members are employers and whosee principle activities include regulating relations between employers and employees. Also a federation of such bodies.

Employment. Level of employment in a community ranging from mass unemployment, when slump conditions are experienced, to full—employment, when the dangers of inflation are present particularly in a laissez-faire economy.

Employment Agency. A firm which finds people to work for other firms. An employment agency usually receives fees from the firms to which it supplies workers. (Also called a 'personnel agency').

Employment Costs. Wages or salary paid to an employee plus the related payments for insurance, pensions, etc., that have to be met by the employer. Overheads related to the employee may also be included.

Employment Exchange. An office at which work people seeking employment and employers requiring work people may notify their respective needs. It is a market palce for labour, intended to replace the unguided individual rearch for work or for employees.

Employment Medical Advisor. A doctor appointed to carry out medical examinations of particular groups of workers—such as those in dangerous jobs or young people—whose health may be affected by their job.

Employment Multiplier. The ratio of increase in total employment (N) to the increase in primary employment (N2) in the same way in which the investment multiplier is the ratio of increase in income to the increase in (primary) investment.

Employment Rate. Usually expressed as a percentage of total population, and sometimes as a percentage of labour force.

Employment Test. Test of questions or exercises or other means of measuring a person's suitability for a particular job, or for working in a particular occupation or a particular organization.

Engineering Change Note. (concession request form: engineering query note). A document which lists any changes or queries to the original design and accompanying drawings in a development project. This provides an up-to-date record of how the design has been altered during its development.

Enterprise. A business undertaking. Unless otherwise qualifies, the entirely of an organization rather than unit or subdivision.

Entrepot Teade. Business consisting of re-exporting of imported goods, with or without any additional processing.

Entrepreneur. A person who is skilled at identifying new products (or, sometimes, new methods of production), setting up operations to provide new products, marketing the products and arranging the financing of the operations.

Environment. Refers to surrounding conditions of an activity, particularly in marketing, the social and psychological conditions.

Environmental Sensor Department. Department in a company which tests the market or provides intelligence helpful to marketing, *e.g.*, market research, economic, customer relations, public relations, legal departments.

Environmentalists. Activists who seek to protect nature from damage by industry and produce articulate pressure groups which present industries with serious PR problems. Topics include pollution, food additives, unclear reactors, hairspray aerosols, disposable plastic containers, lead content of petrol and motor-car exhaust fumes, effluent in rivers and so on.

Equal Pay. Pay this is the same for men and women who perform the same or similar work.

Equilibrium Quantity. The quantity of a good that is bought and sold when a market is in equilibrium.

Equitable Payment. The remuneration which would be generally considered fair (at a particular time and in a particular country) for employees with a particular time-span of discretion.

Ergonomics. The aspect of technology that is concerned with the application of biological and engineering data to problems related to human beings and the machine. Also known as biotechnology.

Escalation. In purchase contracts, a provision for unforseen changes in basic costs—labour or materials or both—that may make it necessary to increase the final price.

Escalator Cards. Advertisemeents placed alongside underground escalators.

Escalator Clause. A cluse in a collective agreement which states that wages should increase at the same rate as a specified cost-of-living index.

Escrow (escrow agreement). Any arrangment in which a bond, deed or other document is adopted by two parties and given to a thrid for safekeeping to be surrendered only when some condition emerges.

Escrow Agreement. An arrangement that may be made during arbitration of wages in an industrial action between a trade union and management under which an employer delivers to the arbitrator a specified sum of money to be used to pay a wage increase if the arbitrator rules the increase to be warranted.

Estimated Work. Work for which standard times have been set without using work measurement (*e.g.* they have been based on practical experience or previous production records).

Estimating. Strictly, producing an estimate of the cost/price of an activity particularly in one-off jobs and in contracting.

Evaluated Maintenance Programme. A form of Planned Maintenance which uses a historical ananysis of previous performance and costs to develop future maintenance plans.

Evening Shift. A shift that is worked mainly in the evening-*e.g.*, from 1600 to 2400.

Ex-ante Investment. Business palns for expansion.

Excepted Provident Fund (EPE). Or retirement benefit scheme or cloth cap pension scheme. A type of pension scheme in which the shole of the benefit may be taken as a lump sum at normal retirement age instead of a pension proper.

Exception Report. A report on a deviation from a plan that is presented to someone practising management by exception.

Excess Capacity. Unused or idle capacity. When the productive factors are not fully utilised, the phenomenon of excess capacity arises. In simple language, the term excess capacity indicates that the output can still be increased with the given factors.

Exchange Management. The term in contradistinction with free exchange market, denotes all kinds of interference by the monetary authorities of a country in the foreign exchange transactions designed primarily to prevent the free fluctuations in the rate of exchange.

Exchange management is one of the devices for correcting disequilibrium in the international balance of payments.

Exchequer Tally. A notched piece of wood, 8 or 9 inches in length, which, at one time, was given in U.K. as a form of receipt to a person who deposited money with the Government. A similar notched stick was retained in the Exchequer Deepartment, and when the depositer wanted his money he produced his portion of stick, and if the two sticks 'tallied', that is, the notches on the one agreed with the notches on the other, he was paid his money.

It is said that a notch of 11/2 inches represented £ 1,000,1 inch,

£ 100,3/8 inch £ 10, half a notch of that size £ 13/16 inch 1s, smallest notch 1d, a small hole 1/2d.

Exclusion Clause. In a guarantee, clause which protects given from complaints over which he has no control, such as exaggerated claims by salesman.

Execution Time. The portion of an instruction cycle during which the actual work is performed, or the operation is executed; for example, the time required to decode and perform an instruction.

Executive. In organizational behaviour, descriptive of a manger how uses a high task orientation and a high relationships orientation in a situation where such behaviour is appropriate and who is therefore more effective. Such a manager sets high standards, treats everyone somewhat differently, prefers team management, and is therefore, often perceived as a good motivating force.

Executive Director. A director of a company who is also a full-time employee of the company. (Also known as on 'inside director').

Executive Gift. Advertising gifts as presented at Christmas to clients. Typical gifts are desk diaries, quality pen sets, calculators, wines and spirits.

Exhibition. Putting on display a company's products or services for promotional purposes.

Exit Interview. Interview of an amployee who has given notice to end his employment in order to gain information about his reasons for leaving.

Ex Officio. By virtue of holding a particular office.

Expectancy Chart. Sometimes used following psychological testing to predict the performance in particular occupations of those being tested. An individual expectancy chart plots the predicted performance of an individual candidate or employee in a particular occupation. An institutional expectancy chart predicts the level of efficiency within a work-force, note being made to such factors as the number of workers expected to be of above average performance.

Expectancy Theory. A broad term that encompasses theories on motivation put forth by Vroom, Lawler and others. The theories hold that an employee's motivation to perform effectively is determined by effort-reward probability and reward-value. The first signifies an individual's subjective view that a given amount of effective effort will result in a given reward. The second refers to the individual's perception of the value of the reward that might be obtained by performing effectively. The concept of reward-value is referred to among behavioural scientists as valence.

Expediter of Expeditor. In manufacturing, a person responsible for considering jobs that are late and, after defining the reasons, taking steps to hasten the jobs through the production facility, using such techniques as overtime labour, acquisition of materials that are in short supply, and resequencing of jobs in a queue.

Expediting. In business and industry, the job of seeing that materials are the right place when needed.

Expenditure. A relinquishment by a firm of money or some other asset or an incurrence of a liability in exchange for a benefit received or to be received.

Expense

1. A disbursement or outlay of cash.
2. (Plural) Money paid out by an employee in connection with his job and reimbursed by his employer.

Expert Witness. A technically skilled and experienced person in a particular field who may be called to give evidence in courts of law, public enquiries, inquests and other examination processes.

Exploitation of Labour. The payment to labour of less than its proper wage. It arises from the unequal bargaining strength of employers and employed.

Export Agent. Person or company acting on behalf of an exporter in another country. Two types of agents are the commission agent and the del credere agent.

Export Declaration. Details, to be submitted within six days, of the export of all goods from the country.

Exposition. Sometimes used as synonym of 'exhibition', but usually to imply a larger or more serious event, often accompanied by a conference or seminar.

Extended Use Tests. Similar to placement tests but used, espically in industrial marketing, where it is necessary for findings to be derived from use of the product in a work situation over a long term period.

External House Journals. House journals produced for a specific external readership such as distributors, users of consumers.

External Labo(u)r Market. The labo(u)r market outside, but affecting, the individual employing organization.

Extractive Industries. Industries which obtain products by exploiting natural resources—mining, oil and gas etc.

Extraordinary Depreciation. Depreciation caused by unusual wear and tear, obsolescence unexpected distintegration, or an inadequacy beyond what can be attributed to loss of physical or useful life through ordinary circumstances.

Extraordinary General Meeting. A general meeting that is not an annual general meeting. The word 'extraordinary' is used because an annual general meeting used to be called an 'ordinary general meeting'.

Extraordinary Resolution. A resoluting of the members of a registered company approved by three-quarters or more of the votes cast on it at a meeting of the mambers of which notice was given specifying that the resolution was to be proposed as an extraordinary resolution.

Extrinsic Rewards (extensive factars). Various kinds of external rewards offered to an employee—salary, bonuses, Fringe Benefits, travel etc—as distinct from the internal rewards of Motivation.

Eysenck Personality Inventory. Type of personality test used to measure an individual's position on the introversion/extroversion spectrum.

Eye-blink Test. By means of hidden camera, eye-blink rate of respondents is recorded to reveal extent of emotional tension during screeing of TV commercials.

Eye Movement Camera. Used in advertising research, this equipment tracks the movement of the eye over press advertisements, showing the path which the eye takes and indicating the sequence of interest that the features arouse.

F

Face Sheet Data. In a questionnaire, personal questions about respondent.

Face-to face Groups. Type of reference group brought together for the purpose of examining consumer buying motives. A face to face group is small enough to ensure that the individuals communicate with each other and that their tastes and values are brought out.

Face-to-face Selling. Personal selling usually on a one-to-one basis, *i.e.* a personal meeting between buyer and seller in which each can state a case and/or hear the other's point of view. Vulgarly referred to as 'belly-to-belly' selling.

Facia. In exhibitions, the headboard above a stand. Sometimes used for advertising purposes, *e.g.*, featuring a brand-name, but usually carries the identity of the exhibitor.

Facial Board. Board or panel bearing shopkeeper's name which may be supplied by a firm whose name or product is incorporated in the design as a permanent and prominent advertisement.

Facilities Management. Planning, installation and operation of a firm's electronic data processing equipment by another, specialist, firm.

Fact Co-ordination Test. Test of psychomotor skills or, more specifically, of speed and accuracy in co-ordination of hand and eye.

Factor Analysis. Study of the component parts of an attitude research programme interview with the aim of discovering more meaningful conclusions than are apparent from the data taken as a whole.

Factor Analysis Chart Technique (FACT). Job evaluation approach to determining the relative worth of management positions within a salary structure. Involves assigning points to the major elements of jobs.

Factior comparison Job Evaluation System. System of job evaluation in which:

(1) a number of benchmark jobs are carefully described and analysed;

(2) a number of factors (such as: skill, effort, responsibility, working conditions) are chosen;

(3) for each factor, the benchmark jobs are ranked according to the degree to which the factor is involved in the jobs;

(4) numerical values are assigned to each ranking position for each factor;

(5) each job to be evaluated is compared with the benchmark jobs, factor by factor, and a total numerical value for each job calculated by adding the numerical values of its individual job-factor rankings.

Factor Comparison Method. Analytical job evaluation technique for defining and assessing jobs in terms of certain common factors. Selected key jobs (having been factor-analyzed) and their wages are taken as datum points and cash values for the factors calculated. Factor comparison method is also known as job factor comparison.

Factoring Company. Firm that does not manufacture goods itself but acts either as a wholesaler or as an agent for a manufacturer.

Factors of Production. The resources required to produce a commodity. They are usually divided into three categories—land, labour, and capital—which however, are admittedly arbitrary, since often a given resource may belong to more than one category.

Factor Rating. Performance appraisal and job evaluation technique in which mangers are ranked in order for each of certain factors selected as indicating the extent to which they have qualities considered desirable. Other management appraisal techniques include controlled report, free report, forced choice approach, ranking system, and task based appraisal.

Factor Rating and Comparison. In performance appraisal procedures etc, a method of reporting on the performance of staff using multiple step scales or linear scales against a series of qualities or characteristics.

Factory. Defined under Factories Act as any premises in which or in precincts of which persons are employed in manual labour in manufacturing or related processes by way of trade or for purposes of gain.

Factory Agreement. Product of collective bargaining on behalf of employees from the whole of a factory, as distinct from work place bargaining on behalf of a smaller group on large scale bargaining such as for company agreements, house agreements, or industry-wide agreements.

Facts Book. File of contact reports Brand manager's book of key information.

Fair. A public exposition or market, usually held at regular intervals, for the purpose of exhibiting, exchanging, and/or selling goods. The practice of holding fairs dates from ancient times and became an important feature of economic life in medieval Europe. Today fairs are used trading for actual trading than for exhibiting merchandise, both to producers within a field or industry and to the public.

Fair List. Type of boycott occasionally used by trade unions against firms not employing or not recognizing trade union labour.

Fair Trade. Also, resale price maintenance. An agreement between a manufacturer and a distributor, or a distributor and a dealer, stipulating that the latter will not resell an item below a specified minimum price.

False Termination. Sometimes the most important answers to be gleaned under depth interviews are towards the end of a session. Thoughts that the respondent hesitates to express through embarrassment or because he thinks them trivial, he is encourged to unload when the termination of the interview is announced. These replies may deserve later investigation.

Family Budget. The term adverts to a detailed statement of the income and expenditure of a family for a period of time, say, a month.

Family Groups. Type of reference group brought together for the purpose of examining consumer buying motives.

Family Life-style. Manner or style of living adopted by a family according to its background, income, or aspirations. Is becoming subject to closer scrutiny in the development of psychograpics.

Family Partnership. A partnership whose members are all of a single family.

Fast-moving Consumer Goods. Small-unit repeat-purchase branded goods (FMCG), *e.g.*, foods, drinks, household goods and toiletries which are mostly bought at least weekly.

Fat Work. Work on which it is relatively easy to earn high bonus under a payment-by-results scheme. May also be known as gravy jobs. Work on which it is difficult to earn bonus may be known as lean work or stinkers.

Fayol Ladder. Henri Fayol, in his promotion of scientific management methods, emphasized the importancee of extensive delegation of authority. He diagramed channels of communications within the hierarchy of an organization. He proposed that direct communications be encouraged horizontally among the branches of an organization tree, and that the procedures and limits for such communications channels shoule be well defined at the superior levels within the organization. The diagrammatic representation of the organization tree or chart with dotted-line paths to indicate communications channels became known as the Fayol ladder or bridge of Fayol.

Fear. Under the General Rules of the Code of Advertising Practice, advertisements should not without justifiable reason pay on fear. It says 'no advertisement should cause those who see it unwarranted anxiety lest they are suffering (or may, without responding to the advertiser's offer, suffer) from any disease or condition of ill health; or suggest that any product is necessary for the maintenance of health or the retention of physical or mental capacities, whether by people in general or by particular groups'.

Feasibility Study. A report containing detailed examination of the inputs, and economic, technical, financial, commercial and organizational requirements of project to determine its viability in principle.

Featherbedding

(1) A term used by opponents of government assistance to industry to describe any assistance they do not like. (Assistance that they do like is known as an 'incentive'

(2) Provision of more jobs, or employment of more workers, than is necessary-usually as a result of union pressure.

Fee. A payment by a person to the Government on account either of a special benefit received from the Government or a special cost imposed upon the Government in connection with a government service performed for the common benefit.

Feedback. In marketing, a return flow of ideas and opinions from buyers and consumers to sellers and producers. Obtaining relevant feedback is a major objective of market research.

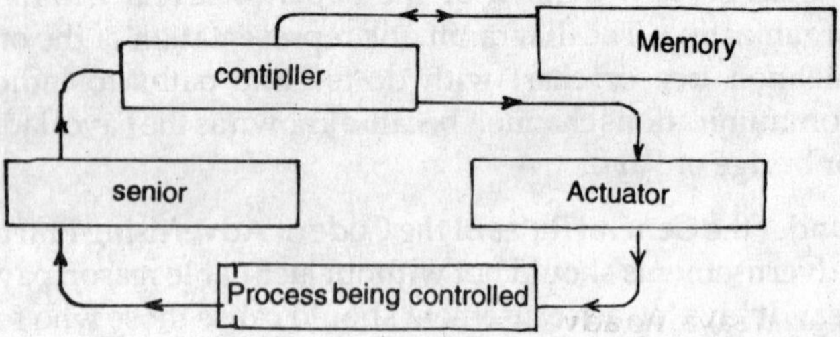

Fellow. An individual in a senior class of membership of a profesional institute.

Felt-fair Pay. Term used by Elliott Jaques for the rate of pay that the holder of a job thinks would be fair for that job.

Fibreboard. Two or more sheets of paperboard pasted together to form a stronger, thicker material. Usually a combination of kraft and chipboard.

Fibreboard Case. Container constructed from either solid or corrugated fibreboard, intended for protection of goods during transit. A transit outer.

Field Salesman. One who works away from base.

Field Sales Manager. Executive responsible for organization, direction, control motivation and training of the field selling force in whole or in part.

Fieldwork. That part of a market research survey which involves face-to-face interviews with respondents by research investigators, as compared with other means of obtaining data, such as postal or telephone enquiries and the searching of relevant published material.

Filler. Pre-perpared advertisement by publisher used to fill the gap left in a page after make-up.

Filter Question. Or strip question. Market research term for a question which an interviewer only puts to an informant if it is made relevant by the answer given to the previous question.

Final Average Pay. In individual's earnings during the final period of employment or participation in a compensation plan, typically the last three, five, or ten years' average pay. It is used particularly in the calculation of pension benefits.

Final Goods. The finished articles which are the end products of production.

Final Goods and Services. The goods and services which are not resold.

Finance. The management of public revenues; the conduct or transaction of money matters generally and particularly those affecting the public as in the field of banking and investment.

Finance Company. General name for a firm that specializes in making loans to business or individuals or both.

Fiancial Report. Fortnightly confidential newsletter containing comment and analysis on world-wide financial matters.

Fiancial Statement. As balance sheet.

Financial System. It consists of those institutions which are mainly concerned with the creation, destruction and exchange of claims.

Financial Year. Also called fiscal year, it is the period of twelve months covered by the budget.

In India the financial year runs from April 1 to March 31 of the next year.

Finder. A person, acting as an individual or as an enterprise, who brings together a buyer and a seller and earns a fee for the service.

Fine Control Sensitivity. Type of psychomotor skill. An individual's ability to make delicately controlled muscular adjustments, particularly where larger muscle groups are involved.

Finished Goods. Final goods which are for the enjoyment of the ultimate consumer and instrumental goods which are for use in process.

Finished goods = Final goods + Investmental goods
= Fixed capital + Hoards.

Fink. A derogatory word, used as either a noun or a verb, to describe a member of a labour who reports to his employer on the activities of the union and of his fellow employees. It was the practice to expel from the union any person behaving in such a way as to be identified as a fink.

Firm. A unit of management operating under a trade name organized either to extract minerals, produce or manufacture goods, sell goods and services or to engage in two or three of these activities sometimes simultaneously. A firm may be a sole proprietorship, a partnership, a private or public limited company, or State owned enterprise. The unit of business activity carried by a unit of management is distinguished from the industry which is the aggregate of manufacturing or technical productive enteprises.

Firm Quotation. Quoted price and/or conditions which will remain unchanged, subject to previously defined criteria.

Firm's Profile. Used in establishing the payment system appropriate to the firm.

First Come, First Served. Decision-making rule for scheduling. This rule places orders in line as they arrive at a processing point. The next order to be processed is the one that is first in line.

First in System, First Served. A rule used in decision-making for production scheduling that is based on the due dates for orders waiting in line. The order that has the earliest planned due date will be assigned first.

First Line. A term used, particularly of supervisory or maintenance management personnel, to describe those who are directly connected with the responsible for keepinng production running on the shop floor.

Fiscal Measures. Government action to counteract deflation or inflation by tax changes. A budgetary surplus, where the government collects more than it spends, should have a deflationary effect-and vice versa.

Fiscal Policy. Refers primarily to taxation proposals which are formulated by a government in order to raise resources to meet its expenditure; the same is also done to influence business activities. An important occasion when the fiscal policy or fiscal measures are enunciated is the presentation of annual budget of the State.

Fisher's Ideal Price Index. An index based on a formula devised by the American economist Irving Fisher (1867, 1947) which is intended to be a 'true' index while the Lespeyre's index indicates an upper limit and the Paasche's Index a lower limit to this 'true' index. It is in fact an index of the Geometric Mean of the Laspeyre's and Paasche's indices. The formula for the Ideal Index as given by Fisher is a follows:

$$\left[\frac{\Sigma P_n q_o}{\Sigma P_o q_o} \times \frac{\Sigma P_n q_n}{\Sigma P_o q_n}\right]$$

where P_o = price in the base year,

q_o = quantity in the base year,

P_n = price in the year being considered,

q_n = quantity in the year being considered.

Five Fold Grading Scheme. Personal selection interview procedure devised by John Munro Fraser under heads of first impression, qualifications abilities, motilivation, adjustment.

Fixed Budget. Budget which is based on a forecast of ideal or normal capacity. It does not take account of possible variations in the level of activiy as would a flexible budget.

Fixed-shift System. A shifwork system where each team of workers always works the same shift.

Fixture. An article that has been installed in or attached to a building or land in a more or less permanent way, so that legally it is considered part of the real estate.

Fixures and Fittings. Items attached to the structure of a building but not forming part of it.

Flat Rate. An overall price for an entire job or group of jobs. For example, a painter may offer a flat rate covering both time and materials, rather than working for an hourly fee plus the cost of the paint.

Flea Market. A market, held either outdoors or indoors, where numerous merchants at separate stalls sell old or used household goods, antiques and curios. Prices are usually subject to bargaining.

Flexible Manning. (fexible working practices.) Alternative arrangements in work organization which permit a greater degree of flexibility within an organization in its use of labour along one more dimensions. Among relevant kinds of flexibility are Flexible Working Hours, levels of manning skill levels (where flexibility is concerned with moving workers around a plant to provide cover for the various operating requirements of machinery), trade union practices (where flexibility relates to removing some of the regidities of demarcation between trades) and in payment systems.

Flexible Manufacturing System. An arrangement of computer-controlled machine tools and transport and handing systems which operates as an integrated system under the supervisory control of a larger computer.

Flexible Time. Term used in an application of flexible working hours(fwh) for the periods during the day when each employee can choose his or her own working hours. The rest of the day is core time when all employees are exepected to be present.

Flexible Working Hours (FWH). An arrangement under which each employee in an organization may choose the times at which he starts and finishes work each day to suit himself. In most arrangements of this kind, an employee must be at work during one or more periods of 'core time' and must work for a minimum number of hours in each week or month.

Flexible Working Time (EWT). Synonymous with flexible working hours.

Floating Currency. A currency is said to flat when it is allowed to find its own level in relation to other world currencies.

Floating Exchange Rate. Where a country ceases to have an official exchange rate for its currency with other currencies but allows its currency to float or find a natural exchange rate. This can in effect be a devaluation.

Floating Labour. Part of the national or regional workforce (usually unskilled) which has no stable employment but which moves around both in terms of job category and geographical location on a short-term basis.

Floating Labour. Workers who change their jobs and/or job locations from time to time.

Floor Trader. Also, competitive trader; registered trader. A member of a stock exchange who trades for his or her own account rather than for customers.

Floorwalker. Store security officer, usually mixing with customers and attempting to spot shoplifters.

Flow Line Production. Method of organizing work used mostly in mass production but also sometimes in batch production. Successive operations on a product are carried out in such a way that work flows in a single direction through the factory or workshop, the product being passed from operator to operator or form section to section for further work on it.

Flow Production (continuous production). Continuous production in which raw materials are fed in at one end of the process and finished products emerge at the other having passed through in an uninterrupted flow through the process.

Flyback Timing. A method of timing a job using a stopwatch in time study in which the hands of the stopwatch are returned to zero at the end of each element of the job. (Also called 'snapback timing'.)

Flying Pickets. Groups of individuals which can at short notice be sent to any location to picket a place of work. Normally used to reinforce local pickets so as to bring more pressure to bear on the management.

F.O.B. Abbreviation for free on board, a price quotation indicating that the seller is responsible for all costs of a shipment of goods, including responsibility for damage or loss, up to a certain named point.

Focal Point Interviewing. Focusing interviews upon certain point or theme in whatever is being researched, *e.g.*, TV commercial, so that respondent becomes more closely involved in a situation in which his responses can be recorded.

Focused Interview. Somewhat misleading term, used particularly in market research, for an interview in which the interviewer seeks to obtain answers to particular questions without specifically asking them.

Folder Technique. Field research technique, used in copy-testing or pre-testing press features, in which respondents are shown alternative advertisements, usually presented in folder containing plastic sleeves.

Folk Media. Traditional media as found in rural areas of developing countries, or used for PR purposes in which areas because it is either traditional or is a means of communicating with people whatever their tribal languages or dialects. Includes folk or village theatre, mime and puppet shows.

Follow Up. Sales contact, telephone call or letter sometimes but not always as a result of an expression of interest by a prospect and usually after his/her receipt of an initial promotional piece, *e.g.*, a direct mail shot.

Fonts. Boxes which rest on bars and from which cans and bottles of beer are dispened.

Food Stamp Program. A program of public assistance to low-income families, which through state and local welfare agencies provides food coupons for needy persons.

Forced Saving. The prevention of spending by individuals, which compels them to save more than they ordinarily would. It may occur through a shortage of consumer goods (as in wartime), or as the by product of a fiscal policy to curb inflation through levying higher taxes, thus limiting consumption.

Forecasting. Predicting future business conditions and the state of the economy on the basis of various statistics describing past and current conditions, particularly those selected as indicators.

Foreigners. Private work undertaken by artisans for the customers of their employers with or without the employer's approval or knowledge.

Foreign Trade Leakage. It means that employment at home increases less than it would if all spending were for products produced within the domestic economy.

Foreman. In manufacturing, construction, and similar industries, a person in direct change of production workers, generally considered a member of middle management.

Foreshift. The morning shift in a three-shift system.

Forefeitures. Funds relinquished by a terminating employee in a qualified profit-sharing or thrift plan.

Forgery. The alternation or false writing of an instrument with the intent of deceiving and injuring another person; for example, signing someone's name to a check without his or her consent.

Formal Agreement. Express undertakings between the various business unit concerning trade conditions or prices, insofar as they do not mean any collective control of the quantity of output to be marketed.

Form Letter. A word processing term for a letter sent to different people with only the name and address and some other particulars changed to give it the appearance of being personally written. The computer automatically inserts a new name and address etc. each time the letter is printed. It is often used in conjunction with a Mail Merge facility.

Formula Pension. The category of pension covering most salaried employees, under which a rate formula is applied to individual earnings to calculate the employee's pension.

Forward Contract. A contract for the delivery of goods at a specified future date (an 'outright' forward contract) or at a date to be chosen by either the buyer or the seller within specified limits (an option' forward contract).

Forward Integration. Where the manufacturer or main supplier of a product or service acquires or takes over certain customer or retail outlets in an endeavour to secure a further part of the market for the product or service.

Foundation. A non-profit organization set up for charitable or other benevolent purposes, such as supporting scientific research, artistic endeavour, educational institutions, etc.

Four-day Week. An arrangement under which employees in an organization work for only four days each week but work the same number of hours that were previosly spread over five days. Also known as 'four-day, forty-hour week' because the number of hours worked is commonly 40 a week.

Four P's. Shorthand way of indicating the principle factors to be included in the marketing mix, *i.e.* product, price, place and promotion.

Fractional (or Fragment) Bargaining. Form of collective bargaining on behalf of a minority of employees or to deal with a particular grievance.

Fragmentation. More sophisticated market segmentation when segments are sub-segmented in a highly competitive market and news source of sales are sought.

Franchise. A right, usually an exclusive right, granted by a government to an individual or firm, to perform some service or activity of a public nature.

Franchising. Manufacturer's products, or to operate a service in which thee manufacturer has a monopoly of equipment or supplies, *e.g.*, washing machines and launderettes.

Franco. 'Franco' price covers the price of goods delivered free of any charge to a specified destination.

Franco Domicile. Price including free delivery to customer's address.

Freedom of Association. Right of workers to organize themselves in a trade union or similar representative body.

Free Enterprise. Production of goods and provision of services only by private individuals (and corporations owned by private individuals) for profit in which individual producers act according to their own judgment and not under the direction or influence of government (thus the government provides no subsidies or price controls).

Free Gifts. Promotional gifts:

(1) Mail-in: inviting prospective customers to send for a gift.

(2) On-pack: gift attached to product at point of sale.

(3) On-pack offer: inviting purchasers to send for gifts, usually with evidence of a minimum purchase.

Free Interview. Harry Henry's name for depth interview.

Freelance. A person who works on an independent basis, taking on assignments from one or more employers.

Free Market. The term may be used in relation to the purchase and sale of any commodity where there is complete freedom to deal.

Freight Absorption. The practice of a seller's paying part or all of the freight charges for goods sold.

Freight Prepaid. This expression means the seller will pay transportation charges to the carrier and the buyer will remit the full amount of the invoice without deduction for freight charges.

Frustration. In human behaviour, the blocking or thwarting of goal attainment, defined in terms of the condition of the individual rather than in terms of the external environment. Frustration may take different forms of expression, including aggression against unrelated persons or objects.

F-test. A statistical test used to decide whether two samples with different sample variances may be presumed to come from normal populations with the same population variance. The F distribution is used for the test.

Fudge. Mistake.

Fulfilment House. Specialist firm which handles response to mailing, sales promotion offers, direct response marketing sales and other postal responses to advertising.

Full-capacity Growth. The 'required' rate of growth to avoid long-run disequilibrium and umployment and to insure the full capacity use of a growing capital stock.

Full-cost Model. Method of determining price by calculating direct costs, adding percentages for average expected overheads and profits.

Full Employment. A situation in which all those persons who are seeking work in a community are able to find suitable work fairly readily, with the consequence that a very high proportion of the working population is actually in work at any one time.

Full Liability. A liability of a sole person or company, not shared with others.

Full-line Strategy. Synonym for broad-line strategy.

Full-service. Describing a bank, wholesaler, or other enterprise that provides all of the services traditionally associated with line of business.

Full Service Agency. Advertising agency offering clients a wide range of activities and expertise over and above the normal creative and/or media facilities.

Function. A group of related activities that contribute to the performance of work by an organization (such as, the purchasing function', *i.e.*, all activities related to purchasing materials for use by an organization). Also the part of an organization that performs such a group of activities.

Functional Budget. Method of budgeting where funds are allocated according to distinct functions within a business, *e.g.* marketing, production, finance, administration.

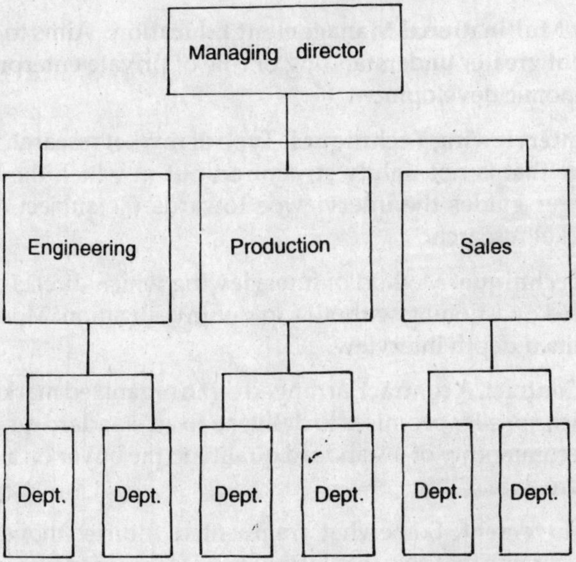

Functional Organization. An organization structure based on dividing tasks to be done into a number of discrete functional areas-for example, research and development, marketing, production, quality control etc.—and giving these areas autonomy under a line manager.

Functional Organization. Organization into departments according to function.

Fund. (1) To provide for a financial obligation by borrowing money for a specific period. (2) To provide for a future financial obligation by setting aside money and lending it to earn interest; to create a sinking fund.

Funds—flow Analysis. Analysis of the flow of purchasing power into and out of an organization. Inward flows include sales revenue, sales of fixed assets and investments, and issues of debentures, loans and shares.

Funds-flow Statement. A summery of the way in which the net current assets of a firm have changed over a period. (Also called a statement of source and application of funds').

Fund for Multinational Management Education. Aims to bring about greater understanding of role of private enterprise in economic development.

Funnel Interviewing Techniques. Type of market research interview that is not tightly structured but in which the interviewer guides the interviewee towards the subject of the market research.

Funnel Technique. Method of interviewing which directs open-ended questioning without topic of investigation. More disciplined depth interview.

Futures Contract. A contract, arranged on an organized market, by which as seller promises to deliver a fixed standard quantity of a commodity of a standard quality to the buyer on a fixed future date.

Future Movement. Somewhat fragmented futurist movement recognizing that new intellectual approaches are necessary to face up to dramatic changes in future development.

G

G77. Group of 77.

Gain-sharing. Operation of a premium bonus scheme in which the incentive payment unit per of time saved decreases as the time saved increases. It is argued that gains from producing at more than the standard rate of performance should be shared between the worker and his employer.

Galloping Inflation. Slow price increase are one thing. But when each increase in price becomes the signal for an increase in wages and costs, which again sends prices up still futher, we may be in the midst of a malignant, galloping hyper inflation.

Galvanometric Response. Change in skin conductivity due to change in moisture content (perspiration); measurement by current flow as indicated on a galvanometer. Such change may have a correlation with psychological stimuli (*e.g.*, fear or other emotion) and arguably may provide a measure of a respondent's reaction to an advertisement.

Gaming, Scientific. Application of business game and other simulation and decision-making techniques, usually with computer assistance, in industry, commerce, government, public service, etc.

Gantt Chart. A pictorial method for displaying and monitoring a process, project, or production schedule so as to evaluate performance against a timetable. Gantt charts, if properly maintained, can serve as valuable tools for planning, scheduling, and controlling the various aspects of a production situation.

Gap Analysis. Methodical tabulation of all known 'consumer wants' of a particular product category, together with a crosslisting of the features of existing products which satisfy those wants. Such a chart shows up any gaps which exist and thus provides a pointer as to where new products might find an unfulfilled demand.

Garibi Hatao. Hindi expression meaning 'banish poverty'. It is an objective of Indian planning. It was coined by (late) Mrs. Indira Gandhi, the former prime minister of India. The phrase having been internationalised with its adoption by the U.N.O. has freely entered into the English language.

Gatekeeper. An individual in an organization who acts as an informal communication focus, collecting inormation from a variety of sources external to the company on passing it on to individuals within the company to whom it will be relevant.

GATT. General Agreement on Tariff and Trade International agreement signed in 1947 by numerous countries to liberalize trade by the reduction and removal of tariff barriers and quota restrictions. The agreement has no legal force but has had considerable influence in postwar developments.

Gazumping. Backing out of a proposed sale of property because another buyer has offered more for it.

Geared Incentive Scheme. Payment-by-results scheme in which incentive payments go up in stages rather than directly in proportion to output.

Gearing. The gearing of a company is the relationships of its total debt, i.e. loan stocks, debentures, bank borowings, etc., to the total equity, *i.e.* issued capital plus reserves.

General Agreements on Tariffs and Trade (GATT). An international commercial agreement signed in 1947 by the

United States and many other countries for the purpose of achieving four basic long-range objectves: (1) non-discrimination in trade through adherence to unconditional most-favoured-nation treatment, (2) reduction of tariffs by negotiations, (3) elimination of import quotas (with some exceptions), and (4) resolution of economic differences through consultation.

General Analysis. General or total analysis as distinguised from partial analysis, is the analysis of the economy as a whole.

General Aptitude Test Battery (GATB) (US). Battery of 12 aptitude tests, presenting results in the form of a profile to be measured against standard profiles of 22 vocational groups. Used widely by occupational psychologists in vocational guidance.

General Clerical Test. Three-part psychological test developed in the USA and measuring verbal, numerical and clerical skills. The test takes about 30 minutes.

General Contractor. A person or firm whose contracts include several types of skilled work in the construction field.

General Depression. A period of situation in which unused resources and employment are general.

General Equilibrium Analysis (Theory). When all prices are viewed as dependent upon one another, the theory of prices become general equilibrium theory.

General Expense. An administrative expense, not identified with a specific process, product, or service generated by the operation of the facility. Also known as burden.

General Index of Retail Prices. An index number computed monthly by the Government and showing changes in the cost of purchasing standard quantities of a wide range of goods and services that are bought by household.

Extensive sampling is undertaken by the Department to obtain prices each month. The index number is a Laspeyres index; the quantities of each item used in calculating it are determined from the Family Expenditure Survey.

General Inflation. The inflation that accompanies full employment of all other resources.

General Learning Ability Test. Term used particularly in the USA in psychological testing for a wide-ranging intelligence test (rather than achievement test). It may be a combination of tests forming a test battery.

General Legacy. A general legacy should be distinguished from a specific legacy and a demonstrative legacy. A general legacy is a gift by will out of the personal estate of the testator but is not necessarily and particular part of the estate. General legacies are usually, but not necessarily, pecuniary legacies.

General Management

1. The work performed by general managers.

2. The general managers within an organization.

General Manager. A manager who determines and influences the broad objectives of a whole organization, determines the resources to be made available for attaining those objectives and has significant responsibilities in more than one major field of activity (usually working through managers who specialize insingle fields of activity). A general manager is especially concerned with the formulation and interpretation of policy and with long-term planning.

General Meeting. A meeting which may be attended by all the members of an association and which gives them some opportunity to control the association's affairs.

General Partner. An active member of a partnership who has unlimited liability for the actions of the partners.

General Planning. Planning may be general as well as detailed. General planning concerns itself with major issues only. It lays down only the broad outlines of future development.

General Price Level. The average of the prices of all commodities and services and property rights currently bought and sold.

General Store. A type of retailing institution that usually sells a limited selection of a wide range of goods.

General Strike. A strike called by all or most of the workers in all or most industries simultaneously. It may involve a city or an entire country. Its purpose usually is not so much one of gaining specific concessions as it is to put political pressure on a government or to demonstrate the unity of the labour movement.

General Union. Trade union whose membership is drawn from all kinds of workers as opposed to the more specialized membership of, for example, a craft union.

Generic Brands. Popular products produced in fairly plain and economically produced packages, *e.g.*, 'thrift packs', and sold in large retail organizations.

Generic Competitive Strategy. Broad company strategies identified by Michael Porter which affect the success of the business in terms of overall cost leadership, focus and market differentiation. He identifies three generic strategies-differentiated, undifferentiated and concentrated.

Generic Term. In marketing, applied to brand name which have come to be adopted as the general descriptive term for a product, often as the result of extensive promotion, *e.g.*, Hoover, Biro. Linoleum.

Gentlemen's Agreement. In business and industry, an informal agreement secured by the word of the parties involved rather than by a written contract.

Geographic Market Concentration. Some industries have classical geographic concentrations while other industries are dispersed according to resources, *e.g.*, paper-making and water. Certain other industries may be located in seaport or airport areas, or close to urban markets.

Geographic Pricing. Occurs when the price for the same product or service varies according to the class of store, retailer or shopping area, whether within one town, or from one part of the country to another, or in different countries. *e.g.* motor-cars.

German Inflation. The German inflation had a very bad reputation. Prices rose with staggering rapidity, until at one time they were one million times the prewar level. This was inflation without recovery with a vergeance. Overnight, every form of property and income lost its real value. Hundreds of thousands of families were ruined. It wiped out the German middle class and made the Nazi revolution possible.

Gestalt Psychology. School of psychology particularly associated with Max Wertheimer is 1912, and basd on promise that human beings perceive things in patterns or wholes. A furnished room is seen, not individual bits of furniture. Similar or associated objects are mentally grouped.

Gestation Period. Length of time which elapse between an initial inquiry for a product and the placing of an order. More often applied to capital goods where it can amount to serveral years.

Ghosting

(1) Providing an inner view of a package or product by cutting away part of the exterior.

(2) Shadow on television film.

Ghost Writer. Journalist who writes speeches, articles or books which are credited to another who has commissioned them.

Giffen Goods. Giffen good is a special case of inferior good and is named after Sir Robert Giffen (1837-1910) who in the 19th cenuary pointed out: "a rise in the price of bread makes so large a drain on the resources of the poor labouring families they consume more and less of it".

Giffen good is an inferior good, but every inferior good cannt be a Giffen good.

Giffen's Paradox. A situation in which consumers by less of the goods when its price falls and more of the good if its price rises.

Gift. A class of public revenue. Voluntary contribution from non-governmental donor generally for specified purpose.

Gift Deed. An instrument that transfers the title to real estate for which the consideration is love and affection, rather than material consideration.

Gifts Inter Vivos. Gifts between living persons. An inter vivos gift is a gift that takes effect in the lifetime of the donor.

Gift Voucher. Special incentive to purchase, usually involving money-off against purchase of qualifying brand or providing an opportunity for a special purchase.

Giles-archer Lantern Tests. Form of colour vision test in which the subject is presented with a number of lights of different colours and different degrees of brightness.

Giri Approach. The plea of V.V. Giri that attempts are increasingly to be made to settle all industrial disputes by mutual negotiations between the employers and the employees failing which conciliation officers are to be approached instead of compulsory adjudication, is referred to as Giri approach.

Gnatt Chart. A chart widely used for monitoring the progress in relation to the target and time horizon in industry for production planning and plant utilization.

Goal Obsession. Term used in T-group training for too great concern with goals and too little concern with existing behaviour patterns.

Goal-orientated Research. Research of practical application as distinct from research for its own sake.

Goldbricking. Term used particularly in the early days of payment by-result schemes where workers find piece work rates tight and hold back their effort, giving up any hope of achieving more than day rate.

Golden Rule Fallacy. Fallacious view in some T-group training that there is a right way for all people to interact in all situations.

Golden Handcuffs. A payment made to an employee as an inducement to him to remain with organization because of his value to it.

Golden Handshake. Colloquial term for severance pay given to a senior executive on termination of his contract of employment or cutting short of his contract of service.

Golden Hello. A payment made to induce a prospective employee to join a firm.

Golden Parachute. A bonus payment which directors of a firm agree to pay themselves in the event of losing a take-over battle. The payment is so-called because one likely consequence of such a battle would be that they would be made redundant.

Go No-go Gage or Go Not-go Gage. In manufacturing, a type of limit gage utilized to measure the dimensions of a mechnical part to determine whether or not the part is within allowable limits.

Good. Material or physical objects, either natural or manmade, used to satisfy human needs or desires.

Good-faith Bargaining. Criteria for good-faith bargaining in labour-management disputes. They require that all parties in a collective bargaining situation genuinely try to achieve agreement and develop a system of communication that will prevent disputes or solve them where they already exist.

Goods in Consignment. An arrangement whereby an agent takes possession of goods but no title to them.

Goods Received Note. A document issued by a firm on receipt of a delivery which sets out what goods and how many items have been delivered.

Goods Returned Note. A document issued by a firm on receipt of goods which is originally supplied and which have been returned because of faults, wrong type or quantity etc.

Goodwill. One of the intangible values of a business beyond its net worth. Goodwill may include such assets as general reputation, brand name recognition, technical know-how, location, and the historic ability of the company to retain its accounts on the basis, for example, of services.

Goon. Slang for a person hired to break up meetings, damage property, and otherwise threaten or terrorize individuals or groups.

Go-slow Tactics. Also called "working to rule" it is an alternative to the strike, in which the labourers work more slowly than usual.

Government Expenditures. Government purchases of goods and services, transfer payments, and net government interest.

Grade Creep. Tendency to re-grade or reclassify employees as surreptitious method of allowing increases in pay.

Graded Hourly Rates. A form of payment system where employees are paid according to their Merit Ratings.

Grapeine. Informtion based on rumour and hearsay, as 'herd on the grapevine', the information becoming more and more distorted as it is passed from one to another. Often the cause of industrial strife, provoked by lack of information from management.

Gratuity. Sometimes known as a lump-sum, it is an amount payable under some pension schemes at the time when the pension is due to commence. It is not liable to income tax.

Gravity Model. Analytical technique employing multiple regression techniques and used to predict distribution of, say, consumer's expenditure between individual stores or competing shopping centres.

Gravy Jobs. Easy piece work jobs or those with loose rates. May also be known as fat work. Jobs on which it is difficult to earn bonus may be known as learn work or stinkers.

Gray Collar. Describing workers whose jobs lie midway between blue-collar and white-collar employment for jobs containing elements of each.

Gray Market. A term for transactions that are conducted outside the usual business channels but are not illegal.

Greenfield Site. A completely new industrial development in a new area, as opposed to being built within an existing facility. Because of the relative ease of escaping from traditional practices the term is sometimes extended to cover progressive union and personnel policies.

Gross Business Product. That part of gross national product produced by business activity.

Gross Fund. A term applied to charities and pension fund and any other funds which are exempt from tax, particularly income tax and capital gains tax.

Gross Profit Margin. Thee ratio of the gross profit acquired by a firm over a specified period from the sale of a specified product to its sales revenue for that product during the same period. (Usually expressed as a percentage).

Gross Profit Ratio. A ratio by which performance of a product or of its management may be measured; it is computed by the formula; gross profit divided by net sales.

Gross Reach. Total number of opportunities for people to see the advertisements contained in a schedule; the sum total of the readership of each publication multiplied by the total number of insertions.

Gross Returns on Net Assets. Gross Profits before payment of interest and depreciation earned from the employment of fixed assets expressed as a percentage of the cost of these assets.

Gross Revenue (ITV). Amount of advertising expenditure which would be spent on television advertising if all of the commercials transmitted were costed at the maximum published rate less any advanced booking discount for the time segment in which they appeared.

Group Incentive Payment. Incentive payment that is related to the value of quantity of work done by a group of workers within a factory or other production unit.

Group Interview. A selection interview at which two or more applicants for a job are interviewed simultaneously-often, conducted as an informal conversation.

Group Problem-solving. Or group decision making. Process in which a manager presents a problem to a group of subordinates in order to elicit a solution by discussion with and between them.

Group Project Training. Project training in which the projects are tackled by students in groups rather than individually.

Group Psychology. People do not just get together; they get together for a purpose.

Group Selection. Selection of perons for employment by observing a group of candidates performing an excercise in; for example, problem-solving.

Group Selection Techniques. Where, in personnel selection, a number of candidates for a vacancy are interviewed or assessed together, and judged partly on their relations with each other.

Group Technology. Arranging batch production so that some of the economies of continuous production can be obtained. Groups of items are identified that require similar operations and the machines for these are grouped together. (Also known as 'group production').

Group Training. Form of group dynamics training in which the trainees meet in small groups and each trainee studies the behaviour and group processes that take place in his own group.

Group Training Methods. Group rather than individual methods of training, including brainstorming, critical incident technique, case histories, case studies, expert witness, instrumented laboratory training, lectures, T-group training, etc.

Group Training Scheme. An arrangement whereby two or more firms have common facilities for training.

Group Working. Organizing of workers to increase the degree of autonomy and responsibility carried by the worker through the delegation of responsibilities to the work group.

Guaranted-wage Plan. That part of a labour contract in which employes are guaranteed either employment or a stated amount of wages during a specific time period.

Guaranted Working Week. An arrangement negotiated between employeers and trade unions guaranteeing workers that they will be paid as for a full working week (usually exclusive of bonuses and other premium payments) even if there is insufficient work for a full week.

Guest Worker. Foreign national who is permitted to enter a country to work, but not settle there with his family.

Guide-book Racket. Obtaining advertisements for guide-books of dubious merit and doubtful circulation, contracts often running for two or more years without change of copy.

Guide-chart Profile Method. Type of job evaluation technique developed in the UK and using three factors: know-how, problem-solving and accountability in the context of a particular salary scale.

Guild Socialism. A moderate form of socialism that advocated social ownership of the means of production but management of industrial activity by the workers themselves, who were to be organized into guilds modeled after the medieval craft guilds.

H

Hackneyed. Words or expressions which are banal or over-used: perhaps the most familiar in marketing is 'new'.

Haggle. Process of discussional bargaining, prior to the negotiating of prices or terms of agreement.

Haggling. Colloquial expression for the process of bargaining or negotiating the price of a sale or purchase. The buyer attempts to buy at as low a price as possible, while the seller attempts to sell at as high a price as possible.

Hallmarks. The impressed stamps on gold, solver and platinum under the authority of the Goldsmiths Company and the various assay offices.

Hallmarking is of particular relevance to silver, partly because silver has traditionally been in more common use than gold, and also because of the facility for converting silver articles into coinage.

Hall Test. Passers-by are asked to test a product and answer questions, the test being conducted in a town hall or other public room. Gives quick results. Method also used *(e.g.,* by Gallup) to evaluate TV commercials, press advertisements, posters and sales literature.

Halo Effect. A tendency toward distortion in an appraisal or performance rating on an individual caused by the reaction of the person doing the appraisal or conducting the interview. A high rating on one factor tends to result in a high rating on all other factors.

Halsey Bonus System. A form of Payment-by-results scheme which includes a bonus element for improving on-target performance. However, the bonus payable is not related to the degree to which performance is exceeded, as with a conventional incentive bonus scheme.

Halsey Constant Sharing Scheme (or Halsey sharing plan or Halsey System). A premium bonus scheme in which time saved is paid for at half the basic time rate. Named after a Canadian mechnical engineer, Fredreick Arthur Halsey (1856-1935).

Handbill. Form of printed advertising delivered personally into the hands of likely prospects.

Handicraft System. The practice of pursuing a craft or trade in a small shop largely by hand or with only simple machinery.

Handout. Inexpensive leaflet for free distribution at exhibitions or for promotional purposes, especially at point-of-sale.

Hand-over Pay. (or Allowance). Payment made to shift workers with particular responsibilities for handing over to, or coupling up with, workers on the next shift.

Hard-boiled, Hard-headed. Buyers, often with long experience, who habitually challenge or reject any new approach, organization, product or opportunity; such behaviour may be natural to the person or assumed in an effort to contain aggressive selling practices. Salesmen must be trained to anticipate and overcome sales resistance of this kind.

Hard Copy. Text or information in a form which can be read by the human eye, as opposed to micros copy or information stored on disc, tape or visual display unit.

Hard Core Control. Small group of directors or senior executives who effectively lead and direct a company usually in long term strategic issues.

Hard-core Unemployed. People who are unemployed because they lack the education or skills required by a complex economy.

Hard Core Unemployment. Another name for structural unemployment.

Hard Goods

1. Same as durable goods;
2. Also, hard-ware. Consumer durable goods made principally form metal, such as most electrical appliances, cutlery and tools.

Hard News. News of value to general news columns of the press as distinct product news which may interest feature writers specializing in say, gardening, beauty, motoring, fashion, food and so on, or trade magazines which report new product news.

Hard Sales Promotion

1. Sales promotion directly concerned with increasing the consumption of a product or service, for example through reduced price offers or increased packet size. Hard sales promotion is usually higher cost but more effective than soft sales promotion such as competitions and personality promotions.
2. Aggressive selling and marketing methods.

Hard Sell. Punchy, persuasive, high-pressure advertising employing five point formula of attraction, attention, desire, conviction and action. Opposite to soft sell. -

Harmonization. Achievement of common international conventions and regulations as with postal, civil aviation, customs and other operations.

Harmony. Essence of an advertisement or commercial reaching the desired theme or objective.

Harmony Doctrine. The thesis that the interest of the community is simply the sum of the interests of the members who compose it; each man, it left alone, will seek to maximize his own wealth; therefore, all men,if unimpeded will maximize aggregate wealth. Smith applying the doctrine argued that the general welfare is best promoted by removing all restrictions on imports and exports.

Harvard Case Method. Teaching of management subjets etc., through the presentation of a succession of case histories and case studies, thus, in effect, providing concentrated practical experience in the classroom. Developed by the Harvard Business School (USA).

Hawthorne Studies. Begun in 1924 at the Chicago Hawthorne Works of the Western Electric Company—with the participation of Harvard University researchers-and designed to determine the effects of lighting on worker productivity. Two groups of workers were selected for comparison and control. Their performance of both groups improved with each increase or decrease in lighting. It became evident that the unusual attention being given to their activities, their knowledge of being tested, their social affiliation as a group, and their interest in the results had a greater effect on their performance than did the environmental conditions. This controlled experiment is considered by many to be the beginning of behavioural science as a profession. The Hawthorne studies were concluded in 1932.

Hay Clerical Battery. Three-part psychological test developed in the USA and covering, in four minutes each, number perception, name finding, and series of numbers.

Headhunter. Recruitment agency which specializes in pinpointing very precisely just those few people known to be suitable for a certain vacancy, and then making personal contact to encourage their interest.

A procedure which contrasts with the more commonplace method of placing recruitment advertisements which will probably attract more responses but may be missed by the most suitable people for the job.

Head-on Position. Outdoor advertising position directly facing traffic.

Heavy Users. Consumers or customers whose purchases of a product are larger than average.

Hedging. A method by which wholesale dealers in basic raw materials and food-stuffs or manufacturers of certain products can transfer risks of adverse price fluctuations to professional speculators in the commodity exchange.

Heir. The heir or heir-at-law was the person entitled, by law, to the real property of a deceased person who left no will.

Henrigram. Graphical representation devised by Harry Henry to show that a minority are responsible for a majority of actions or consequences, 'small proportion of people.....responsible for......more than proportionate share of consumption'.

Heroic Theory. There are essentially two different theories of the process of invention: the heroic theory and the systematic theory.

According to the heroic theory, the credit for a particular invention belongs completely or mainly to one individual who has the unique inspiraion. Thus the invention of the spinning mule is attributed to Crompton, of steam engine to Watt and so forth.

Heroic invention also called spontaneous invention can be explained only in terms of chance happenings, the curiosity of an individual inventor or what Taussig called the "instinct of contrivance."

Herzberg's Theory. Findings of research by Frederick Herzberg in US in late 1950s and early 1960s on motivation at work. His findings lead to general theory that two sets of complementary factors can be distinguished. First, the 'motivators' or 'satisfiers' which create job interest and encourage the application of willing effort to job tasks. Second, the 'dissatisfiers' or 'hygiene' (also known as maintenance) factors associated with the environment in which the work is carried out. Although these hygiene factors do not create job interest, if they reach an acceptable level they prevent frustration and help individuals to justify their 'putting up' with work, *e.g.* good working conditions, status, job security, 'high'pay, etc. Both types of factors need to be satisfied ideally.

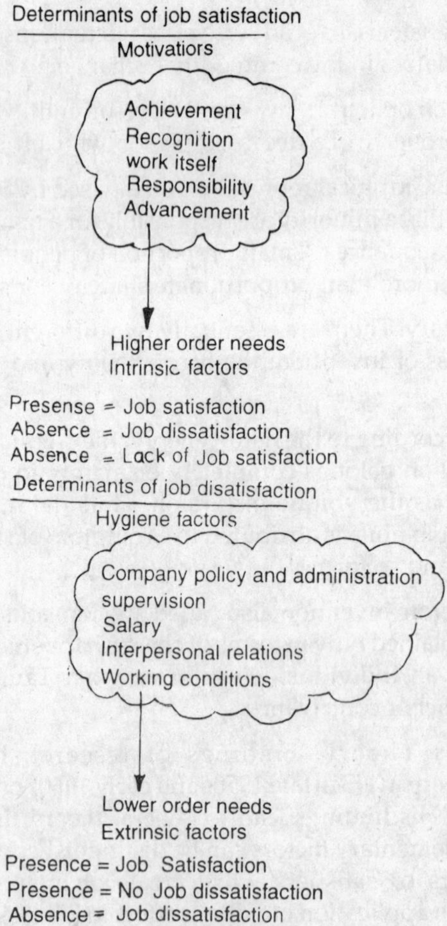

Herzberg's two factor theory

Heuristic. An adjective used to describe an exploratory method of tackling a problem, in which the solution is discovered by evaluations of the progress made towards the final result, *e.g.* guided trial and error. Contrast with alogrithm.

Heuristic Method. Training approach.

Heuristic Method Programming. Means of discovering best possible solution to a problem obtaining estimations of the correct answer, through analogies, and other forms of search, without exhaustive study of all possibilities. Means of reducing by adopting rule of thumb assumptions. Computer can be employed in this way.

Heuristic Models. Use of mathematical modelling technique that takes into account the fruits of practical experience of actually getting the work etc. in question done.

Hindden Agenda. The matters that are important to an individual at a meeting (*e.g.* of a committee) but which he cannot discuss or deal with, either because the matters are not on a formal agenda for the meeting or because they are personal emotional matters relating to the meeting (*e.g.* intense dislike of another member of a committee).

Hindden Decision. Any decision taken automatically and without question; for example, renewing a contract when due without reviewing its continued usefulness.

High Frequency Work Sampling. Variation on work sampling in which the time/output relationships for a group of workers are calculated on the basis of observations by work study officers and, particularly in the case of machine times, records kept by the workers themselves.

High Pressure Selling. Aggressive selling activity to achieve sales revenue irrespective of a consumer's real need or resources.

High Street Redemption Schemes. Redemption of cash vouchers at shops which has proved more successful than when customers are expected to claim cash by post. Saves customer's postage a promoter's handling and mailing charges.

Hind Mazdoor Sabha. (*Economics of labour). One of the major trade unions of India. Founded in 1948, it stands for the establishment of a democratic socialist society.

Hinterland. Area external to store or shopping centre from which custom is drawn.

Hire Purchase. The equivalent of instalment buying. The buyer pays an initial deposit, takes possession of the goods or receives the benefits of the services, and then makes regular payments the cover the reminder of the purchase price plus interest or carrying charges. The buyer does not take title to the goods until the last periodic payment or instalment is paid in full.

Histogram. In statistical analysis, a graphic representation of a frequency distribution by means of a vertical bar graph with no space between the bars. The class boundaries are of equal size and are depicted on the horizontal axis, while the frequencies are depicted on the vertical axis. Thus each bar is equal in width to all others; height varies in accordance with the reference data. It is also known as column diagram or bar chart.

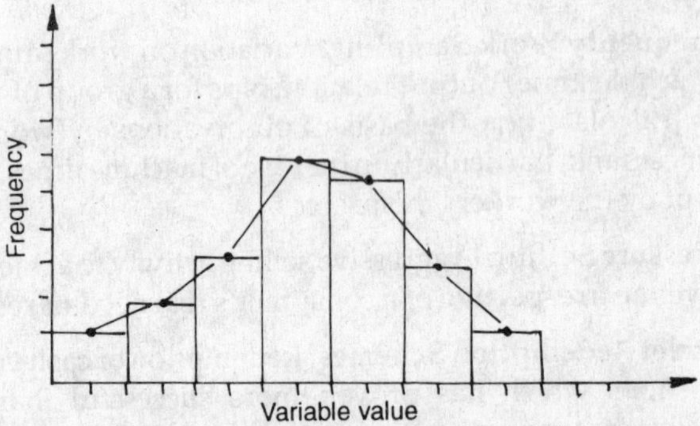

Historical Method. Spending same amount on advertising as in the past but with adjustments to meet changing costs of different needs.

Hoarding Site. Parcel of land or a building used for posters.

Hobbesian Model. Organizational factors model showing balance between advantages to consumer and manufacturer.

Hold-back Pay. Wages with held by an employer for the purpose of calculating payroll periods.

Holding Company. A company controlling one or more other companies by virtue of stock ownership; a corporation that owns the majority of stock or securities of one or more other corporations for purposes of control rather than of investment.

Holding Out. Pretending that a partner who has in fact left a partnership is still a member of it and obtaining credit on the strength of his name.

Hold Order. In manufacturing, a written order directing that certain operations or work activities be interrupted or cancelled, pending a change in design or material.

Home Audit. Market research for waht is normally a combination of dustbin check and pantry check to obtain data on households' choice and volume of consumption of consumer goods.

Hosting. Continental system of selling editorial space.

"Hot Cargo" Agreement. A form of secondary boycott whereby an employer agrees not to handle, use, sell, or transport the products of another employer to whose labour policies a union objects.

Hot Shop. Creative studio which puts high value on novelty and topicality in the preparation of its advetising copy and designs.

Hot Shop Agency. Opposite to a modern service agency. Small executive team buying creative and other services and required and so keeping down overheads while not being inhibited by the limitations of regular staff.

Hour-for-hour Pian. Payment-by-results system in which pay is directly related to the achievement of standard performance.

Hours of Work. The time during which an employee should be doing his job.

House Account. Significant customer, usually serviced at management level; because of the volume of business transacted, prices are keen and leave little or no opportunity for the payment of commission on sales.

House Agency. An advertising agency wholly owned and operated by a large business organization to which it provides services which are, however, not necessarily exclusive to that organization.

Household Goods Warehouse. A warehouse that specializes in storing household articles and furniture.

House Journal. A regular publication, in the form of a newspaper or magazine, that is distributed to all employees of an organization and contains information of common interest.

House Journal (or Magazine). Published by an industrial or commercial organization or company for the information of its own employees as part of personnel policy, and/or for the information of its customers as part of marketing policy.

House Mark. A brand used by a firm or by group of firms on all products.

House Organ. Also, company magazine. A periodical issued by a business enterprise either for its own employees or for its customers, distributors, stock-holders, or other outsiders with whom it has regular dealings.

House Style. The image which a company presents of itself in written material in its dealings both internally and externally. House style may be formally specified to cover the way in which news and other information is sritten up and published.

House-to-house. Calling direct on potential consumers and users at their own homes for purposes of distributing or collecting information, leaving samples or direct selling.

House-to house Distribution. Door-to-door distribution or direct advertising. Hand delivery of one or more samples or promotional items. Maildrop.

Housewife Time. On radio, the time between the morning and afternoon Drive times.

Hundi. An indigenous bill of exchange in India.

Hurdle Rate. A figure, set by the management of a firm, for the minimum internal rate of return that an investment project must have if it is to be accepted.

Hygiene Factor. An aspect of a job that can contribute to the dissatisfaction but not the satisfaction of the job holder according to the motivation-hygiene theory. (Also known as a 'maintenance factor'.)

Hyper Employment. An alternative term for overall employment. It means that situation in which the demand for labour greatly exceeds supply. This situation generally arises during inflation.

Hyper-inflation. The condition when all the equilibrating effect of inflation is lost and the value of the monetary unit sinks almost to zero.

Hyper market. Larger self-service unit with minimum sales area of 2500 square metres offering an assortment of food and non food merchandise at popular prices; often provides extensive parking facilities and associated with out-of-town shopping; often called superstores but to be distfinguished from discount houses.

Hyping. Promotional activity. Usually used with derogatory implication that claims are being made that will not be fulfilled. (Probably derived from 'hyperbole').

Hypothecation. The pledging of property as collateral for a loan, the lender is not given title to the property but is given the right to sell it in case of default.

Hypothesis Testing. Determining the correctness of assumed parameters, usually by sampling techniques.

I

IAA. International Advertising Association.

IBA (India). Indian-Bank's Association.

IBM. International Black Market. Term used in West Africa, *e.g.* number of Ghanaian cedi to the pound sterling.

Iceberg Principle. Psychological concept suggesting human personality is similar in appearance to that of an iceberg, with innate desires hidden deep down under the surface. Advertisers recognize that influencing people to move in any given direction frequently demands an appeal to their less apparent desires.

Iconic Models. Laboratory simulations of real-life situations, particularly in engineering. These are models that look like the systems they represent.

ICTFE. Indian Council of Trade Fairs and Enhibitions.

IDBI. Industrial Development Bank of India.

Idem Sonans. Latin for "the same sound." A doctrine holding that absolute accuracy in the spelling of names in legal documents is not required.

Idle. In cost accounting, equipment or labour that is not being used productively and hence represents a loss to the firm.

Idle Capacity. In manufacturing, unused productive potential, in reference to machinery, operations, or a factory's facilities that are not in use or are used only partially. Idle capacity may be expressed in units of output capability that could be realized through full usage, or in hours available for use.

Idle Poor. Habitually lazy people.

Idle Time

1. Part of attendance time when a worker has available work but does not do it.
2. Synonym for machine idle time.

Ignorance Effect. A situation where commodities may be mistaken for other commodities for many reasons *e.g.* deceptive lables as well as price.

IIM. Indian Institute of Management.

IIPA. Indian Institute of Public Administration.

Illustration. Any visual or pictorial representation such as a figure, chart, model, drawing, map, diagram, cartoon, photograph, or painting, especially when reproduced in print.

Illustrative Case Method. Form of motivational research, using group depth interview, to discover what motives different types of people. Group is told about a number of people who use the same product or service differently or more or less frequently. Then respondents are asked to fill in other characteristics of people who behave in these ways. What sort of person smokes five cigarettes daily compared with a chansmoker, and so on.

Imitative Entrepreneurship. It is characterised by readiness to adopt successful innovatioons inauguarated by innovating entreprenuers.

It is one of the four types of enterpreneurship, the other three being:

((i) Innovating entrepreneurship.

(ii) Fabian entrepreneurship, and,

(iii) Drone entrepreneurship.

Imperfect Competitor. Anyone who buys or sells a good in large enough quantities to be able to affect the price of that good.

Imperfect Market. The market is said to be imperfect when some buyers or sellers, or both are not aware of the offers being made by others.

Impingement Pay (or Money). Special payment to employees for working during what is normally holiday time. Originated in the printing industry.

Implied Contract. A contract that is inferred from actions of the parties who fulfill promises without the existencee of an expressed contract.

Import Licence. Items for which restrictions are imposed against their importation could be had only when the Government permitted the party to do so.

Import Prohibition. Prohibiting by law or allowing only under defined conditions thee importantion of certain commodities.

Import Quota

1. A system in which a fixed amount which may be imported cannot be exceeded.
2. The practice of disallowing the importation of a commodity after a limit which is arbitrarily fixed by the government during a given period.

Import Substitution. Efforts by countries with poor trade balances, especially developing countries, to reduce imports by encouraging home production.

Impoverished Style. A style of managerial leadership that exerts a minimum effort to get the required work done with the minimum of control considered to be appropriate to sustain organization membership.

Impression Cover. Number of insertions it takes to cover the required percentage of population actually seeing the advertisement or commercial.

Impulse Buying Goods. Phenomenon of self-service, items being displayed to induce extra, unplanned purchases.

Impulse Goods. Consumer goods that are normally bought by consumers without any previous planning (i.e. on impulse).

Impulse Purchase. One made without careful prior consideration, i.e. on the spur of the moment or even in contradiction to normal buying behaviour and sometimes without apparent rational or logical justification.

Inc. Abbreviation of Incorporated when the word is part of the name of a corporation.

Incentive Engineer. American term for a work study officer/ engineer or rate fixer responsible for setting payment-by-results targets.

Incentive Marketing. Marketing of products which companies may use as premium offers, gifts, prizes, or staff incentive awards. Some products may be specially created as incentives; others-like cameras—may be specially promoted to incentive market.

Incentive Payment. Part of an employee's reemuneration that is related (according to a known rule) to the degree to which he has achieved an objective desired by his employer (such as an increase in the quantity or quality of output or an improvement in timekeeping).

Incentive Payment System. A payment system of which incentive payment is a principal feature.

Incentive Schemes. Awards for ideas, increased productivity, record sales. Special organizations offer packages incentive schemes, particularly suitable for sales forces.

Incentive/Reusable Packs. Promotinal device offering attractiv containers available for some subsequent use by the consumer. Frequently encountered in food and drink products.

Income of a Person. The value of the goods and services which an individual can consume during a given period and still have the same amount of wealth (assets) at the end of the period as at the beginning.

Incomes Policy. A policy aimed at reducing inflation by limiting incrases in wages and prices, and therefore the income of workers and poducers. It may be carried out through various measures, ranging from very mild (such as suggestions that union wage demands and manufacturers' price increase be kept down; Guidelines), to moderate (through tax cuts and similar incentives to hold down prices), to very forceful (mandatoy price and wage controls).

In-company, In-house. Work handled inside the company's, not put out to an agent or consultant. House magazines, exhibitions and print may be internal responsibilities.

In-company, Training. Training for the employees of a company held on the company's own premises. May be put on by outside bodies such as consultants. Also known as in-plant training, in-farm training in-house training.

Incoterms. Terms for use in international trade contacts drawn up by the international Chamber of Commerce. Incoterms include c and f, cif, ex-works, fas, fob and for.

Incorporate

1. To form into a corporation.
2. To make one object or substance a part of anothor-*e.g.*, as pat of a mixture or as one of a number of components or as a mateial that is changed in form.

Incoterms. A set of intenational rules for the interpretation of the chief terms used in foreign trade contracts. The rules were drawn up by the International Chamber of Commerce.

Incremental Payment System. Giving pay increments arising from increased merit, age or service in accordance with a predetermined scale.

Indemnify. To promise to someone that if he should suffer loss as a result of some specified event then he will be reimbursed (but he cannot claim more than he loses).

Indemnity. The legal production or security whereby a person or an organization is obligated to make good a loss or damage another has suffered. The compensation for that loss or damage. Also, legal exemption incurred by one's actions.

Indemnity Fund. Used by an employers' association, to compensate member firms for losses incurred by adhering to association policy during industrial action.

Indent. A purchase order to an exporter or middleman to import certain goods within a specified time.

Independent Union. A labour union that is not affiliated with any federation of labour organizations. It may be national or international, and not limited to workers in any one firm.

Independent Worker. One who works on his own account and not for an employer.

Index. To arrange that the size of cash payments to be made in the future (*e.g.* payments of pension or of interest on a loan) should be in proportion to a specified index number (especially, a cost-of-living index).

Index Linking. Systematic adjustment of the value of transactions in line with changing prices, particularly in times of inflation.

Index Numbers. A statistical measure used by economists and business managers to gain an overall view of such areas as prices, volumes, and rates of change. Econometricians develop and use index numbers to establish a reference base for depicting growth or decline in a condition of micro-economic. An index number may be a ratio or other number derived from a series of observations and used as an indicator or measure of a condition or a phenomenon.

Indian Council of Trade Fairs and Exhibitions (ICTFE). Government body responsible for organising trade fairs and exhibitions to promote the trading of industrial products of India. Address: Jhansi Castle. Cooperage Road. Bombay-400039.

Indian Institute of Management (IIM). Major qualifying body in the area of Management Science. In India, there are three IIM located one each at Ahmedabad, Bangalore and Calcutta.

Indian Labour Conference. Tripartite body, comprising the representatives of the Government, Employers and Labour, set up by the Government of India for consultation and discussion relating to questions affecting labour.

Indian Management. Monthly publication of the All India Management Association. Address: Management House, 14, Institutional Area, Lodi Road, New Delhi 110003.

Indian National Trade Union Congress (INTUC). Founded in May 1947 it is one of the four central all-India trade union organisations. It "aims at establishing an order of society which is free from hindrances to an all-round development of its individual members; which fosters the growth of human personality in all its aspects".

In further aims at progressively eliminating social, political and economic exploitation of labourers and inequality and anti-social concentration of power in any form. It covers over 2000 trade unions with approximately 2,25,000 members.

Indirect Materials Cost. An indirect cost that relates to an expenditure by a firm on materials or supplies.

Indirect Question. Oblique approach to gain information which might otherwise be withheld.

Indirect Review. Where management reviews the progress of work, not by direct monitoring or inspection (direct review) but indirectly through feedback in the form of complaints returned work.

Indirect Wages. Synonym for indirect labour cost.

Indirect Worker. An employee of a firm whose work does not directly contribute to the manufacture of one of the firm's products. (Also known as an 'indirect.')

Individual Consumer. The term usually refers to a family.

Individual Expectancy Chart. Sometimes used following psychological testing in an attempt at predicting the degree of success a candidate or employee would have in a particular occupation. Another form of expectancy chart is the institutional expectancy chart on which the predicted levels of efficiency within a workforce are charted, note being made of such factors as the number of workers expected to be of above-average performance.

Individual Training Methods. Individual as opposed to group training methods, including programmed instruction and personal job instruction.

Indoctrinated Desire. Encouragement of the sales of products, devices and ideas which may have no value or necessity, perhaps no genuine desirability, yet are an integral part of modern life. Such desire created, and is inherent in the desire for material benefits.

Illegal Contracts. Certain classes of Contract which are not legally binding. Examples include those between firms in countries at war with each other.

Induction Method. Films, videocassettes, slide presentations and literature to introduce new recruits to an organization.

Induction Procedure. (or Induction Programme) Activities taking place when a new employee joins an organization of which the objectives are to acquaint the individual with the organization and his colleagues and to ensure that all the organization's records concerning the employee are complete.

Induction Training. Devised for school leaver entrants or other new employees in a firm to familiarize them with company practices (practises) and procedures.

Indulgency Pattern. Terant and lenient style of management.

Industrial Accident. Accident suffered at work.

Industrial Action. Action taken by employees collectively to air either a grievance or a demand, usually on questions of pay and/or conditions of employment. Industrial action that goes as far as with drawal of labour or refusal to work is a form of strike (see its various forms). Action to limit the effectiveness of work rathar than refusal to do it, includes go-slow, overtime ban and work-to-rule, and is sometimes categorized as cut-price industrial action (that is, 'cutprice' to those taking the action since it does not involve total loss of pay).

Industrial Advertising. Advertising of products or services to industrial, commercial or business organizations.

Industrial Democracy. The concept of giving workers a voice in how they do their jobs, so that to some extent they help manage a firm or industry.

Industrial Diseases. A range of disease and illnesses which are caused by some aspect of work or its environment—for example, asbestosis, silicosis, dermatitis etc.

Industrial Dispute. A dispute between, on one side, one or more employers or organizations of employers and, on the other side, one or more employees or organizations of employees. Industrial dispute is a feature of capitalist civilisation.

Industrial Espionage. Planned attempts by a company or its agents at obtaining secret or confidential information from within or about a rival company.

Industrial Relations. Rules and regulations governing the relations between a labour union and management. They often deal with such matters as contract negotation, the type of recognition accorded the union, the financial arrangement for collecting membership dues from employees, the methods of controlling the quantity and kind of union membership through apprenticeship requirements, licensing provisions, initiation fees, seniority rules, and the handling of grievances.

Industrial Trade Union. Where a single trade union represents all the workers in an industry (see industrial unionism) instead of the more common situation, known as multi-unionism, where union represent particular skills or types of worker whatever the industries in which they are working, many commentators have pointed to the multiplicity of trade unions in several industies as a root problem of industrial relations.

Industrial Union. A labour union that admits membership people who work within an industry, irrespective of their occupatin craft.

Industry-wide Agreement. Or national agreement. Collective agreement or bargain between employers and trade unions on an industry-wide basis. At the other extreme is workplace bargaining. In between are company agreements and factory agreement.

Industry-wide Bargaining. A process of Collective Bargaining which takes place at a national level between empolyers and trade union representatives of an industry and may lead to an Industry-wide Agreement.

Inertia. Resistance to change in individuals and / or organizations; considered one of the major problems confronting marketing effort.

Inertia Selling. Practice of delivering goods to people who have not ordered them and living them either to pay for the goods or to return them within a specified time.

Infant Industry. The newly established industrial units.

In-firm Training. Training that takes place on the premises of the employer of the trainees. (Also known as 'in-plant training').

Inflation. Any increase in the general price level that is sustained and non-seasonal in character. The effect is to decrease the consumer's purchasing power.

Informal Agreement. Also called "Gentlemen's agreement" the term refers to an agreement added by the members of a traded association to conform to certain trade practices.

Informal Group. Association of individuals brought together by common association, without any formal organizational structure but not necessarily lacking leadership.

In-house Training. As in-company training.

Inner Pack. One of a number of packs which are then stored in multiple containers, *e.g.*, twenty individual cartons of cigarettes might be wrapped as a unit, a number of which are then packed in a fibreboard case.

Innovating Entrepreneurship. Clarence Danhop classifies entrepreneurs into the following types:

1. Innovating entrepreneur,
2. Imitative entrepreneur,
3. Fabian entrepreneur, and
4. Drone entrepreneur.

Innovating entrepreneurship is characterised by aggressive assemblance of information and the analysis of results deriving from novel combination of factors. Men in this group are generally aggressive in experimentation and exhibit celerity.

Innovation. Introduction of new thoughts, policies, products, markets, distribution, merchandising or other deliberate change.

Innovation Peripheral. Another company's contribution to same product group, such as a different kind of nylon shirt with different properties and sales appeal.

Innovator. Experimental buyer, first to try a new product or service.

In pack Premium. Gift offer contained within a pack, as opposed to appearing on the outside of the container, in the media or within the sales oulset.

Input/Output Analysis. A statistically-based technique used particularly in economics and marketing in which tables of inputs to and outputs from a system—for example, an industry—are produced which show the changing nature of their relationship over time.

Inquiry Test. Method of testing advertisements or media by comparing the number of inquiries received.

Instability. Departure from full employment at stable price levels.

Installment Buying. Also, buying on time. Purchasing consumer goods, usually relatively expensive ones, and paying for them over a period of time, in periodic partial payments called installments.

Installment Selling. Involves taking an initial deposit against goods purchased and collecting the balance of the selling price over an agreed period of time in fixed instalments.

Institutional Expectancy Chart. Sometimes used following psychological testing in an attempt at predicting the levels of efficiency within a workforce, note being made of such factrs as the number of workers expected to be of above-average performance.

In-store Interview. Consumer research where respondents are interviewed while shopping. As conducted by British Market Research Bureau.

In-store Promotion. Sampling, demonstration and sales promotion event organized by manufacturers in stores for foods, wines, washing machines, chewing gum, ironing boards, etc.

Instr (Test). Ability to follow instructions test.

Instrument

1. A document intended to have a specific legal effect, *e. g.*, written contract, a financial instrument or a statutory, instrument.
2. A device for measuring or testing either physical or mental attributes (*e.g.*, a questionnaire or an achievement test).

Intangible Asset. In accounting procedures, any asset having no physical existence; examples are goodwill, patents, trademarks, formulas, licenses, franchises, and research-and-development costs.

Integral Job Evaluation. Job evaluation approach in which whole jobs are compared as a whole, as opposed to the approaches of analytic job evaluation Integral job evaluation uses such techniques as job grading and job ranking. Sometimes known as whole-job evaluation.

Integrated Learning System. Combined and planned use of a variety of methods of instruction and teaching aids (e.g., audiovisual aids) to achieve specified goals.

Integrated Manager. A term describing the manager who likes to become part of the people, things, and processes he or she manager. Such managers are joiners and take pains to get involved with individual and groups about their work.

Integrated Pension Plan. A plan that adjusts the employee's pension benefits downward to reflect the company's contribution to social security.

Intelligence Tests. Form of psychological testing used for a wide range of applications but having a special usefulness for personnel selection purposes where those taking the test have no previous experience of the work in question so that it is necessary to identify which of them can be trained for the work.

Intensive Interview. Technique developed by Dr. William Belson to overcome problem of validating respondents replies, especially on readership surveys, suggesting serious errors in interviewing on the former National Readership Survey. Showed that intensive interviews could produce more accurate responses.

Intensive Selling. Selling a greater volume to present customers through energetic promotional derive.

Interaction Matrix. Design tool used in arranging plant layouts, activity relationships, etc., particularly where physical positioning is a vital consideration.

Interactive. Refers to the ability of the system to handle immediate-response communications between the user and the machine.

Interactive Behaviour. Behaviour between members of a group.

Interactive Medium. Medium which permits the recipient to participate or to demand information, such as TV system where by the viewer can communicate with an information base, terminals or other viewers.

Interactive Skills. Skills in interacting with others in a group and in making a goup work more effectively through the development of the social sensitivity of the individuals. Clashes of interest between the group members and their functions are said to raise questions of territorial rights. Interractive skills are involved in such group training methods as group dynamics and T-group training.

Interchangeability. Removal of demarcations between types of labour and job, having the advantage for employers of more economical use of labour and for employees of greater job security.

Intercompany Comparisons (interfirm comparisons). Comparisons made between firms on a number of dimensions to ascertain how well firms perform relative to each other and to identify areas for improvement or development.

Interference Pay (or allowance). Payment made to an employee on a payment-by-results scheme where he has to interrupt his work to carry out other work the employer requires to be done.

Interlocking Directorate. A situatioon in which an individual serves on the boards of directors of two or more competing corporations. This tends to create a monopoly by bringing the management of these corporations under a single control.

International Advertising Association, Inc. (IAA). Set up in 1938 to promote advertising standards and the free market concept at the internatioonal level.

International Forces. It refers to the role of the poor countries in the world economy.

Interview. In market research, a face to face meeting or telephone conversation in which a person is asked to give opinions and views relating to a product, service, company, etc. In a quantitative interview the questioner asks a series of fixed questions so designed that the answers lend themselves to statistical analysis. In a qualitative or depth interview the respondent is encouraged to talk freely about the issue rather than answering set questions, and the answers are open to more subjective interpretation.

Interviewer. Conducts research surveys, whether in the field or in discussion groups. For fieldwork, matronly, self-effacing intelligent women and those with social science training preferred. Discussion groups usually led by people with psychological training. Men usually conduct industrial interviews.

Interviewing Procedures. General types of interview include the connected conversation interview, the directive interview, and the non-directive interview. types of Interview used particularly in personnel section include the seven point plan, the five fold grading scheme, the panel interview, and group selection interviews.

Interview Technique. When writing feature articles interviewer shuld have written or unwritten questionnaires of information to be sought. First questions should not require act of memory, and should be simple, personal ones.

Interview Tension. Condition suffered by respondent according to proocess adopted, *e.g.*, anxiety during a tape-recorded interview. Interviews often more satisfactory if there are no obvious clumsy and inhibiting factors such as large notebooks, clipboards or tape recoders and microphones.

Intrapreneuship. A name coined to describe the process of generating new business ventures within an existing company—usually large—often involving a break with the bureaucratic traditions of the parent firm. The name originated in the Xerox Corporation in the USA but has been widely used to describe such internal innovation within large firms.

In Transitu. On the way.

In-tray Exercise. A training exercise where an individual is given the role of a manager and required to make decisions about various items which are presented to him as the contents of a fictitious in tray. This simulates one aspect of the typical business of management-dealing with memos, complaints, enquiries and other forms of paperwork.

Intrinsic Rewards. Rewards which are internal to the employee-such as job satisfaction or self-actualization, rather than external such as pay or Fringe Benefits.

Inventory. Part of an enterpriser's working assets consisting of raw materials to be used in the manufacture of a product; goods in process of manufacture, and finished goods ready for delivery to customers.

Inventory Control. Also, inventory management, material requirements planning. The management of inventories so that there is always enough rock on hand for prduction yet n capital that could more profitably be used otherwise. Inventory control involves determining how much stock must be kept on hand, the rate at which stock will be consumed, the most Economic Order Quantity for purchasing or manufacturing, and the lead time required to obtain the needed materials.

Inventory Management. As stock control, but possibly taking into account plant, equipment, etc., as well as stocks and products.

Inventory Shrinkage. Losses that result from such non-productive process and actions as deterioration, disposal as scrap, and pilferage.

Investment Adviser. A person who on a professional service basis gives advice to another person on investment situations.

Investment Appraisal. An assessment of whether investment in a proposed project will show a satisfactory rate of return; various alternative projects may be examined to ascertain which should give the greatest return on capital invested over any given period of time.

Investment Counseller. An individual or firm whose principal business consists of guiding the investments of its clients, generally making for them all decisions to buy and sell securities and/or commodities and seeing that these decisions are executed.

Investment Deepening. Investment which increases the total output of a given labour force by increasing the productivity of that force, within a given framework of technical knowledge.

Invoice. A itemized statement of goods or services bought or sold, usually including (or implying) a request for payment. The same invoice is called a sales invoice by the seller and a purchase invoice by the buyer.

Issue Management. PR activity to present an organization's position or views on a public issue.

Issue Readership (average). Number of readers, on average, who read a publication.

Item Analysis. Technique for selecting the items to be included in a psychological test so that they are relevant to both the purpose of the test and the people taking it.

Item Number. I manufacturing procedures, a number assigned to each line item, part, or assembly in a bill of material for purposes of identification. Item numbers are normally assigned sequentially for each bill of material.

J

Jar

1. A wide mouthed container, usually of glass, stoneware, or plastic.
2. Glass container usually for high viscosity materials such as pastes and greases.

JCL. Abbreviation of job control language.

Jenning's Corollary. A satirical principle holding that the chance of bread falling with the buttered side down is directly proportional to the cost of the carpet on which it lands.

Jerque Note. Certificate issued by Customs when they are satisfied that cargo is in order.

Jet Propelled Inflation. A name employed by F. Benham to refer to hyper inflation.

JEMIP. Joint Financial Management Improvement Programme.

JIC.

1. Abbreviation of joint industrial council.
2. Abbreviation of job instruction and communication.

Jig and Tool Design. Design of new jigs, tools and equipment to meet the requirement of a new production run, or the design improvement of existing jigs and tools for use in existing or modified production runs.

J-index. Index giving proportion of jurors to all electors in polling district.

Jingles. Catchy tunes to which slogans or doggerel are set to gain memorable effect, as in TV and radio commercial. May often be extended as slogans in press and poster advertising.

JIT. Abbreviation of job instruction training.

JM. Abbreviation of job methods.

JMT. Abbreviation of job method training.

Job.

1. The collection of tasks, duties and assignments that an employee is employed to perform.
2. A piece of work. A single item of work, complete in itself, performed by a person, or by an organization or by a machine (especially, a computer); especially, a piece of work that separately identified for purposes of accounting, costing, work study or paying wages.

Job Analysis. Examination of of a job, its component parts and the circumstances in which it is performed. Purpose and slant of job analysis very between job evaluation, vocational guidance, personnel selection, training, equipment, design, etc. Can be known as job study.

Job-in-finish. System under which workers are free to leave work when they have completed an agreed amount of work rather than waiting until the normal knocking-ff time.

Jobber. In the distribution of goods, an individual or a firm that intervenes between a wholesaler-distributor and the retailer. jobbers may act exclusively as brokers or sales agents, carrying no inventory of the goods purveyed, or they may so organized and finance their activities as to provide warehousing facilities for the goods.

Job classification. The process of describing the duties, responsibilities, and characteristics of a job, point-rating it (sometimes through the use of formulas based on-time studies of workers already in such jobs), and then grouping the jobs into graduated classifications with corresponding wage rates and wages ranges.

Job Classification Method. Non-analytical job evaluation technique involving the allocation of jobs into pre-determined job grades/and or levels the characteristics of each grade will normally be defined in terms of level of responsibility or skill involved. Job classification schemes are often developed by means of job ranking.

Job Clinic. Technique used particularly in sales training where specific problems encountered by an individual are discussed with two or three colleagues and solution suggested.

Job Costing. Practice or activity of allocating costs to specific jobs or items of production.

Job Cover Plan. Usually drawn up following manpower analysis in manpower planning in the individual firm. Such a plan, often presented in the form of a chart, carries a note of all the jobs and tasks in the firms or unit, both at present and in the predictable future, and of the extent to which each employee is capable of carrying out each of them.

Job Cycle. The complete sequence of operations that a worker has to perform in order to complete a unit of his output.

Job Description. A document that outlines in broad terms the purpose, scope, duties, and responsibilities of a job for which a person is hired. Also known as position guide.

Job Design. Process, or activity, of deciding on the tasks and responsibilities to be included in a particular job and of deciding on the methods to be used for carrying out those tasks.

Job Engineering. Adapting responsibilities, methods, procedures and equipment of a job so changing its skill level.

Job Enlargement

1. Training and encouraging emplyees to perform a range of jobs related to the ones they hold so that manpower can be used more flexibly.
2. Assigning additional tasks to an employee in order to make his job more varied and interesting.

Job Enrichment. Changing features of a job other than compensation, physical working conditions and the essential tasks of the job in order to increase the job satisfaction of the person performing it.

Job Evaluation. A complete analysis of all the positions in a company, with a view to establishing their comparative value to the firm. Each job is ranked according to such factors as physical and/or mental effort required, responsibility, skill and working conditions.

Job Order System. Also, job cost system, job lost system, order cost system. A system of cost accounting in which costs are collected separately for each job order, or job lot accepted by the plant.

Job Price. The price quoted or paid for completing a specified task without regard to time required for completion.

Job Price Contract. System of paying employees or contractors an agreed price for completing a specialised job irrespective of how long it takes.

Job Production. Manufacture of an articles according to the specifications of a customer, or against specific order.

Job Relations (JR). One of the programmes in traning within industry. It is designed to provide an understanding of human relationships with particular emphasis on the prevention of problems and effective handling of problems that do arise.

Job Requirements. Characteristics required of a worker to perform a particular job successfully.

Job Rotation. A technique of training employees by moving them from one job to another in a systematic way.

Job Sample Test. Use of a simulator to test performance, actual or potential, in job or range of jobs.

Job Satisfaction. The gratification (in the sense of mental pleasure follwing from the satisfaction of needs, desires or hopes) that a person derives from the job that he is employed to perform.

Job Selling

1. Disposing of unwanted remainders in bulk and at a low price.
2. Selling units, usually capital equipment produced in low volume, against limited demand and established specification.

Job Shop. A functional organization whose departments or work centres are organized around particular types of equipment or operations, such as drilling, forging, wave soldering, and assembly.

Job Shortage. The total quantity of items or parts that is short or lacking for work in process.

Job Spoiler. Term used of a member of a work group who does not conform with that group's informally agreed fiddle or restricted output.

Job Time. In work measurement the time for completing all the elements in a job.

Job Title. The name given to a particular job.

Job Valuation. A logical and to some extent, objective method of ranking jobs relatively to each other.

Joint Consultation. 1. Arrangements in which employees and employers can discuss issues of concern where there is some measure of consultation by management, although there may be only limited scope for negotiating the outcome of management decisions—as distinct from Collective Bargaining.

Joint Consultation. Structure or procedure developed in the circumstances of a particular organization for promoting understanding and common purpose between management and employees.

Joint Consultative Committee. A committee established for the purposes of joint consultation.

Joint Consultative Machinery. Institutions and procedures that enable regular joint consultation to take place.

Joint Demand. The simultaneous demand for two or more goods or services than generally are used together.

Joint Industrial Council (JIC). A voluntarily established permanent body for the consideration of terms and conditions of employment in a particular industry or sector of an industry.

Joint Life Policy. A policy of insurance under which the sum assured is payable on the death of the first of two or more lives.

Joint Negotiating Panel (of Trade Unions). Representatives of two or more organizations of workers or trade unions authorized by those organizations to engage in collective bargaining and enter into collective agreements on their behalf.

Joint Probability. The probability that two outcomes will both occur together.

Joint Product. Two or more products that inevitably result from processing a single raw material and that are of equal importance, so that none can be designated as the major or primary product.

Joint Product Offer. A form of sales promotion in which consumers are offered a banded pack of two or more different products from the same or from different manufacturers, at a reduced price.

Joint Rate. A transportation rate between two points on the routes of different carriers that is quoted as a single rate.

Joint Regulation. Concept that managerial autonomy becomes modified in practice (practice) by a kind of balance of power between management and trade unions, imposing contraints that both sides come to accept.

Journey Cycle. Frequency of salesmen's visits.

Journeyman. A skilled craftsman. The term derives from the fact that such a craftsman was independent rather than employed by a firm and often journeyed around seeking work for his skills.

Journey Planning. Organizing the salesman's route, rate(s) of call, and customer priority rating so as to make his selling as cost effective as possible.

Journeywoman. A female journeyman.

Judgement Sample. Group selected without use of statistical methods inorder to obtain its views and ideas.

Jumbo Packs. Promotion of bulk sales of small unit items such as confectionery by packing a number in one wrapping, usually with price reduction.

Junior Board. A committee of people in a company below the status of top management (often trainee managers) which meets like a board of directors, reviews the progress and plans of the company and makes recommendations to top managememt.

Jurisdictional Dispute (or issue). Question of which trade union should have the right to organize a particular group of workers.

Jurisdictional Strike. A strike caused by a dispute among craft unions over which shall have jurisdiction over a specific job.

Just-in-time Production (JIT). An approach to management originally developed in Japan which emphasizes very low inventories, frequent deliveries by suppliers, operator involvement and quality awareness. JIT also encompasses a philosophy of production organization and management within the firm, based on reducing inventory and batch sizes which involves a problem-solving approach to those bottlenecks which prevent the smooth flow of work through the factory.

K

Kabmobile. Porta Kabin trailer for product displays, demonstrations. AV shows and other promotion.

Kaiser Plan. Scheme adopted by the American Kaiser Steel Corporation and the Steel workers Union to guarantee employees against possible loss of earnings or employment as a result of technological changes.

Kangaroo Court. Informal court with no legal standing, such as one conducted by workers to 'try' a colleague.

Kelley Repertory Grid Test. Obective test to provide exhaustive list of attitude scales used by public in differentiating between certain products or brands. Basic test procedure requires informant to compare a series of sets of three products of brands (trade) and clearly state the terms in which he can differentiate between one product and the other two, with the restriction that the terms must be different for each new set of products or brands compared. Developed by W.A.K. Frost from the work of G-Kelley.

Kerbside Conferences. Post-interview discussion between a salesman and his sales supervisor, involving analysis of selling method, performance and achievement.

Keyed Advertisement. Advertisement designed to cause an enquirer to indicate the source of his information, for instance by including a code of number or a particular 'department' within the return address.

Keyed Advertising. A method of identifying the source of an advertisement that prompted a customer's order or inquiry.

Key Industry. An industry that, by virtue of its size or the importance of its product or service, is vital to a nation's economic activity and whose condition is therefore considered a barometer of the entire economy.

Kendsian Unemploment. In contrast to Marxian unemployment, Keynesian unemployment denotes a situation in which the flow of investment is insufficient to mop up the savings that would be forthecoming at full employment levels of income.

Keypad. Means of calling up information on TV, and for interaction in ordering and making payment, simply by pressing numbers on magnetic key pad.

Key Points/Factors. Factors in job analysis vital to the performance of work and therefore of special note.

Key Prospects. Groups of buyers within a market who hold the greatest proportionate potential purchasing power.

Key Question. Varied between control and experimental groups in experimental research.

Key Results Analysis. As key task analysis.

Key Results Analysis

1. Activity of identifying the areas (usually 5-8 of them) of a manager's job that are crucial to the sucess of the job in the organization (`key areas or result areas') and of quantifying the results that the manager must achieve in each area. Also a record of such an analysis.
2. Activity of identifying the objectives that it is crucial for an organization to achieve. Also a record of such an analaysis.

Key Task Analysis. Or key results analysis. Analysis of key tasks to be performed, levels of performance required and methods of checking actual against desired performance. Used chiefly in management and supervisory traning, though also in other training.

Kickback. A portion of a fee, salary, sales commission, or other payment that is given to a third party for having assisted—or refrained from preventing—the payment in the first place.

Kicked Upstairs. Term used of someone who is promoted in order to remove him from a position in which his inefficiency is creating problems.

Kill. Action of media in deciding not to carry an available story or news items.

Kind. Goods or commodities as opposed to mony. (As in`payment in kind'.)

Kinship Ties. Extent to which a family stays together. Small communities have strong kinship ties. In Western civilization families break up, move to cities, creating loneliness problem of the avandooned agred.

Kitchen cabinet. Group of personal aides gathered around a senior person in industry, politics, etc., having responsibilities to that person rather than to the organization to which he belongs.

Knocking Competition. Deciding the quality of competitors products or services.

Knocking-off Time. End of a working day or period.

Know-how. Skill or ingenuity usually of a kind derived from practical experience.

Know-how Agreement. An agreement by which the possessor of know—how promises to disclose it to someone else. When the disclosure is made to enable the other person to perform his own research or to evaluate the usefulness of the know-how, the agreement is called a 'secrecy agreement'. When the disclosure is made so that the other, can use it in commercial production, the agreement is called a 'known-how licence' (US spelling:know-how license).

Know-how Licence. (US spelling: know—how license).

Kuehn Model. Stochastic learning model developed by Alfred A.Kuehn and used for analysing consumer choice as recorded by consumer panel data.

Kuder Preference Record. Interest test or inventory used in personnel selection, careers guidance, etc., to build up a picture of the personal interests of a candidate or employee. The person being tested indicates his first and second choices in each of a number of groups of three activities. The items selected are scored according to the category to which they relate.

Kuznets Cycle. A long swin in building construction and certain other activities, averaging between 15 and 25 years in length. First observed by Simon Kuznets in 1930, such swings may be associated with fluctuations in immigration, population growth rate, and growth rate of the money supply.

L

Laboratory Training (T-group). A form of Group Dynamics training in which content is relatively unstructured, although carefully controlled by the trainer. The emphasis of this training is on participants learning form their own experience as they form a group, begin to adopt its norms and experience and try to resolve conflicts which develop. The training is designed to develop participants' interpersonal skills over, a period of time through regular meetings in which the relationships between group members are analysed.

Labour. The element of production represented by those hired workers whose efforts or activities are directed toward making the product; also, all personal services including the activities of wageworkers, professional people, and independent businessmen. Laborers may thus receive compensation in the form of wages, salaries, bonuses, commissions, and so on. Labour includes the vary highest professional skill of all kinds as well as the labour off unskilled workers and artisans and of those emloyed in education, in fine arts, in literature, in science, in the administration of justice and in Governments in all its branches; and we must include also not the labour that results in the firmament form but also that render services which persists in the act

Labour Contract. Also, collective bargaining agreement, union contract. A formal contract between a union and one or more employers concerning wages, working conditions, job security, and numerous other issues of mutual interest. Most labour contracts are negotiated in a give-and-take process called Collective Bargaining and are in effect for a limited period, most often one year.

Labour Code. Used in some countries to regulate the relationship between employee and employee.

Labour Cost. In a business, the total slaries and wages paid to workers. (Excutive and clerical salaries are usually considered sparately, as administrative Overhead).

Labour Cost Ratio. Standard costing of direct labo(u)r divided by its actual cost.

Labour Efficiency. The relationship between the planned labour requirements for a tesk and the actual labour time charged to the task.

Labour Exchange (US spelling: labour exchange). (Now obsolete) Synonym for employment office.

Labour Force. The labour force or working force denotes that part of population which is economically active or "gainfully employed".

Labour Force Participation Rate. The percentage of available individuals of working age who are actually in the labour force.

Labour Hoarding. Where a firm employs more labo(u)r than immediately necessary (creating a concealed surplus) to guard against the possibility of being caught with insufficient labo(u)r later.

Labour Hour Rate. Hourly payment.

Labour Injunction. A court order requiring an individual or a group to perform or case to perform certain actions that have been deemed injurious and for which money damages are not a suitable remedy under law.

Labour-only Subcontracting. (US spelling: labor-only subcontracting). Practice of employing people under a contract for services in circumstances where a contract of employment would be more appropriate. The workers do not provide any of their own tools or equipment (thus the contract is for 'labour only') and claim to be self-employed.

Labour Organization (US). As trade union.

Labour Problems. The economic and social issues that grow out of work for pay. They include not only industrial unrest, labour unions, and slowdowns or strikes but also threats of wage loss from unemployment and other forms of economic insecurity.

Labour Relations. Also labour-management relations. The relations and transactions between employers and groups of employees especially labour unions concerning such matters of mutual interest as wages working conditions job security etc.

Labour Saving Invention. One that raises the marginal productivity of capital more than that of labour.

Labour Stability Index. An index sometimes used to express Labour Turnover which relates the number of employees who recently joined the firm (up to a year ago) to the number who were employed in the previous year.

Labour-standard Rolled-up Cost. The total labour cost required to build an assembly. This figure includes the labour cost of both the assembly and its subassemblies.

Labour Turnover. The number of workers who leave or are replaced in a given period expressed as a percentage of the average number of workers employed during the period. Usually measured by the ratio:

$$\frac{\text{number of employees leaving durable the year}}{\text{average number of employees during the year}}$$

(Also known as 'manpower turnover'.)

Labour Union, Trade Union. An independent and voluntary association of workers having no organic affiliation with any employer and organized for the purpose of maintaining or improving the conditions of their employment.

Labour Unit. A hypothetical unit used or adopted for analytical purposes. The term was used by John Maynard Keynes in the sense of a unit of ordinary labour that labour that was for exaample paid twice as high as ordinary labour was counted as being two labour units. By this device labour could be made homogeneous for analytical studies.

Ladder Activities. In project Networks, overlapping or interdependent activities.

Laity. Persons in a profession who are not skilled with respect to the profession.

Lame Duck. A colloquial term for an individual or organization which performs consistently badly and relies on or is seeking some form of government subsidy.

Land Reform. Government-enforced changes in land ownership. In most countries, land reform mean breaking up large estates worked by landless peasants in to smaller plots that can be owned and worked individually.

Latin Square Design. Term used particularly in market research for a survey or test designed to measure the effect on sales of a number of different factors. The different factors are plotted against each other. This technique makes for a considerably shorter overall survey or test than would be possible if separate tests were run for each factor.

Law of Large Numbers. A law of probability, commonly but incorrectly called the law of averages. This law states that if we increase the number of trials if we repeat whatever we are doing a great number of times, it is practically certain that the relative actual frequency of successes will come close to the assumed probability of success.

Leader Effectiveness. The extent to which a leader influences his co-workers in the achievement of group obectives.

Leadership. The characteristics and behaviour of individuals who are responsible for leading groups within organizations and the field of studies of those factors.

Lead/Lag Method. Technique used particularly in marketing. In preparing forecasts in a particular area, an anlysis is made of trends or economic indicators that are known to be related to the data being forecast and tend to vary upwards or downwards in advance of this data. This can provide useful advance warning.

Lead Rate. Extra or premium payment made to an employee called upon to use exceptional skill or to take extra responsibility.

Leasing. Practice in business whereby a firm may for a continuing consideration, obtain the use of a piece of equipment or other plant without purchasing it. Of particular interest where new technology is likely to lead to premature obsolescence.

Least Squares Method. A mathematical technique used in Regression Analysis to identify the best fit for a line through a set of data plotted on a graph.

Legacy. A gift of money or of a specific item bequeathed by will.

Legal Entity. Any individual, partnership corporation, or organization empowered by law or custom to own property or engage in business transactions.

Legalized Invoice. A copy of an invoice on which a chamber of commerce has certified that the details are accurate.

Legatee. The person to whom 'personal' property is left or bequeathed, in a will. The person who takes all the personal property remaining after all legatees have received their shares is called the residuary legatee.

Legislative Budget. Budget prepared by or for a committee of the legislative branch or adoption by that branch.

Less than Full Employment. The phrase introduced by Lord Keynes while repudiating the Classical assumption of full employment relates to underemployment. While many economists call it a significant contribution of Lord Keynes, Keynes's severest critic W.Hazlitt calls it 'pure nonsense".

Letter of Credit. A letter of credit is a document issued by banker authorizig the banker to whom it is aaddressed to honour the cheques of the person named to the extent of a certain amount and to charge the sums to the account of the grantor.

Letter of Indemnity. Document guaranteeing to cover another party against loss or default.

Levelling. In time studies the use of the best judgement of the persons engaged in the study to adjust the performance of an observed worker to the level that is considered average or normal..

Levelling Effect. In a management meeting, the effect created by a dominant person who, by force of personality or rank and title, causes others in his group or among his peers to tend to agree with his views, that is come to his level.

Level of Living. The nature of the satisfactions that the individual is actually enjoying at a given time.

Levy. A tax assessment. In management a request made on members of an organization or contributions of capital.

Licence. A permit to do something for example to use a Patent granted to someone else—to produce or sell goods or offer services originally produced by someone else, or to import or export items which are subject to government control of some sort.

Licensee. A person who is entitled to do something (that is otherwise ulawful) under the terms of a licence (1).

Lien. A right one perons has to keep possession or control of the property of another in satisfaction of a debt.

Lieu Bonus. A payment made to a worker who, for special reasons, is not able to participate in an incentive payment system or who is unable, because of abnormal circumstances, to do the work required to entitle him to an incentive payment.

Lieu Days. Holidays taken in lieu of unpaid overtime.

Lieu Payment (lieu bonus). If an employee is not able to join a Payment-by-Results scheme, he may be entitled to lieu pay, in lieu of the Bonus he would otherwise have enarned.

Life Annuity. An annuity whose payments terminate on the death of the beneficiary.

Life Assurance. An arrangement under which an insurer promises to pay a fixed sum if a named person (called the 'life assured') dies within a specified period ('term life assurance') or to pay a fixed sum when a named person dies ('whole life assurance') or to pay an annuity to a named person if he does not die. Payments after death go to the estate of the decased person for payment to his heirs.

Life-Style Concept. Distinctive or characteristic mode of living of a whole society or section of it. Location, religion, nationality, culture, occupation, industry, climate, soil, politics, education, history, habits and traditions all have a bearing on this.

Likert Scales. Scales often ued in questionnaires and surveys which allow the respondent to indicate the degree of agreement or disagreement with a set of statements. This allows them greater choice than a simple either/or choice, and allowds a wider range of opinion or attitude to be axamined. The idea originated with Rensis Likert in work at the Survey Research center at the University of Michigan.

Limited Company. A company whose members are required to contribute capital to the company but only up to a known limited amount agreed between member and company. No further contributioncan be required even if the company is unable to pay its debts.

Limited Editions. In advertising, limited editions are usually limited by preannounced number, or by application or subscription within a stated period of time.

Linear Decision Rule (LDR). Developed in 1955 by C. S. Holt, F. Modigliani, J.F. Muth, and H.A. Simon as a quadratic programming approach for making aggregate employment and production rate decisions. The quadratures are: (1) regular payroll, (2) hiring and layoff, (3) overtime, and (4) inventory holding, back-odering, and machine setup costs.

Linear Responsibility Charting. Analysis of job functions on a large chart. Titles are listed across the page and all major job titles down the left-hand side of the sheet. A symbol is used to indicate which functions are covered by which jobs and the nature of this involvement (actual performance or supervison, etc. of the work). The object is to provide a flexible type of organization chart which indicates functions and responsibilities, establishes overlapping duties, improves decision—making and highlights training needs, etc.

Line Authority. Authority that is, or is like, the authority exercised by a line manager.

Line-by-line. Method of selecting outdoor advertising positions site-by-site from a contractor's list.

Line Management (line functions). A type of management associated with taking executive responsibility for a particular functional area—production, marketing, design, quality control etc—within an organization. It given rise to the traditional pyramid model of mangement—as opposed to Matrix Organization or other structure.

Line Manger. Functional head, with power of command and carrying executive responsibility as compared with staff appointments with merely advisory powers.

Line of Command. The sequence of people in an organization through whom instructions from the chief executive pass before reaching particular employee. (so knowns chain of command.)

Line Relationship. Relationship between two members of an organization, one of whom may issue instructions and delegate authority to the other.

Line Responsibility. Responsibility of, or like that of a line manager.

Liquidated Damages. A sum payable as damages for brech of contract the amount of which is not left to assessment by a jury, but is previsously agreed by the parties to the contract.

Liquidator. An individual appointed to manage the winding up of a company.

List Broker. Organization or individual supplying on commission mailing lists of specific categories of people representing markets of sements of a market, *e.g.* teachers, garage owners. doctors.

List Broking. Hiring mailing lists to direct mail users. The broker compiles and maintains lists, usually offering personalization techniques and computerized control methods to reduce or eliminate duplication.

Litter-bin Advertising. Provision by contractor of litter-bins in mani thoroughfare, bins being colourful and carrying one or more advertisements painted on or as attached metal plates. Usually attached to lamp-posts or bus-stop pillars.

Living Person. The advertisements or advertisement features should not portary or refer to living persons, whether in their public or private capacities, unless their prior permission has been obtained. (Special considerations apply to television commercials or persons prominent in politics even with their permission).

Living Wage. A wage sufficient to ensure to the workman food, shelter, clothing, frugal comfort and provision for the evil days.

Load Chart. Visual display of work loading of plant or production equipment.

Loaded Question. One which suggests a particular answer, thereby introducing bias, and should not be included in a market research questionnaire.

Loaned Employee. Loaned or temporary employee who is owned the usual employer's duty of care by his temporary employer.

Loan Shark. Person or organization making loans at extortionately high interest rates.

Lock Out. The closing of a business or wholesale dismissal of employees by the employer because of a disagreement over terms of settlement; the refusal of an employer to admit his employees to their place of work.

Logo. A distinctive symbol used repeatedly by an organization for identifying itself. Often consists of the organization's name in distinctive lettering. (Originally, a shortening of logotype' *i.e.*, one piece of printers' type with a whole word on it-practice of supplying a printer with a logotype when a name in distinctive lettering is to be included in, *e.g.*, an advertisement).

Logotype. Commonly used to describe a company symbol, badge or name style.

Long-term Contract. Any contract for goods or services that extends beyond one year.

Long-term Lease. An obligation for rental payments on real or personal property over an extended period, in excess of one year.

Loose Inserts. Advertisements distributed separately with a publication, and usually inserted loosely within its pages.

Loose Rate

1. A piece rate that is high enough to enable a worker to earn a lot without too much effort.
2. Synonym for loose time value.

Loose Rein. A term for a style of management also known as laissez-faire. Laissez-Faire.

Loose Time Value. In work measurement, an inaccurately measured time for a job which actually requires less time. (Also known as a 'loose rate').

Loss Adjuster. An independent consultant who, for a fee, will advise an insurer on the extent of his liability to pay a claim from an assured.

Loss Assessor. An independent consultant who will, for a fee, advise an assured on the presentation of a claim to an insurer.

Loss Leader

(1) In marketing, a product or service which is sold at, or even below, its cost price as an incentive to customers to buy other products or to use other services offered by the firm.

(2) In retailing, items offered at low prices to attract customers into a shop.

Lost-time Accident. An accident that injures an employee and prevents him from continuing his normal work on the day or shift after that on which the accident occurred.

Lot Tolerance Percent Defective (LTPD). In statistical quality control the decision on how many items should be inspected in a given batch or lot, in order to check on quality and determine rejection or acceptance of the total batch quantity.

Ltd. Abbreviation for Limited, an Indian term equivalent to "incorporated" in the United States, indicating the limited liability of stockholders.

Luddite. An individual who resist the introduction of new technology. The name derives from the Luddities, a group of 19th century textile workers who rioted and smashed new machinery which they saw as a threat to their traditional craft skills.

Lump Labour. Type of labour met particularly in the construction industry, and sometimes known as labour workers are self employed and are paid a lump sum per day's work or per amount of completed work either by the contractor or by an agent or so-called labour master who in turn is paid by the contractor a lump sum for work done.

Lump of Labour Fallacy. The attitude of workers that their job and livelihood are at constant threat by events like replacement of labour by machine, women's entry into labour market, unwillingness of old workers to retire etc., is sometimes called by economists lump of labour fallacy.

Lump-sum death Benefit. Payment to dependents etc., of a lump sum in the event of an insured peron's death as in life assurance (or insurance).

M

Machine Down-time. When a machine is not being used for production work because of breakdowns, maintenance, etc.

Machine Idle Time. When a machine is available for production work but is kept out of action by lack of materials or labour or orders, etc.

Machine Loading. In manufaturing the process of compiling the load or quantity of work assigned to each machine for a given period.

Machinery for Consultation. Parts of proccedure agreements providing for consultation on terms and conditions of employment and for settlement by negotiation or arbitration of points of contention between employers and emloyees.

Macro-specification. Scope and implications of market as a whole in contrast to micro-specification of numerous decisions necessary to produce a product for this market.

Mahalwari System. A system of land tenure that prevailed in India. Mahal means village land. This system puts the responsibility for the payment of the land revenue not only on the individual co-shares of the village land but legally speaking jointly on the village community.

Maildrop. More precise form of door-to-door delivery in which shots are delivered to actual addresses or kinds of premises, *e.g.*, all grocers' shops.

Mailing List. Classified list of names and addresses suitable for distributing mailing shots. May be purchased or built up over time but requires careful maintenance to keep in an up-to-date condition.

Mail Order. Distribution channel. Customers buy direct by post either in response to an advertisement or from a sales promotional catalogue.

Mail-order Advertising. Advertising intended to persuade people to buy goods by mail order. Note that mail order advertising may or may not be direct—mail advertising though the terms are often confused.

Mail Order Publisher. One engaged in selling books, magazines, gramophone records, cassettes and other publications by post. Includes book and record clubs and subscription publishers.

Mail Order Selling. Selling against orders received through the post directly from consumers/purchasers or agents. The order may be in response to advertisements of the direct response promotion or coupon advertising kind. Alternatively the orders may be made from catalog(us)s.

Mail Order Trading. Retailing by mail order house goods c services sold by post.

Mail-order Wholesaler. Serving as a middleman in the distribution of goods this merchant substitutes mail-order catelog and order forms for a personal sales force.

Main Question. Where a motion and amendments to it are move at a meeting or conference the main question is the resulta issue to be finally debated and voted on. If all amendmer fail the main question is the original motion. It amendme are carried, the amended motion or substantive motion comes the main question and has to be put to the v separately after the vote(s) on the amendment(s).

Maintenance Shift. A special shift laid on specifically for the purposes of maintaining a plant at times when it is not production.

Make-up Pay. In payment by results each-worker is usually guaranteed a minimum weekly wage Make-up pay is given if the worker fails to do the work that could earn him the minimum wage and is the difference between the payment for the work he has done and the guaranteed minimum.

Make-work Practices (Practises). Form of restrictive labo(u)r practices (practises) to make work take longer.

Manage. To carry onthe task of ensuring that a number of diverse activities are performed insuch a way that a defined objective is achieved—especially the task of creating and maintaining conditions in which desired objectives are achieved by the combined efforts of a group of people.

Manage Change Technique (MCT). Approach developed by Westinghouse Electric Corporation (US) concerned with obtaining real involvement and commitment by managers and employees to implementing effective changes within an organization.

Managed Costs. Those over which there is some degree of management discretion during the progress of a proect/enterprise to that there is some scope for varying expenditure once the project/enterprise is under way (*e.g.*, reducing costs to cut losses if things go badly).

Managed Expenditures. Items the levels of which are currently controllable by management, as opposed to items bequathed by previous management or determined by external influances and factors.

Management. The process activity or study of carrying out the task of ensuring that a number of diverse activities are performed in such a way that a defined obective is achieved especially the task of ceating and maintaining conditions in which desired objectives are achieved by conbine efforts of a group of people (Which includes the person carrying out the management). Also a group of people within an organization who are primarily concerned with the management of the activities of that organization.

Management Accountancy. Analysis of monthly trading figures to assess age of debt cost of serving trade-in goods, profitability of individual salesmen, bank situation.

Management Accounting. Branch of accounting geared to making the decision making of management better informed by providing detailed information, present and projected, on the costs of individual products departments and activities.

Management Appraisal. As perfomance appraisal.

Management Audit. Systematic assessment of all management functions an techniques to establish the current level of effectiveness, and to lay down standards for future performance.

Management Buy-outs. Purchase of business by management with loans from financial groups such as ICFC. Managers buy between 10% and 85% of the companies they manage or of a subsidiary/division. In early 80s about 100 or more management buy-outs annually.

Management by Crisis (or Drive). Management style that concentrates on crash program(me)s intended to rectify apparent weakness as they arise. It tends to be unconstructive and to lose sight of the overall objectives of the organization.

Management by Exception. An approach to management in which senior managers are called in only to make decisions exceptional circumstances which fall outside a previously agreed plan. The responsibility for day-to-day decision-making is delegated to subordinates.

Management Pregative. Traditionally, exercising of complete authority by management, an authority that might become qualified during collective bargaining though not during joint consultation.

Management Ratios. Means of keeping an eye on company and management performance by identifying relationships between quantifiable aspects of the company's activity and continuously recording these relationships, sometimes by plotting them on a graph.

Management Science. Application of scientific techniques, research and results to problems of management. Virtually synonymous with operational research although it is sometimes suggested that management science is concerned with general theories while operational research is concerned with solving particular problems.

Management Services. A group of services provided to management, such as Work Study, Organization and Methods and Data Processing.

Management Style. Or managerial style. Approach adopted by management to exercising authority, encouraging participation in decision making, movtivating staff, delegating authority, communicating information and maintaining control.

Management Succession. Process of assessing the management needs and hierarchy an organization will require in the future and of ensuring that there are junior managers able to succeed more senior management.

Management Threshold. State in personal development which marks the transition period from specialist to a generalist centered with managing the work of others. It is characterized by dramatic changes in the individual's outlook to work, its rewards, and social and family life.

Management Trade Union. Part of the general growth of white collar trade unions, such unions have deliberately set out to recruit a 'middle class' memberships.

Management Training. Planned experience and training in the practices (practises) and techniques of management. Often in company or even on-the-job. Can merge with management education.

Management Union. A trade union concerned with the interests of white-collar managerial workers.

Manager. In the most fundamental interpretation of the word, a person who occupies a formal position in a formal organization, is responsible for the work of at least one other person, and has formal authority over that person.

Managerial Economics. The part of the theory of economics that is concerned with, or applicable to, the management of business enterprises.

Managerial Effectiveness. The extent to which a manager achieves the productivity or output requirements of his or her position.

Managerial Grid. A concept developed by Robert Blake and Jane Mouton used in management and organizational development work. It provides a way of measuring managerial behaviour along two dimensions which express concern for the task and concern for the people. A 9.9 score would indicate a high degree of concern for both.

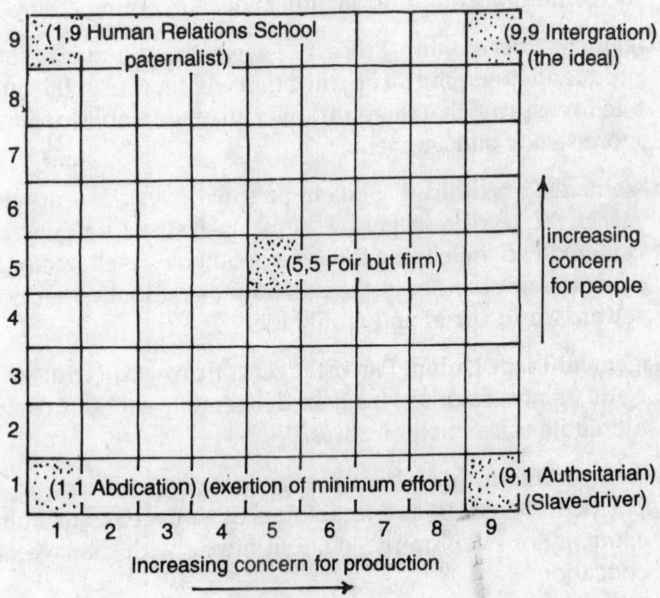

Managerial Marketing. Management function of marketing, total marketing requiring planned use of research and budgeting.

Managerial Structure. The established relationships between managerial positions in an organizations—usually described in terms of responsibility and authority.

Managerial Style. The way in which a manager characteristically conducts his dealings with his subordinates. (Sometimes called 'management style").

Manager's Guide. Synonym for management guide.

Manager's Letter. Used in some organizations as a statement of the manager or executive's repressibilities under management by objectives.

Managing Agent

1. A firm which is entrusted with the task of managing an industrial concern under an agreement with the parent company, subject to the directions of the Board of Directors.

2. A person, firm or company entitled to the management of the whole affairs of a company by virtue of an agreement with the company and under the control and direction of the directors except to the extent, if any, otherwise, firm or company occupying such position by whatever name called.

Managing Director. The chief executive of a company. The title is generally preferred in areas outside the North American continent. Boardly equivalent to president of a company, the title preferred in the United States.

Managing System. A system (of individual people) that is concerned with regulating the transactions between the operating systems in a firm and the environment of the firm.

Mandate. Instructions given by an organization to its delegate or representative on how he should vote on particular issues at a meeting or conference.

Man-hour. A unit of measure used in business and industry to estimate labour cost, productivity, the amount of spervision required, defects in products, etc.

Man Power. Human resources available to the economy.

Manpower Analysis. First stage in manpower planning in the individual firm, it is an analysis of all the employment in the firm or unit by, for example, age, length of service, job title and wider occupational category.

Manpower Budgeting. Balancing of future supply and demand for labour.

Manpower Deficit. Excess of jobs available over manpower available. Opposite of manpower surplus.

Manpower Inventory. Summary of information about the quality of manpower than an organization employs.

Manpower Mobility. See labour mobility.

Manpower Planning. Estimating how many employees and what types of employees an organization or a nation will require at sometime in the future and making plans to meet those requirements.

Manpower Ratios. Management ratios for monitoring employee costs and manpower utilization, including a total payroll costs as a percentage of sales revenue, by sales per employee, c net profit as a percentage of payroll costs, d added value per 100 of employee pay, and e the ratio of direct to indirect labour).

Manpower Surplus. Excess of manpower available over jobs availe. Opposite of manpower deficit.

Manpower Turnover. Synonym for labour turnover.

Manual. Printed document (of any number of pages) usually containing specific instructions, *e.g.*, sales manual, operating or service manual, relating both to products and services as well as company policies, regulations and practices.

Manual Dexterity. Ability of a person to make controlled skilful movements with his hands and arms.

Manual Dexterity Test. A test of which the purpose is to measure a person's ability to perform tasks with his hands.

Manual Labour. Predominantly physical work, usually of a kind that requires little or no special skill and considerable supervision.

Manual Worker. Also known as a blue collar worker, is employed in manual work, whether skilled, semi-skill, or unskilled.

Manufacturers Agent. Unlike sales agent who distributes products (perhaps entire stock of manufacturers agent will distribute a portion of production, perhaps in a limited area.

Manufacturers' Sales Branch. A whole sale establishment operated by a manufacturing firm to market its own products, eliminating the need for middlemen between the producer and the industrial user (or ultimate consumer).

Manufacturing. General term for the process of producing or assembling goods,. by hand or machine, for sale to other.

Manufacturing Industry. Industry concerned with changing the form of raw materials.

Manufacturing Management. See production management.

Marginal Productivity of Capital. The size of the reqard paid as interest. This is the ntraditional view.

Marginal Productivity of Labour. Amount per labour by which a small change in the number of labourers changes the total product.

Marginal Productivity Theory of Wages. The theory states that under conditions of perfect competition every worker of the same skill and efficiency in a given category will receive a wage equal to the value of the marginal product of tat type of labour.

Marginal Service of A Commodity. The service which we should have to forgo if the supply of the commodity in question were slightly contracted.

Marginal Testing. A test carried out on equipment to diagnose some intermittent fault or to see whether the equipment operates within specified operating to earners.

Manufacturing Resources Planning (MRP2). A system of production management developed by the Oliver Wight Company in the USA. It extends the concept of Materials. Requirements Planning by introducing the idea of a Master Production.

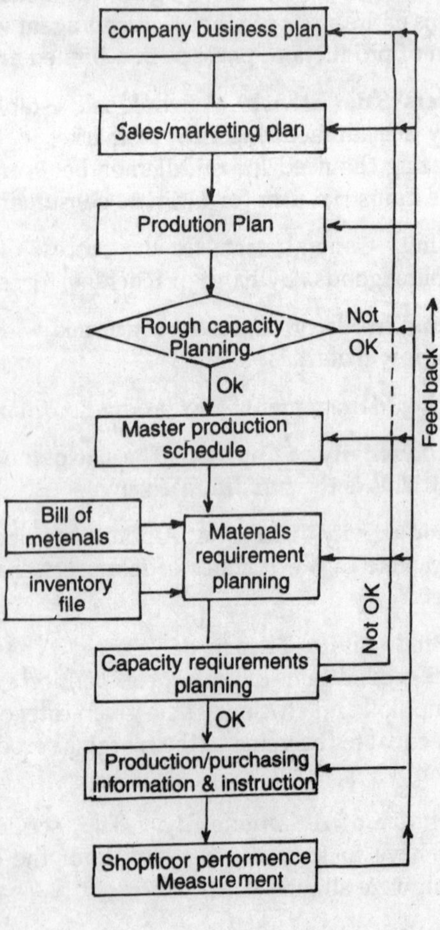

Schedule, which is generated by a mixture of forecasting of sales demand and actual customer orders. From this master schedule, a materials requirements plan and a capacity requirements plan are generated and used in connection with the Bill of Materials to produce orders for materials. MRP2 differs from Materials Requirements Planning in its strategic nature, taking into account the entire operational resource base of the company.

Margin of Safety. Extent to which sales volume or revenue exceeds the breakeven point on a break-even chart.

Markdown. A reduction in retail price, usually because an item cannot be sold at the original markup.

Marked. The conditions determining the number and nature of transactions for leasing or sale of particular goods or services, for performance, of work.

Market Follower. New product, introduced, to compete with existing products, as distinct from a poineer prouduct, which is one of entirely new design and/or function, or a brand leader that is already in a dominant position in its field.

Market Forces. Various forces which affect attitudes, wants and needs of customers. Population income leisure, career, sex, age, life—style, may all impinge on the market, or concern market segments.

Market Identification. Process of a identifying existing or potential customers: (b) establishing the characteristics by which customers are grouped together in separate market segments; (c) establishing why and how the product or service's bought.

Marketing. The range of activities involved in identifying demand for goods or services and providing the facilities and channels for their efficient distribution and sale.

Marketing Budget. Part of an overall budget appropriation earmarked for marketing expenditure, covering items like advertising, sales promotions and the costs of the sales team.

Marketing Expense to Sales Ratio. A ratio indicating the efficiency of marketing by relating the expense of marketing to the value of sales generated for the company.

Marketing Game. A management game in which the management problem that is simulated is primarily concerned with marketing.

Marketing Mix. Method used to market a product (*e. g.,* price, distribution channels, quality, advertising etc.). It is sometimes referred to as 'the four Ps,—product, price, position (in the market) and place.

Marketing Mix. Way which the different parts and techniques of a company's markting effort are combined and stressed.

Marketing Model or Operational Research Method. Basing advertising appropriation on a scale showing various costs for different quantities of a product resulting in a certain net profit. Opposit to unit method since advertising costs rise or fall in relation to sales.

Market Niche Strategy. A marketing strategy which aims to identify small gaps or niches in the market and then provide suitable products or services to exploit them. It is a useful strategy for smaller firms competing with large firms in mature markets.

Marketing Orientation. Used to describe concerns which seek to identify and quantify customer requirments and to plan output and profitability accordingly.

Marketing-Oriented Company. One that tends to manufacture what the consumer or customer needs rather than what best suits its production and technical facilities.

Market Push. Pressure from a companys, market which forces it to follow a particular cours seat action.

Marketing Research. Any research activity which provides information relating to marketing operations. Whilist the term embraces conventional market research, motivation studies, advertisement attention value, packaging effectiveness, logistics, and media research are also included, as well as analysis of internal and external statistics of relevance.

Market Segmentation. The breakdown of a market into a number of differentiated segments based on factors like price, quality, delivery, performance etc., Markets are segmented in an attempt to find chunks which are small enough to become the subject of a niche strategy but large enough to provide a viable business opportunity for the firm.

Marketing Services. Term sometimes used to cover all marketing activities in a company other than the sales function *e.g.*, marketing research, advertising and public relations.

Marketing Society. Membership consists of senior marketing executives, two—thirds of new membership restricted to marketing companies.

Marketing Strategy. Written plan, usually comprehensive, describing all activities involved in achieving a particular marketing objective, and their relationship to one another in both time and magnitude.

Marketing Tools. Activities, processes and techniques used for implementing service. Or a product be may launched to sell to a specific segment, usually a new segment, of the market.

Market Segmentation Study. Research into segmentation of markets so that manufacturers can supply specific targets groups. Seeks to define consumer groups and marketing targets.

Market Segment Capacity. Amount of a product or service that could be absorbed in the future by a specialized segment of a market irrespective of price considerations.

Market Share. Percentage measure of the share obtained by an individual company from the total market available. Usually calculated upon a national basis but some international measures are in use.

Market Sharing Agreement. One made between two or more companies organizations producing and/or marketing similar products. They agree that each shall deal only with a particular part of the available market rather than competing with each other in the market as a whole.

Market Stability. Product qualities such as durability (for example, how much in danger of obsolescence in the product?), breadth of use (is it used locally, nationally or internationally?) whether it has a captive market, and the security of any.

Market Structure. The term usually refers to the factors which significantly affect the constituent firms of the industry. The main feature which indicate the market structure are:

(a) concentration and concentration ration;

(b) Product differentiation;

(c) barriers to the entry of new firms;

(d) growth rate of market demand;

(e) price elasticity of market demand; and

(f) ration of fixed to variable costs in the short-run.

Market Supply. Instantaneous supply with no time given for supply to adjust itself to a change in demand. Also called in stantaneous supply, it is the sale of goods already produced and in existence.

Market Supply Schedule. The schedule which shows the relation between the price of the commodity and the total quantity which people are willing to sell at each price.

Market Theory. Based on David Ricardo's 19th century theory of an international division of labour. He explained that if Britain specialized in textiles and Portugal in wine, both would benefit. That goods will be produced where it is most efficient to do so. Theory of customs union, although not a fact of the Common Market as presently constituted. In effect, labour and capital should move to where it can be best employed. Britain's advantage is that it has larger firms, such as indesit Fiat and Necchi in Italy, base their production on European or world markets. Probably the best modern example of the market theory in operation is the aircraft industry which is dominated by American manufacturers such as Douglas and Boing, making the British Aircraft Corporation less viable despite the brilliance of its innovations. Hence joint venturers such as concord and European airbus. Not to be confused with marketing concept which is sometimes called marketing theory.

Market Trend. Direction of developments in a market.

Market Value. The market value of something at a particular time is the price that any buyer might removably be expected to pay for it at that time if he was able to make a considered judgment of its value and was not influence by any special relationship with the seller.

Market Visit. As field inspection.

Market Penetration Proportion. It is usually expressed as a percentage, of the actual market volume (that is, total sales by all suppliers) that is met by a particular company or its product.

Market Weight. Used for weighting advertising expenditure; means of varying expenditure according to the pattern of consumption by different market groups.

Mark of Origin. A mandatory indication of the country of origin on imported goods.

Mark Process Model. Stochastic model which assumes that brand about to be bought it influenced by previously purchased brand in same product group.

Marque. Distinctive brand or make used to segment the market, or to retain market loyalties following company mergers and takeovers.

Mass Advertising. Using the mass media to each markets.

Mass Market. Popular market for mass-produced goods are distinct from custom-built, made-to-measure, and other individual products.

Mass Media. Principally, television, radio and newspapers, *i.e.* those channels of communication which reach a very large market.

Mass Merchandiser. Discount store selling great variety of merchandise. Usually out-of-town.

Mass Production. It refers to:

i) the scale of production for an item of goods and services to be large;

ii) the item of production must be standard, that is, of standardized specifications;

iii) the labour required for the production of the item must be specialized; and

iv) there should be intensive use of capital equipment.

Mass Retailing. Selling through large-scale outlets such as supermarkets, hypermarkets, discount stores and mixed retail business.

Mass Unemployment. Sir William Beveridge is responsible for the phrase. It refers to for a number of men, over many months of several years. It is also called cyclical unemployment on account of its association with the trade cycle.

Master Budget. Overall or final control budget of a company or organization, co-ordinating the various sectional budgets.

Master Production Schedule (MPS). A production schedule that indicates which products will be made using which sequence of operations, which are materials, which human resources, and so on. It is used as the basis of several production planning systems.

Master Clerical Data (MCD). A predetermined motion-time system developed by a firm of management consultants. It is based on methods-time measurement and is intended for use in measuring office work.

Master Sample. Assembly of sampling points maintained by a number of research establishments and used as a basis for final selection of samples. This practice eliminates the expensive selection processes which would otherwise be required each time a survey or research study is commissioned.

Matched Area Tests. The marketing using compatible test towns in one of two ways:

i) one as a control town, one as a set test town, or

ii) testing a different advertisement or promotion in each town

Matched Orders. A method of creating a false market in which two orders are given by one persons to two different brokers who deal in the same organized market. One order is to sell a quantity at not less than a stated price (above the prevailing market price); the other order is to buy at up to that price. The brokers carry out the deal which is then reported to the public and gives the impression that market prices are rising.

Matched Sample. Describes a technique where in two or more samples with matching characteristics are used to provide realistic comparisons on different test subjects.

Matching. Refers to the technique of comparing the keys of two records to select items for particular stage of processing or to reject invalid records.

Matching Item. Test question requiring the testee to match individual works, statements or figures from one list with others from a second list.

Materials. The goods that a manufacturer buys for conversion into manufactured products. Also the value of a manufacturer's stock of unconverted materials.

Material Control Schedule. A delivery reduest issued by Material Control in accordance with a blanket order. The schedule is normally for some long-term period (*e.g.* three months) with varying degrees of firmness (*i.e.,* the period over which indicated requirements will not change).

Master Sample. Assembly of sampling points maintained by a number of research establishments and used as a basis for final selection of samples. This practice eliminates the expensive selection processes which would otherwise be required each time a survey or research study is commissioned.

Materials Handling. The activity, or study, of moving materials to a factory, moving work-in-progress throgh the factory and moving finished goods to customers.

Materials Management. A concept of organization that places under a single, manager functions concerned with the movement of materials, production control, inventory control, traffic, storage, materials handling, purchasing, and other similarly related activities.

Material Requirements Planning. Also, MRP. The process whereby industrial firms work to optimize the conflicting objectives of having a minimum investment in inventory with that of always having material on hand to meet the needs of manufacturing departments within the company and of customers of the company's end—products. Although companies have long engaged in this process, the term became widely used only when the planning process involved the use of a computer.

Matrix Management. The idea of both vertical and horizontal relationships in business organization. For example, a purchasing director would have a vertical relationship with members of the purchasing department and a horizontal relationship in working with members of the engineering department on their purchasing-related problems or in working with purchasing departments in other divisions of the same company. The matrix organizations is perceived as a successor to the older form of line of staff organization.

Mature Student. One who enters further on higher education after a period in employment, rather than straight from school.

Maturity. The date on which a loan, bond, debenture, or other obligation falls due and is to be paid in full (redeemed) be the borrower.

Maturity Basis. The method of calculating the values of bonds and their rates of return, based on the assumption that the bonds will be held until maturity.

Maturity Curve. A graph which is sometimes used when determining salaries. In the method a survey is made of all people working in a particular kind of professional or technical carreer. The survey establishes the salary of each individual and the number of years he has been working in his profession (or sometimes number of years since first degree, or sometimes just chronological age). The distribution of salaries is plotted for each year. The 90th percentile (for example) maturity curve can then be derived by plotting all the 90th percentiles of these distributions of a graph of salary against years in profession. Similar maturity curves are derived from other percentiles. The salary of an individual working in that profession can then be determined by assessing which percentile the individual corresponds to (assessing him as corresponding to the 90th percentile, for example. is equivalent to saying he is better than 90 per cent of the other people in his profession with the same experience) and then reading off his salary according to his years of experience from the maturity curve for that percentile. (A maturity curve is also known as a 'career curve').

Matrix Organization. One such as a research laboratory or management consultancy in which there are a number of funtions or disciplines, of members of which may be assigned to special project teams.

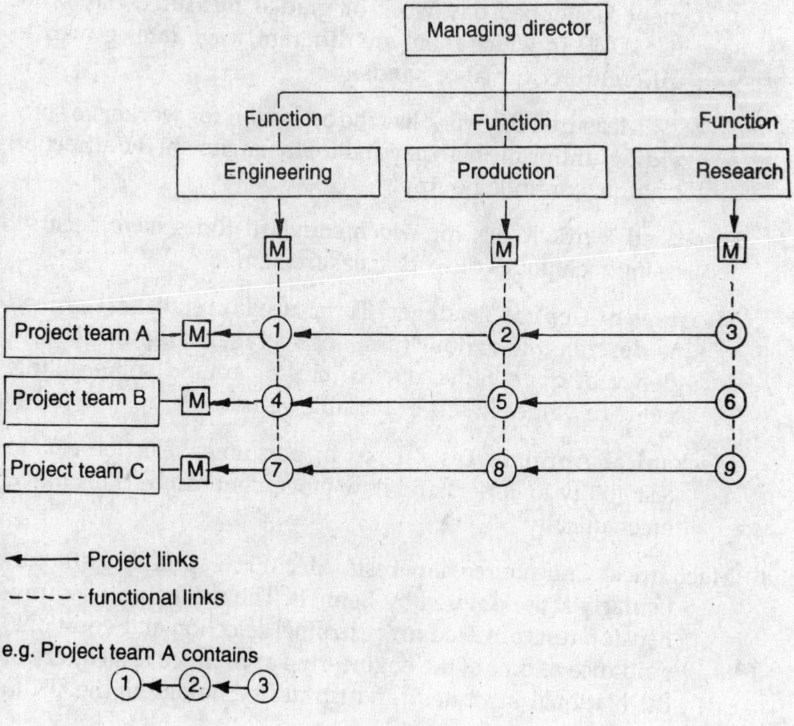

Mean Repair Time. In a given time period it refers to the ratio of time spent in corrective maintenance of a unit to the number of unit failure.

Mean Time Between Failures. In a given time period, it refers to the ratio of the total time in the period to the number of failure in the period.

Mean Time to Repair. Synonymous with mean repair time.

Measured Day work (MDW). Management technique which involves defining a target daily rate of productivity but then, instead of employing conventional direct payment-by-results, establishes a regular wage level to be paid for each day that the operative or production unit concerned reaches target. Targets set under measured daywork are often established upsing work measurement and, when this is so, the technique may be called controlled daywork. A further refinement is stepped day work or graded measured day work (GMDW) in which there are different wage rates geared to different performance bands.

Measured daywork has the attraction for workers of providing uniformly high pay and for management the attraction of high, controlled output.

Measured Work. Work for which standard times have been set using techniques of work measurement.

Measures of Central Tendency. Term used in statistical method to describe the various forms of average, based on the tendency of quantitative data to cluster around some middle value or values in sets of variable values.

Mechanical Aptitude Tests. Used in personnel selection etc., to test ability to understand how movement can be transmitted mechanically.

Mechanical Comprehension Tests. Mechnical aptitude tests, particularly those devised by Bennett. The mechanical comprehension tests are used for personnel selection and vocational guidance as part of the engineering apprentice test battery of the National Institute of Industrial Psychology in the UK in this latter battery they are coded (m). Bennett's mechnical comprehension tests also have a much wider use internationally.

Mechanic's Lien. A lien that has been created by statute to assist labourers in collecting their wages. Its purpose is to subject the land of an owner to a lien for materials and labour expended in the construction of buildings. Having been placed on the land, the buildings become a part of the land by the law of accession.

Mechanisation. The use of tools of equipment of any kind to aid human brain and muscle.

Mechanistic Organization. In their pioneering work on organization structures. Tom Burns and George Stalker found two forms which were suitable under different conditions—mechanistic and Organic. Mechanistic organization structures are based on a bureaucratic model (*i.e.*, one involving high division of tasks and allocation of clear responsibility and vertical hierarchies) and are approprite for activities such as production with high levels of predictability requiring a high degree of control.

Member. One of the persons who are associated together as a corporation.

Member Corporation. A securities broskerage firm organized as a corporation.

Members of the Disguised Unemployment. Phrase coined by Mrs. Joan Robinson. It signifies the workers who are transferred or displaced from shrinking industries in depression period, to less productive enterprises like agriculture and other occupations.

Membership Group. Types of reference group brought together for the purpose of examining consumer buying motives.

Memorandom of Association. One of the documents of a company to be formed. It contains the title of the company, the nature of the business to be undertakem the amount of the authorised capital, the address of the registered office, particularly of the shares and a statement that liability of the share-holders is limited.

Mensualization. Term of French origin for extending to blue collar or manual workers terms and conditions of employment associated with staff status. Strictly speaking, the term means switching to monthly payment though this is not necessarily a condition of staff status. The process of levelling up the terms and conditions of blue collar and white collar employment is also known as integration or harmnonization. Where staff status applies to both blue and white collar workers they are said to have single status.

Merchandise Planning. Defined by Drucker as 'the systematic design of quality goods for mass distribution, the systematic development of mass producers for them.

Merchandise Programme. In-store advertising, policy regarding goods bought and their promotion. May be topical, seasonal innovatory or traditional.

Merchandiser. Sales promotion expert who sets up in-store promotions, special displays, sampling facilities at point-of-sale. May be specially engaged from contact sales force organizer.

Merchandising. Tactical advertising. Any kind of special sales promotional scheme or activity such as in-store promotions, competitions, free gifts, sampling, premium offers and premium vouchers. Loosely used term.

Merchandising Area. Part of large supermarket or store set aside to promote a product or range of product.

Merchant. Type of wholesaler, and sometimes retailer, who is not committed to handling goods from a particular supplier or selling to particular outlets.

Merchantable Quality. Implied condition that a reasonable person would, after examination, accept goods as satisfactory to complete a contract for their purchase or sale.

Merchant Middleman. An intermediary that takes possession and ownership of goods. (Also known as a 'reseller').

Merchant Wholesaler. A general term for a trader who takes title to goods for sale to retailers who in turn resell them to end users.

Merit Increase. An increase in pay given to an employee if his performance satisfies some criterion.

Merit Pay. Extra pay or salary awarded to an employee, executive, etc in recognition of particular qualities, of value to the employer.

Merit Payment. An addition to a standard time rate, for a particular type of work in an enterprise, that is paid to individual workers because of their special skills or responsibilities.

Merit Rating. Techniqe for rating individual operators. Recognizes thast different people doing the same job can have different values to their firm and theorefore merit different pay. Merit rating factors can include absenteeism, punctuality, length of service, adaptability, health and safety records, attitude to management, etc.

Merit Salary Increase. The increase in base pay granted a salaried employee, theoretically intended to reward increased job competence and good performance.

Merit System. Where promotion is by examination or other objective demonstration of ability. Different, for example, from spoils system.

Metamarketing. Application of marketing concepts and tools to marketing or products, services, organizations, individuals and places inorder to achieve an exchange relation.

Meter Advertisements. Advertisements on parking meters. Passers by are able to see a message repeated every 15 seconds.

Methodology. Strictly relating to the basis of a research design application and analysis. Commonly used as a synony for 'method', but more properly should apply to a set of methods.

Methods Manual. Detailed information developed as sets of instructions for the routing and operations to be performed in the processing or manufacture of a part or a product.

Methods-time Measurement (MTM). In manufacturing procedures, a methods engineering technique for acquiring data that may apply to all classes of work involving manual motions.

Micro Marketing. Meeting the needs of the individual firms in terms of its objectives and its actions to achieve them.

Micromotion Study. A work analysis method that uses motion pictures with a timing device to obtain times for each motion.

Micro-specification. Each decision point within the marketing macro-system, *e.g.*, purchasing, production and labour devisions.

Middleman. Wholesaler, agent or other businessman coming between the producer or the manufacturer and retailer in the sales chain. His basic role in the distribution of goods is to buy from the producer and sell to the retailer.

Middle Management. An intermediate management position, such as that of a foreman who supervises production workers and in turn is responsible to the works manager.

Middle Manager. A manager in an organization who is not a first-line supervisor and is not in a general-management position. Also a person in an organization with the same status as middle managers in that organization.

Middle-of-the Road Style. A style of managerial leadership based on the belief that adequate organization performance is possible through balancing the need to get out the work with the need to maintain the morale of people at a satisfactory level.

Midnight Shift. A shift that begins about midnight.

Migrant Labour. Also, migratory workers. Workers who regularly shift from one job to another throughout the year.

Migrant Worker. Synonym for migrant.

Migration of Labour. Movement of labour into and out of a particular area.

Milk Bottle Advertising. Advertisements silk screen printed on milk bottles by bottle manufacturers (*e.g.*, Rockware) for advertisers such as breakfast food manufacturers.

Milk Round. An annual tour of universities made by representatives of large employers for the purpose of interviewing students who have expressed interest in working for those employers.

Mineral Rights. A right to extract minerals from a given piece of land.

Mini-magazine. Small circulation periodical serving a specialised readership.

Minimum Charge. Also, minimum rate. A price charged for a service even if it is not performed or used in full.

Minimum Demand Survey. In industrial market, research, particularly, eliminating irrelevant or unnecessary initial investigations to arrive at a preliminary stage, when data so far discovered is sufficient for go/no-go decision to be taken.

Minimum Duties. As opposed to maximum duties, they are the which are usually laid down by Parliament in the tariff law and which fix a lower limit to any concenssions which the Administration may make.

Minimum Earnings Level (MEL). Nationally agreed minimum wage applicable in indistries where wage levels are largely determined by local agreements.

Minimum Entitlement. Minimum pay an employee can receive under a particular payment system, including a payment—by-results scheme.

Minimum Movements. Movements which, while natural, are the minimum necessary for the job.

Minimum Piece Work Standard (MPS). Level earnings in the engineering industry as that which should be obtained by the worker of average ability on payment-by-results schemes.

Minimum Planned Start Date Per Operation (MINSD). In this rule for production scheduling, the order assigned next is the one with the earliest planned start date for the current operation.

Minimum Wage. Wage level below which the workers cannot be paid. It is the establishment of a uniform or differentiated "wage floor."

Minimum Wages Act. The Minimum Wages Act, empowers the government to fix minimum wages of employees working in specified employments.

Minimum Wage Legislation. A situation of statutory fixation of wage-rates below which no payments can be made for employing the specified workmen. Its introduction was based on the assumption that the employers often appropriated the labour power of the workmen without adequately remunerating them for the same mainly because of the helplessness of the latter.

Mint. A place where money is coined, usually under government auspices.

Minute Book. A book containing the minutes of meetings specifically one containing the minutes of meetings of directors of a company or of general meetings of a company.

MIS. Management Information System (acronym, pronounce letters individually).

Misfeasance. The improper performance of a duty that has been imposed by law or contract and that injures another person.

Misfeasance Proceedings. Court action during the winding up of a company to recover property of the company that has been misapplied by persons.

Mixed Strategy. In game theory, a rule adopted by a player specifying probalities of his selecting each of a number of choice.

Mobile. POS advertising device suspended from ceiling so as to attract attention by its movement. Ideal for supermarkets where display space is scarce.

Mobile Shop. Research technique. Copies of a magazine containing an advertisement for a new product are delivered on a housing estate. Then a mobile shop tours the estate, and purchases by residents are noted to see whether the new product or existing rival products are bought. Tests both advertisement and pack.

Mobility. Movements of a factor of production between industries or occupations or places.

Mobility of Labour. Movement of labour between countries and within the country between occupations, industries and places.

Mode of Production. The term refers to a particular social arrangement of production in a society which is uniquely characterised by the following components : (i) the organisation of labour in a scheme of division and cooperation, the skills of labour and the status of labour in the social context with respect to degrees of freedom or servitude; (ii) the geographical environment and the knowledge of the use of resources and materials; (iii) technical means and process and the state of science generally.

Modular Advertising. The concept of providing clients with one or a few specialized advertising services, instead of a complete package of all services (market research, creating ads, styling and packaging help, media selection, etc.

Module Training. Training involving units or modules of knowledge which can be learnt piecemeal by the student. Typically, each module involves a combination of experience, formal training and on-the-job training.

Modus Operandi. Methods and manner by which an organization etc., operates.

Modus Vivendi. Manner and style of living, particularly one arrived at by a compromise between clashing interests.

Monadic. Single product test. Used as a test of acceptance or validity as an alternative to a comparative assessment.

Monadic Product Test. A market research term for a consumer test of a single product.

Money demand Schedule for Labour. A list of demand prices that are offered for hiring various quantities of labour.

Money Manager. Manager of investments and related financial matters.

Money Order. An order for payment of a particular sum of mony drawn on a bank, telegraph company, post office, express company, or other agency from whom the drawer purchased it. It is used primarily to make payments over a distance without mailing cash or personal checks.

Money Shop. Offers banking and consumer finance services including instalment credit and hire purchase.

Monopolistic Competition. A type of market structure in which a relatively large number of the sellers of products that are similar but not identical possess some degree of control over their selling price.

Monopoly Agreements. When there are more than one firm controlling the total production of any specified commodity which could be used as near substitutes, they often enter into agreement with one another in order to safeguard their own interests and to obtain the maximum gain.

Monopoly Profit. The difference between average cost and average revenue, multiplied by output.

Monopoly Profit. A monopolist is able to control the price of his product, so he does not fix the price epqual to the point where his marginal cost and marginal revenue are equal; he restricts his production to the level where the average cost and the average revenue are equalized which gives him the maximum profit which would be greater than what it would have been under the conditions of perfect competition.

Monopony. A market situation in which a single firm is the only buyer of a product, although there may be more than one seller also known as a buyer's monopoly.

Monte Carlo Method. A technique for simulating a long sequence of states of a system that has uncontrollable variables that occur in known probability distributions.

Monte Carlo Simulation. A statistical technique using Random Numbers (as might appear on a roulette wheel; hence the name, traditionally associated with gambling) to determine whether an actual set of values is random or non—random.

Monte Carlo Techniques. Simulation, sometimes using a computer, of a work situation that is complicated by random elements.

Most-favoured Nation Clause. This means that each state binds itself not to impsoe high duties on imported from a third country.

Most Favoured Nation-Clause. Used in treaties and international trade agreements, meaning that tariff rights given by one country to any other are also given to counmtry with which new agreement is being made.

Motion Study. Synonym for work study. This area of motion and methods study has many names. It is known as methods analysis, methods engineering, methods research, work study, and work analysis. F. B. and L. M. Gilbreth define motion study as the science of eliminating wastefulness resulting from using unnecessary, ill-directed, and inefficient motions. the aim of motion study is to find and perpetuate the scheme of least waste methods of labour.

Motivate. To ensure that people carry out effectively and willingly the tasks assigned to them by providing them with reasons for behaving in certain ways.

Motivation. Psychological stimulus behind the acts of courses of action adopted by individuals or groups of individuals. Applied in marketing both to individual and organizational activities as well as to consumer and user behaviour.

Motivational Research. Study of psychological reasons underlying human behaviour particularly in relation to buying situations.

Motivation-hygiene Theory. Also known as the duality theory, proposed in 1959 by Frederick Herzberg of Case-Western University and expanded to include a theory of work motivation, Herzberg argues that when people feel dessatisfied with their jobs they become concerned about the work environment, or about hygiene factors. When people feel good about their jobs, it may be due to the work itself, the motivators. From another perspective, the hygiene factors are not necessarily motivators. The job itself, according to Herzberg, is effective in motivating people to superior performance.

Motivation Research. Research to discover underlying motives, desires and emotions ehich provoke human behaviour and, in market research, true reasons why people buy or donot buy certain goods as distinct from reasons they express or even imagine they act upon.

Motivation Study. Market research technique for identiying the motivation responsible for the behaviour pattern of a market.

Motivator. An aspect of a job that can contribute to the satisfaction but not the dissatisfaction of the job holder according to the motivation-hygience theory.

Motor Skills. Those connected with the motor activity of muscles.

Motor Speed and Accuracy Mechanical Test (Motor Spd Acc). Personnel selection and vocational guidance test devised as part of the engineering apprentie test-battery of the national Institute of Industrial Psychology.

Mover. Someone moving a motion at a meeting or conference.

Moving Average. A technique for studying the behaviour of a time series in problems in which the trend of the series is obviously not a straight line and in problems in which the analysis are interested only in the general motion of the series, be it a trend, cycle, or both.

MPS. Minimum piece work standard.

MRA. Abbreviation of multiple regression analysis.

MRG. Abbreviation of Management Research Groups.

MRTPC. Monopolies and Restrictive Trade Practices Commission.

Multi-client Survey. Market research survey financed jointly by sponsors of subscribers. Usually, such surveys are not mounted until a certain minimum number of subscribers have been recruited.

Multi-employer agreement. An agreement between a labour union and several employers, from a handful to many or even a whole industry. By combining for collective bargaining employers—particularly small firms—are able to hire skilled lawyers to negotiate on their behalf, prevent a union from picking on one firm at a time and using agreements of other firms against it, and generally gain the benefits of collective action.

Multi-employer Bargaining. Or association bargaining. Form of collective bargaining in which a number of employers participate, as in industry-wide bargaining, sometimes, through an employers' association.

Multi-factor Incentive Scheme. An incentive payment system in which the incentive payment depends on several factors *e.g.*, performance, quality of output and wastage of materials.

Multi Grade Salary Structure. Salary structure with a relatively large number of grades. A structure with a small number of grade is a broad-banded slalary structure.

Multilateral Trade. The sale of goods in any country while its proceeds are used for the purchase of goods from another country leading to multilateral trading: it is trade between several countries.

Multilateral Treaty. Sometimes it is known as collective agreement or international convention.

Multi employer Bargaining. Collective Bargaining taking place at an industry or sub-sector level involving several employers.

Multi-minute Measurement. A form of work measurement where samples are taken at short intervals.

Multiple Correlation. Marketing reserarch tool used to measure the effect of several independent variables on one dependent variable.

Multiple Cutoff Approach. Where, in psychological testing, a candidate is given a number of tests (*e.g.*, a test battery), but it is necessary to ensure that a weakness in one test score is not compensated for and obscurred by high scores in other tests.

N

Named Vote. Vote taken at a meeting by recording by name the way in which each voter votes. This procedure is usually reserved only for critically important issues.

Name Screening. Market research technique for checking that the prospective name of a product or service conveys the intendes image, does not imply unfortunate associations, and voids confusion with other brand names.

National Agreement. As industry-wide agreement on wages, conditions of employment, etc., usually made between the appropriate employees association and trade union(s).

National Campaign. Marketing operation covering the entire country.

National Claim. Claim for more pay or improved conditions, etc. lodged by trade unions as the first move in industry-wide bargaining.

National Industrial Tribunal (NIT). Quasi-judicial authority for the adjudication of industrial disputes, in India, which involve questions of national importance or of such a nature that industrial establishments situated in more than one state are likely to be interested in, or affected by, such disputes. NIT is constituted by the Central Government as and when the need arises.

Nationalised Industry. Commerical and non-commerical organization *e.g.*, National Coal Board and atomic Energy Authority, owned and controlled in the name of the nation.

Nationalisation. It is a process by which the government assumes control of firms and organizations operating in the private sector with or without compensation.

Nationalise. To transfer ownership of something (usually compulsorily) from private individuals to the government of a country.

National Labour Institute Bulletin. Indian quarterly. Reports empirical and action research of interdisciplinary nature. Address: AB-6 Safdarjang enclave, New Delhi-110029.

National Procedure Agreement. Made between the employers associations and the trade unions in a particular industry to lay down the procedure to be followed in the event of industrial disputes, etc.

National Wealth. The value of a nation's total resource, including both reproducible tangible assets (buildings, machinse, inventory) and non-reproducible assets (land, natural resources).

Included are all structures (residential, institutional, farm, etc.), all equipment (producer and consumer durables), inventories and land.

Natural Break. Requirement in broadcast media that commercial breaks occur only between normal gaps in the continuity of programmes.

Natural Business Year. A fiscal year that ends at the annual low point of business activity or at the conclusion of a business season.

Natural Monopoly. A monopoly created by the nature of an enterprise, which is such that competition is self-destructive and contrary to the public interest, so that one firm can, through economy of scale, produce more at lower cost than two or more firms.

Natural Resources. These comprise both the raw materials and the conditions of nature that are required in production. They include mineral wealth, soil, climate, waterways, and topography.

Natural Wastage. Process of reducing number of people employed in a firm or organization by not taking on new employees to replace those leaving of their own accord.

Nature's Remedy. It is a rise of prices sufficient to divert real resources out of the pockets of the main body of consumers into the pockets of entrepreneurs and thence to the Treasury, party in the shape of a higher yield from existing taxes particularly Excess Profits Tax and partly in contributions to loans out of the increased savings and reserves of the entrepreneurs.

Near Cash. Something that can be converted into a known amount of cash at very short notice—for example, a demand deposit.

Nearest-neighbour Analysis. Study to discover mean distance between shops, factories, businesses or other located units of similar class.

Near Money. Anything that can be readily turned into money at a known value, predominantly savings accounts and savings bond. Bank deposits. Bills of exchange, are some of the examples of near money.

Needs Analysis. Term used in training management for analysis to establish the instructional programme required by a particular trainee to bring him/her to the standard laid down in the relevant job description.

Needs Satisfaction. Fulfilment of a want. When a need is satisfied, it may no longer serve as a motivator. For example, a hungry person is highly motivated to acquire food and will perform a difficult task in moving toward that objective.

Negative Cash Flow. Where less cash is flowing into a project or enterprise than out of it. Where the larger flow is into the project/enterprise there is said to be positive cash flow.

Negative Income Tax. A form of welfare payment whereby all low-income individuals and families recieve a direct cash subsidy from the government that is sufficient to raise them to subsistence level. The subsidy itself in the negative tax.

Negative Motion. One moved at a meeting or conference with entirely negative intent. It should not be accepted by the chairman because it makes no more contribution to the work of the meeting than if it has been left unsaid.

Negative Self-selecion, Personnel selection term for the situation where a candidate decides to withdraw his application for a job.

Negative Strike. Industrial action to fight against a worsening of wages and/or conditions.

Negative Wealth. Things which are injurious to man.

Negotiable. A document of title is said to be 'negotiable' if, according to custom, anyone who becomes a holder of it for value and in good faith will not be affected by prior calims to it.

Negotiable Instruments. Claims or rights to payment that are readily transferable from one person to another, that is, capable of being bought and sold. There are four principal kinds of negotiable instrument: the Bill of Exchange (on draft), Check, Promissory Note, and Certificate of Deposit.

Negotiate. To discuss with someone with whom one has a difference or dispute possible terms for the settlement of the difference or dispute.

Negotiated Environment External variables over which management has no control: political, economic, legal, social, technological and the competition. Area in which management is obliged to negotiate.

Negotiating Machinery. The institutions for conducting negotations between employers and trade unions and the rules governing such regotiations.

Negotiating Rights. Or full regotiating rights. Traditionally, where a trade union has the established right to enter into full negotations and collective bargaining with employer.

Negotiation. The formal process of reaching an agreement by discussion. In Industrial Relations, negotiation has an important role to play in Collective Bargaining and other form of bargaining procedures.

Net Audience. Number of unduplicated homes, readers or viewers, *etc.*, also known as net readership.

Net Avails. The net proceeds of a discounted note.

Net Cover. Percentage of the target audience receiving at least one exposure to a commercial or advertisement.

Net Effective Distribution. In Market Research, the number of retail outlets which have a certain product in stock on a ceretain date.

Net Rate. Publisher's rates after deduction of agency commission.

Net Realizable Value. The price at which something could be sold less the expenses of selling it.

Net Requirements. In manufacturing procedures, the actual production or purchasing requirements for a particular item, part, subassembly, or assembly.

Net Terminal Value. The terminal value of the cash inflows associated with an investment project minus the terminal value of the cash outflows at a specified time (usually the time when the investment is likely to be abandoned).

Net Weight. For packaged goods, the weight of the items contained in the package, not including the weight of the wrapping material, container or other packaging. For canned goods, especially foods, net weight includes all the liquid as well as the solid material contained in the can or jar.

Network Analysis. Breaking down a complex project into component requirements and recording these in a diagramatic form which incorporates a critical time scale, so that planning and control can be effected in the most expedient manner.

Net-worth Turnover. A ratio for determining an aspect of the financial worth of an enterprise, calculated by dividing net sales by dividing stockholders' equity.

New. Word often applied to indicate a novel market opportunity. Newness may vary from very slight to very large, the risk factors increasing with the actual amount of innovation, so that many 'new' products fail to achieve market acceptance.

New Plant and Equipment Expenditures. The total value of private business spending for new plant, machinery, and equipment,an important baro meter of general business conditions.

News Agency. News gathering and distributing organization. Each agency specializes in news of a certain kind.

News Desk. Section of newspaper office which handles intake of news by telephone, Telex, wire service tape or Unitel Prestel service.

News Editor. The working editor-proper of a newspaper the editor as managing editor a big newspaper being more a business and policy director. The night editor replaces the news editor at night on a morning paper.

New Technology Agreement (NTA). An agreement between a Trade Union and an employer on the introduction of new technology, containing details of implications and impacts on such factors as employment levels, working practices, status differentials etc.

News. Information that is not already known to recipients. However, the late American newspaper owner, William Randolph Hearst, said 'News is what someone, somewhere doesn't want you to print—all the rest is advertising'.

News Agencies of India. India has 4 news agencies—Press Trust of India (PTI)., United News of India (UNI)., Samachar Bharati and Hindustan Samachar. The four news agencies were merged in 1976 to form Samachar. Two years later, Samachar was dismantled and the news agencies regained their separate identity from 14 April 1978.

Next Business. Motion moved from the floor of a meeting or conference with the object of ending discussion on the item of business in hand. If the motion is seconded and then carried, the meeting abandons the item in hand and moves immediately to the next item on the agenda. The chairman has discretion to reject a motion for next business but if he accepts it, it must be put to the vote immediately, usually without discussion. A motion for next business has much in common with a previous question motion.

Next Matter. Advertisement next to editorial matter.

Next-to-reading Matter. Advertisement position immediately adjacent to editorial.

Nielsen Index. Retail audit of brands within predetermined groups, classified geographical area within regular time periods. Standard format is available to subscribers in large and steadily increasing number of Countries.

Night Shift. A shift that is worked mainly at night. (Colloquially known as a 'graveyard shift').

Night Shopping. In many advance countries stores have late closing night on Thursdays, while in the suburbs and provinces super-markets are open during the evening. Not strictly speaking a new idea.

Nightwork. Work performed at night. The conventions adopted by the International Labour Organization for the control of nightwork define 'night' as 'a period of at least 11 consecutive hours including the interval between 2200 and 0500'.

No-benefit-to Payee Clause. A clause added to their bills of lading by many transportation companies and agencies such as railroads and motor carrier lines. It provides that any insurance payable in connection with the property being transported shall be payable to the transporting company.

No-change Strategy. Continued serving of existing customers with existing products, plus increasing market share through extra market penetration.

NOI. Initials for Not Otherwise Indexed, with reference to tariff classification.

NOIBN. Initials for not otherwise Indexed By name, with reference to tarif classification.

Nominal Partner. An individual who lends his or her name to a partnership but is not actually a partner. The value to the partnership is in the promotional value of the nominal partner's name and reputation for which the nominal partner receives a fee in payment.

Nominal Wage. Earnings regarded in terms of their face value rather than their purchasing power.

Nominee. A person who is in some legal relationship in name only, having under taken to exercise all rights and duties attached to the reltionship in accordance with another person's directions.

Nomographic Chart. The term nomograph is derived from the Greek noms, law, and grapho, to write. The term has come to be associated with one particular type of chart that uses functional scales for the solution of numerical problems.

Non-aligned News Agency, 1976. Encourages co-operation between news agencies in member states, and in Tunis general assembly, 1982, adopted Iran's proposal to launch a non-aligned communications satellite.

Non-analytic Job evaluation. Methods used to establish the relative worth of jobs by comparing whole jobs and either placing them in rank order or assigning them to pre-determined grades.

Non-assisted area. For research purposes, not an Intermediate Development, Development or Special Development Area.

Non-competing Groups. a country's labour force consists of different groups of labour (technical, skilled, semi-skilled and un-skilled, to mention one common classification) among which mobility is far from perfect. These distinct categories of labour, with rather well-marked and enduring differences in wages became known as "non-competing groups."

Non-contributory Pension scheme. A scheme run by an employer to provide pensions for employees who are not required to make payments towards it.

Non-cost Payments. Payments which reduce the usable funds of the treasury, but reduce correspondingly the debit obligations.

Non-directive Interview. Where, particularly in attitude surveys, the interviewer encourages a free exchange of views instead of working to the detailed and tighter structure of a directive interview. The non-directive interview has points of similarity with the connected conversation interview sometimes used in personnel selection.

Non-durable Goods. Goods that can usually be used only once or a few times or have a useful life that is very much less than one year.

Non-employed Person. One who is neither in employment not seeking it. A term used, for example, for national insurance purposes in the UK and many other advanced countries, other categories being employed person, self-employed person and unemployed person.

Non—executive Director. Or outside director. Director who is not a full—time employee of the company or corporation conerned and is not therefore an executive director.

Non-labour Income. According to Karl Marx, it refers to capitalists income.

Non-material External Goods. Relations beneficial to a person with other prople such as labour dues and personal services of various kinds.

Non-material goods. Services, goodwill of business etc.

Non-material Internal Goods. One's own qualities and faculties for action and for enjoyment such as business ability, professional skill.

Non-revene Receipts. Receipts which increase the usable funds of the treasury, but increase correspondingly the debt obligations.

Non-sampling Error. Error resulting from imperfect selection, bias in response, observation or recording but not attributable to the sample itself or its design.

Non-standard Material. Raw material or other goods whose quality standard differs from that appearing in a standard engineering specification.

Non-stick Corporation. A Corporation in which membership, with its rights and liabilities, is acquired through an agreement rather than through ownership of shares of stock. Examples of non-stock corporations include mutural companies, and some public coprorations.

Non-tariff Barriers. Sagfeguards which some countries impose to protect sensitive home industries, but which are often contentious. Include long term quotas, pricing agreements.

Non-transferable Good. The goods that or their ownsership cannot be transferred from one person to another, e.g. personal skill.

Non-verbal intelligence Test (g). Personnel selection and vocational guidance test devised as part of the engineering apprentice test-battery of the National Instiute of Industrial Psychology in the UK.

Normal Profit. The average rate of reward per unit of output in an industry or sector of the economy over a period of time. Normal profit is the minimum rate of profit necessary to ensure that a sufficient number of people will be prepared to invest, undertake riskes and organize production. The rate differs from industry to industry according to the degree of risks and difficulties in the enterprise.

Normal Results. Those results which can reasonably be expected as the outcome of a given situation.

Normal Table. In statistical analysis, a tabular presentation of selected values calcualted from a normal curve.

Normative Forecasting Techniques. Types of technique used, for example, in technology forecasting, which begin with a consideration of the likely future structure and needs of society, and then consider the developments necessary to create that structure and meet those needs.

Normative Model. Includes prose, mathematical, logical flow and similar models.

Normative science. Also called regulative science, it is a body of systematised knowledge relating to crieria of what ought to be and concerned with the ideal as distinguished from the actual.

Notary Public. A licensed public officer whose principal job is attesting or certifying the validity of signatures on certain documents that require such approval. Such a document then bears the notary's signature and seal, indicating that it was signed in his or her presence (but making no claim concerning the content of the document).

Note. A very general term for any kind of Paper, that is, acknowledgement of a debt and, by inference, a promise to pay.

Note of Hand. As promissory note.

Note Payable. A promissory note of the maker held by the payer as a liability.

Note Receivable. A promissory note held by the payee as a liability.

Noting. Term used in advertisement research. Indicates that a reader's attention was drawn to an advertisement when first looking through the newspaper or magazine in which it appeared, through not necessarily that he read, fully understood or acted upon this stimulus.

Noting and Reading Test. Gallup Poll technique of evaluating recall and impact of press advertisement, each part of advertisement being investigated and percentage male/female awareness being recorded.

Noting Score. Average number of readers found to have noted a specific advertisement or editorial item expressed as a percentage of total readership.

Novation. An arrangement by which a contract between two persons A and B is rescinded and replaced by similar contract between A and a third person C.

NPC. National Productivity Council.

Number Completion Test. Sometimes used in psychological testing. The subject has to compete or continue a series of numbers related accordings to a definite principle or principles.

Numerical Analysis. Refers to use of computing systems to solve mathematical problems; for example, equations and matrix manilpulation in contrast to record keeping.

Numerical Control. Also, NC, N/C. Automatic control of production processes particularly of machine tools such as lathes and milling machines, usually carried out by means of magnetic tapes that contains a series of prerecorded singals sent to electric motors and controls.

Nursed Account. A supplier who is favoured by a customer in terms of payment of invoices and preference for new business, particularly over other regular suppliers.

Nursery Unit. small factories on new industrial estates, set up by developers or local authorities, to help knew small businesses to find suitable premises in which to begin operations.

O

Objective Budgeting. Allocating expenditure according to established objectives, rather than arbitrarily by historical precedence.

Objective Function. In manufacturing procedures, the function that is to be optimized in a linear or nonlinear programming proble.

Objectives, Management by. Focusing management efforts on the ultimate goals of a business enterprise. The chief goal generally is to make a profit (for private companies; for the non-profit sector it is not forming at a loss). In addition to this basic economic objective, most organizations have goals that, even if seemingly non—economic, may be basic to their prosperity or even survival. Among them are favourable community relations, good customer service, pleasant working conditions and opportunities for advancement for employees, and technological leadership in their industry.

Objective Selling. Selling against predetermined arms., *e.g.*, to obtain an interview or a demonstration, where an immediate sale is not always possible.

Obligation. In law, a duty to perform (or not perform, some act, or to pay a sum of money. The person or persons who bind themselves, or are bound, to perform an obligation are called the obligor(s); the party in whose favour the obligationis assumed (for example, a creditor) so oblige.

Obligee. The person for whose benefit a promise is made in a bond.

Observation. Research technique, in which data is collected by researchers witnessing or recording the actual events which take place.

Observational Research. Marker research involving observation of evidence, *e.g.*, purchases discovered in kitchen and larder, and not answers to questions. In sociological research can involve participation in group activities to study by actual observation of behaviour. Known as covert observation as opposed to non-participant observation.

Obsolescence. Indicative of a significant relative decline in a product's usefulness or competitiveness in the market. This occurs when alternative products become available which have a better performance or lower.

Occupational Health. Prevention and treatment of illness or injury suffered by employees during or as a result of their work.

One-stop Shopping. A retailing concept which attempts to group the main types of retail outlet together so that the customer may buy all that is required within one area.

Occupational Profile. Analysis of breakdown of skills or occupations(s), for example within a firm, expressed as ratios or proportions. Sometimes qualified as 'ideal' (the profile a firm requires) or 'real' (the profile it actually has)

Occupational Psychology. The study of psychological problems associated with work and which arise in connection with, for example, vocational guidance, design of aptitude tests, personnel selection, training, work study or ergonomics. (Also known as 'industrial psychology').

Occupational Role. A role adopted by someone in order to pursue his occupation *e.g.*, a specific job or an arrangement for practising a profession.

Occupational Strucuture. Pattern of occupations, usually meant nationally but might be used of an industry or even of an individual firm.

Occupational Title. The name given to an occupation.

Occupational Union. Trade union for people working in a particular occupation(s).

O'Connor Finger Dexterity Test. Pegboard test of psychomotor skills, originating in the USA. The test involves sorting out small brass pins and placing them in groups of three in holes.

Off-card Rate. Special negotiated price for media advertising, *i.e.* other than that published in the official rate card.

Offending Images. Those in advertising which are likely to up set prople such as feminists non-smokers, immigrants, animal lovers, teetotallers, environmentalists, and other sensitive group.

Offer. A proposal made by one person (called the 'offeror') to another person (called the 'offeree') of the terms of a contract and an indication that if the offeree accepts the proposal then the offeror will consider himself bound by the contract.

Offer by Tender. A method of making a public offer securities:

1) in which the public is invited to submit tenders
2) for purchasing the securities.

Offeree. A person to whom an offer is made.

Offeror. Someone who makes an offer.

Offer Price. The price at which the management company sells a security.

Officer. In business management, any principal executive of a corporation to whom authority has been delegated by the board of directors or by the bylaws of a corporation.

Official Receiver. Officer appointed by the Department of Trade and attached to the High Court or a country court to investigate the causes of insolvencies that are dealt with by the court to which he is attached.

Official Strike. Traditionally a withdrawal of labo(u)r or strike by workers with formal trade union approval and support.

Offshore. The ocean waters and bottom within a given distance from a nation's borders which may be leased or sold to individuals, companies, or other nations.

Offshore Company. Company registered in a country where there is little government control over its financial dealings and where there are usually low tax rates.

Off the Books. The payment of wages for services performed but not recorded in the books or on the payroll records of the employer. Paying an employee off the books may be illegal, depending on rules and regualtions pertaining to the number of employees actually working for the employer.

Off the Books Payments. Payment for labo(u)r, services or goods which are not recorded in the business accounting books. Usually illegal payments since they avoid taxation and other statutory changes etc.

Off-the-job Training. Training organized in training centres etc.,. away from work/production, usally in conjection with complementary on-the-job training and further education.

Off-the page Advertising. Maill order trade advertising which seeks sales direct from press advertisements. Women's Clothing usually most popular merchandise.

Off-the-record. Statement made to the medial by an authoritative person who does not wish to be named. Could be a politician who is prepared to provide information from a non-attributable source. Media reports use various expresions like a usally reliable source to indicate that the information is authentic if anonymous.

Off-trade. Modern abbreviation of off-licence trade in beers, wines and spirits.

OJT. On-the-Job Training.

Ombudsman. An official of a government who is responsible for receiving and answering complaints and queries related to administrative practices and for making recommendations for corrective measures where indicated. In many countries, this function is filled to some degree by the comptroller-general.

Omnibus Motion. Motion put to a meeting or conference, each clause covering a different topic or subject. It differes from a composite motion, which is a combining of a number of different motions on the same subject.

Omnibus Questionnaire. One containing both opinion and preference questions or as, in an omnibus survey questions on different topics for different sponsors.

Omnibus Survey. Survey for a group of different clients enabling them each to ask a limited number of questions, sharing the overall cost.

On-air Testing. Depth interviwing of a sample of housewives after transmission of a commercial or series of commercials, as conducted by the British Market Research Bureau. Aternatively, recall testing can be made next day on a sample of housewives who had no expectation of researcher's call.

On Call. Available to perform work immediately a request is made.

On Consignment. Transmitted to another for the purpose of sale, display, demonstration, or similar use withoutactual transfer of title, as in merchandise delivered on consignment.

On-demand Guarantee. A contract guarantee under which the compensation must be paid on a demand being made by the buyer without further proof that the seller has defaulted.

One Man Pension Arrangement (OMPAs). Discretionary endowment pension scheme designed to arrange a pension scheme designed to arrange a pension for an individual employee.

"One Off" Production. The producing of an article to suit the particular requirements of a customer; opposite of mass production.

One-stage Advertising. Direct response off-the-page advertising which seeks to sell immediately from one independent advertisement.

One-stop Shopping. Out-of-town gaint store where all or most shopping needs are met.

On Order. In manufacturing, the total of all outstanding replenishment orders. For example, the on—order balance increases whenever a new order is released and decreases whenever an order is canceled. The releases and cancellations may be for the ful quantity ordered or for partial quantities.

On—pack. Gift or other offer or information printed on the outside surface(s) of packaged goods, particularly relating to premiums or competition entries.

On-pack Sales Promotion. Sales promotion offer printed on the product pack, such as sell-liquidating premium offers cash premium dividend and refund tokens, cross-coupon offers etc.

On-site Training. See on-the-job training.

On the Air. Indication that broadcasting is taking place.

On-the-job Training. Training or re-training carried out at the employee's work place and during the period of work (*e.g.* operating a new piece of equipment under the supervision of a specialist). This is the opposite of Off-The-Job Training.

On-the-record. Statement made to the media by an authoritative person, such as politician, who is willing to be named.

Open-door Policy. A management policy whereby any individual has unrestricted access to his or her immediate supervisor during working hours.

Open-end Contract. A contract in which some of the terms remain unspecified, or open.

Open Pricing. General circulation of pricing practices with a view to achieving conformity of prices within an industry.

Open Prospectus. Prospectus which seeks support or investment without spelling out clearly the purposes for which the support is to be used.

Open Shop. A work place in which no one union is recognized as representative of all employees and in which membership of a trade union is not compulsory.

Operating Marginal Analysis. Study of market potential for new entrant; time it will take new entran to win crucial market share, and at which cost; market segments likely to be most economic, *i.e.*, quickest to develop, most profitable.

Operating Rate. Also, capacity utilizaion rate. The ratio of actual physical output to potential production, that is, the proportion of output of current operations to output at full capacity.

Operating Ratio. Any comparison of an item from a financial statement with net sales; in calculations, the dollar value for net sales is placed in the denominator.

Operating Results. Net income or net loss.

Operating Revenue. The gross sales of goods and sevice less, returns and allowances and cash discounts, together with gross amounts, received from any other regular source of income; net revenue from sales.

Operating Statement. A detailed income statement that displays financial operations over a stated accounting period.

Operating System. A system that includes people performing work and which has been identified for purposes of discussion and analysis that concentrat attention on the performance of work.

Operational Marketing. Application of a corporate operational marketing system which, having carefully planned a marketing operation, now places product on the market, tests reactions of consumers, measures performance against initial plan, and has a built-in system of handling and rectifying problems.

Operations Management. The management of the central function of a business organization, whether in the manufacturing or service sector. This covers the management of materials, equipment, plant, and people with the objective of matching the activity of the enterprise to its market.

Operation Sheets. Precise specifications and descriptions of manufacturing methods telling in detail how an operation is to be performed.

Opportunity Analysis. Study of what market has to offer. Analysis of market potential and prospects for future profitable growth.

Opportunity to See (OTS). Average number of exposures experienced by the audiene covered by a particular medium.

Optimum Allocation of Resources. The direction of resources towards their most productive uses, ensuring that the maximum satisfaction or gain is being obtained by the individual, firm, or community allocating these resources.

Optimum Image. One most desirable in keeping with policy and objectives.

Optimum Location. Industrial location ideally suited to company's economic needs such as labour, room for expansion, transportation, linkage with components, fuel and raw material supplies.

Optimum Output. Output at which factors of production are combined in the most efficient way, that is, the output at which the average cost of production is at its lowest point.

Optimum Population. Ideal population. Population which combined with the other available resources or means of production, will yield the maximum return.

Optimum Price. Price giving highest profit potential, found by relating movements of sales volume to increases and decreases in selling price.

Optimum Production. The greatest output that can be reasonable achieved given the general social and organizational structure of society at that time.

Option. Also, option contract. In business law, a binding promise to keep open a specific offer for a given period of time.

Option Money. The fee paid by the holder of an option for the option. The holder is semetimes called the 'giver' of option money and the other party is called the 'taker' of option money.

Orario Flessibile. Italian term for flexible working hours.

Order/Call Ratio. Relationship between the number of orders obtained and the number of calls made to get them over a particular period of operation. Establishes a useful comparative tool for sales efficiency supervision.

Order-point Control. Also, max-min system. Any system of inventory control in which material is ordered when stocks drop to a predetermined level, called the order point, which is presumably equal to the amount that will be needed until stocks can be replenished, plus a little extra for sefety (the so-called Safety Stock). Both the two-bin and perpetual inventory systems are of this type.

Order Quantity. The amount of any material or item being ordered, which is influenced both by its price and by the company's ordering and carrying costs.

Ordinance. The legislative act of a municipality; a law of a city; an authoritative decree of direction promulgated by a government.

Ordinary Depreciation. Decrease in or loss of the usefulness of a fixed asset as a result of normal wear, tear, and aging and the normal action of the elements.

Organismic Theory. Theory developed by Andras Angyal that there is a continuous interaction between that organism (the customer) and the environment and the because of the continuity of this interaction it is impossible to differentiate one from the other. The theory is used as a means of analyzing buying behaviour by directing attention to the likelihood that customers in a given market segment are influenced by similar forces to similar degrees.

Organization. Sub-division and delegation of the overall management task by allocating responsibility and authority to carry out defined work and by difining the relationships that should exist between different functions and positions.

Organisational Behaviour. (US spelling: organizational behaviour). The behaviour of people when they are acting as members of organizations.

Organisational Change. Change in the organbization structure or in the usual forms of organizational behaviour in a particular organization.

Organisational Climate. The points of view, particularly on how employees should be treated, that are common to most senior people in an organization.

Organisational Purchasing. Relating to any purchase by an organization as opposed to an individual.

Organization and Methods (O & M). The study of how methods employed and arrangements made in organizing work lead to differing levels of achievement, efficiency and development.

Organization, Company. The apportionment of authority and responsibility among the employees of a business.

Organization Development. The activity of improving an organization, such as the legal and accounting fees for incorporation and promotional costs created by the issuance of capital stock.

Original Motion. Motion in the form in which it is intitally moved at a meeting or conference before any amendment to it is moved. I an amendment is moved and carried, the amended motion is knows as a substantive motion.

Origin Period. In statistical analysis, the period of time within a time series selected as the base period.

O'Rourke Mechanical Aptitude Test. Early psychological test of the mechanical comprehension kind. Of US origin, it is basically an achievement test but has also been used as an aptitude test.

Outdoor Advertising. Mainly poster and transport advertising, but including illuminated signs and outdoor displays.

Outdoor Publicity. Advertising by means of posters on hoardings, on or inside buses, bus shelters, telephone kiosks or by similar methods.

Outer Pack. Container which holds a number of units and whose function usually is one of protection during distribution. It may also be used to carry an advertising message.

Outlay. An expenditure, particularly a cash expenditure, or the incurring of a liability to pay cash. Also, the transfer of property in exchange for goods or services.

Outlet. Selling or trading unit.

Outlet Store. A retail store that specializes in selling low-priced overstocked goods, discontinued lines, absolete merchandise, or distressed goods (inventorie seized for nonpayment).

Out-of-pocket Cost. In accounting, an expense that requires a current outlay of cash, such as wages, power bills, supplies, or taxes.

Out-of-town Shopping Centre. Shopping centre established away from city centre where land is cheaper and car parking space plentiful.

Output Budgeting. As programme budgeting or planning, programming, budgeting system.

Output of A Country. Goods and service consumed at home and exported.

Output Per Manshift (OMS). A unit of efficiency, mainly used in the coal mining industry, to measure the productivity of an operation. The total output for the shift is divided buy the number of men working during that period to obtain the average OMS.

Output Response Function. Hypothesis that the Aggregate Effective Demand for goods and service if within an economic system steadily increases, output will also increases but ultimately at a diminishing rate of response.

Outright Forward. (or outright forward contract). A contract for the delivery of goods at a fixed future data.

Outside Director. Synonym for non-executive director.

Out-turn. Output, particularly in the petroleum and certain other processing industries.

Outwork. Work done outside of a factory, epecially work done, for a factory owner, in the home of the worker.

Overall Market Capacity. Amount of a product or service that could be aborbed in an overall market without taking into account price or market segmentation considerations.

Overcharge. A charge on a freight bill based on an error in rate, weight, or rating, resulting in excessive freight charges.

Overdue. Any item that remains unpaid after the due date for payment.

Overevaluating. Term used in psychological testing where too much reliance is placed on test results.

Overmake. Production in excess of the required or ordered quantity. Also an item that is part of such excess production.

Overnight. Of or relating to a deposit of money made at the end of business on one day for repayment with interest on the following day.

Overnight Money. Money that is repaid the next morning.

Over-priced. More than most customers would be prepared to pay.

Overrejected Style. In organizational behavior, the basic style a manager uses far less frequently than the average manager.

Overrun. The quantity manufactured or received from a manufacturer that is in excess of the quantity ordered.

Overseas Company. A company incorporated outside the country.

Overselling

1. Persuading distributor or customer to order more goods than they can reasonably handle or consume.
2. Overstating the case for buying a product or service.

Oversold

1. A term describing the market as a whole or a particular security, in the belief that excessive selling activity has driven down prices in general, or an individual price, to an unreasonably low level.
2. Discribing a business that has committed itself to more than it can deliver.

Overstaffing. As overmanning, though possibly with an emphasis on white collar workers.

Overtime Ban. A Restrictive Practice technique designed to expose the extent to which a company is reliant upon overtime to complete its operations (and thus how under-resourced it is in terms of labour) and to create operating difficulties which will bring pressure to bear on the company, in support of specific cause.

Overtime Multiplier. The ratio of the time rate for overtime to a basic rate. Often expressed as e.g., 'time and a half' (*i.e.* overtimehours are paid for at $1\frac{1}{2}$times the rate for normal hours)

Over-turning. Training and/or education to a higher level than is necessary for the performance of the work of the trainee.

Own Brand. A retailing technique of packaging goods with the retailer's name as the Brand, often sold at a lower price than proprietary brands.

Own Brand, or Label. Selling of goods usually by a retail outlet under their own brand name. Also known private brand.

Owner. A user or process which is having overriding control over resources or data.

Own Label. Branding of products by the outlet itself rather than the manufacturer or distributor.

Own Shop. A shop, or chain of shops, in which the manufacturer sells his own goods.

P

pa. Abbreviation of per annum *i.e.,* yearly.

Pacer. A fast worker sometimes used by management to set' the pace for other workers in a factory, or to establish piecework rates.

Package Goods. In the retail trade, merchandise that is bought and sold prepacked in containers (cans, bottles, jars, etc.) as opposed to bulk (pickless from a pickle barrrel, beer on draught, etc).

Package Mortgage. A mortgage financing a home purchase that also covers the purchase of some equipment, such as a refrigerator, stove, washing machine, etc., that makes the property more livable.

Package Pay. Also, pay package. The joint consideration of salary or wages together with various Fringe Benefits, such as pension plans, profit sharing stock, options, etc.

Packaging. Monthly journal about packaging materials, machinery, equipment and methods.

Packing Note. A document enclosed with a parcel of goods sent to a customer, which informs him of what the parcel contains.

Pack Test. Market research technique for checking the effectiveness of a product's pack, functionally, aesthetically and in establishing the product's identify and image.

Paid-in Capital. The total amount of cash, property, and services contributed to a corporation by its stockholders. Synonym for contibuted capital.

Paired Comparison Test. Test in which a pair of products are compared by a sample or group of test consumers.

Panel. Sample of retail establishments or consumers specially recruited to provide information on buying, media, and consumption habits and sometimes to test potential new products.

Panel Interview. In personnel selection, interviewing a candidate by an inteviewing panel rather than by an individual interviewer.

Panel Methods. Or audit methods. Market research term where product testing panels of consumers or users are used to obtain views on products and product acceptance.

Pantry Check. Observational market research survey, brands being recorded as found in actual kitchens and pantries.

Paper Set. Setting of advertisement by publisher instead of being supplied with complete block or camera ready copy.

Paper Setting. Setting of an advertisement by the printer of a periodical, usually free of charge.

Parta. Indian system of short-term business planning and control based on operational cash flow.

Parachute Salesman. Inexperienced businessmen who descend on a foreign market, think they can sell quickly and go home, not realising that it takes time and patience to create credibility and be taken seriously.

Paradigm. Large-scale model representing a stable pattern of scoentific activity. Smetimes described as 'super model'.

Paradigm Shift. Change in the aims of an organizations as when it acceepts social responsibility for its effects on the environment including pollution and social hazards, or is involved in political issues, or minority and ethnic situations.

Parallel Pricing. Practice of increasing the price of a product that is sold by several manufacturers by the same amount approximately the same time by all manufacturers.

Parallel Readership. Reduction of the average claim period for readership research, where a second reading event occurs during original claim period so introducing error into estimated average readership figurres leading to understatement of readership.

Parity of Authority. The management principle holding that a superior within an organization has the legal and moral right to issue orders to his or her subordinates.

Parity of Responsibility. The management principle holding that a subordinate within an organization has the obligation to be responsive to orders from a higher authority. The principle also holds that the degree of authority and responsibility must be equal if a manager is to be effective.

Parkinson's Law. A semi-serius observation, originated by the UK author C. North-cote Parkinson, that 'work expands to fill the time available for its completion'. It is often borne out by experience, especially in related senses (*e.g.*, required space increases to fill available space and expenditure rises to meet income). There are several variations on the theme, causing the above to be known as 'Parkinson's First Law'.

Parole Evidence Rule. A legal rule stating that, once parties have entered into a written agreement in writing, they are bound therby and cannot offer proof of an oral agreement that contradicts the terms that have been written into the agreement.

Partial Equilibrium Analysis. An analysis of a market that assumes that the price of one commodity can change without significant repercussions on the prices of other goods.

Partial Release Clause. A part of a mortgage or trust deed that provides for removal of certain property from the effect of the lies on payment of an agreed-on sum.

Participative Management. Refers to a managerial style characterized by extensive use of the groupdicision method and in which each person is given wide opportunity to excercise discretion in his work. The style represents a complete contrast to authoritarian management. People practising participative management usually believe that people can be emotionally committed to doing jobs well.

Participation. Generic term for a variety of ways of increasing the involvement and commitment of employees to their own jobs and to corporate goals.

Participatory Leadership. Refers to a style of management in which the leader plays an active consulting and advising role but gives subordinates a considerable amount of independence in making final decisions.

Part Method. Refers to a method of training in which the operation to be learned is divided into small parts and the trainee practises each part separately and combinations of parts.

Partnership. Business organization which is owned by partners who are responsible for all debts of undertaking, even to extent of their private assets.

Parts. A general term for components that will be incorporated into a company's end-product.

Partsman. Refers to a storekeeper or salesman who handles orders for spare parts, particularly in the motor vehicle business.

Part-time Director. Synonym for non-executive director.

Part-time Shift. Refers to a shift that is shorter than 8 hours, especially when it is always worked by a group of part-time workers.

Passbook. Also, bank book. A booklet which is given to bank depositors in which their deposits, withdrawals, and interest earnings are recorded.

Passing-off. Occurs when one product so resembles another, usually by its "get-up" or packaging, but also by misleading similar spelling of the brand name, that it is bought mistakenly for the original.

Pass-on Readership. Refers to the number of people reading a publication over and above the primary of original readers.

Patent. Refers to a document by which an individual or a corporation (called a 'patentee') is granted certain rights (called 'patient right') to prevent, for a defined period of time, anyone else from making, using, or selling goods made in a defined way or using a defined manufacturing process without permission of the patentee.

Patentee. Refers to a person to whom patent rights have been granted for a specific invention.

Patent Exchange. Refers to an arrangement under which two firms in different countries grant each other licenses to operate patents each onces.

Paternalism. An attitude of managers to employees based upon the belief the subordinates can make only token contributions to decision-making (*i.e.* that a manager must take a parental role). Paternalistic management assumes that empoyees respond to generous conditions both in the workplace and in their personal life.

Paternalistic Management. A management style which is characterized by provision of wide range of valuable rewards for employees and a belief that employees will work well out of gratitude, and out of fear that they could lose the important benefits if they did not work well.

Pattern Bargaining. A negotiating tactic which brings pressure to bear by referring to agrements made in other forms and/or unions.

Patterned Interview. Technique of planned selling where interview is conducted by salesmen according to a predetermined plan.

Pay Differential. Refers to variance in pay of different types of employee.

Payment-by-results (PBR). A payment system which links the level of remuneration to quantity of Output.

Payment Pause. Refers to the temporary freezing of pay by government order or decree.

Payment System. Refers to the pinciples, rules and procedures by which the rate of pay of employees in an organisation are determined (Also known as a pay plan).

Payment Patrixoff. A matrix which is formed from the payoffs of all the combinations of courses of action and events in a given situation.

Payola. A colloquial term referring to corrupt influence is business deals involving a paid information or other form of bribery.

Pay Package. As total remuneration.

Pay Pause. A period during which a government attempts to prevent and increase in wages as part of an incomes policy.

Payroll

(1) A list of all emplyees who must be paid by a company.

(2) The total amount of money required per period to pay a workforce.

Pay Scheme. A formal arrangement of pay within a company explaining grading levels, Salary Ranges, Merit Ratings etc.

Pay Structure. Refers to the fixed arrangements or formula by which an employer determines the pay of individual employee within a defined group.

PBR. Abbeviation of Payment By Results.

PDM. Abbreviation of 'Physical Distribution Management'. It means management of a physical distribution system.

Peak Listening Hours. Refer to times when there are the largest radio audience, *e.g.*, breakfast time, mornings (housewises) lunch time, late night (teenagers).

Peddler. Refers to the earliest kind of traveling salesman, who travelled through rural regions selling whatever as light enough to carry.

Pedlars. Door-to-door or street salesmen carrying stock of wares or services for immediate sales on demand.

Pegboard. Refers to a device for measuring a person's psychomotor skills (*i.e.*, skills involving mental control of bodily movement).

Pegging. Refers to the act of fixing a price during the initial distribution of a security.

Pegging Requirements. In manufacturing, a statement of the relationship between the requirement for end products and the requirements these end products generate for lower-level parts or components.

Penetration. Refers to extent to which a product or an advertisement has been accepted by, or has registered with the total of possible users. It is usually expressed as a percentage.

Penetration Policy. Introduction of new product at low price, which is meant to be product's regular price.

Penetration Pricing. The introduction of a new product to the market at a low price in order to maximize the volume (though not the value) of sales in the early stages.

Pension. Regular payment which is made to a person who has reached retirement age (when the pension may be known as superannuation) or who has suffered a disability, or to dependents of a person dying before or after retirement.

PER. Abbreviation of Professional and Executive Recruitment.

Per Capita Income. Refers to the total income of a nation averaged over its population, thus giving an arbitrary but comparative measure of income per head of the population.

Perfect Market. Refer to the situation (condition) where all the potential sellers and buyers are promptly aware of the prices at which transactions take place and of all the offers made by other sellers and buyers and where any buyer can purchase from any seller and vice versa.

Performance Appraisal. Refers to systematic assessment of an individual's performance in order to assess training needs, potential for promotion, eligibility for a merit increment as part of a pay or salary review or for management succession planning.

Peripheral Media. Advertising media, especially some small circulation journals, which may have limited advertising value.

Perishable Dispute. Refers to strike over issues which the management would win by default if the workers did not act immediately and before being overtaken by events.

Permanent Night Shift. A group of employees who always work a night shift.

Perms. Permanent emplyees as distinct from those who may be hired on a casual or temporary basis.

Personality Promotions

(1) Use of well-known persons to endorse a product or service.

(2) Use of readily identifiable, often gaily dressed, persons from whom a prize can be claimed if approached with the use of a promotional phrase or saying.

Personality Test. A procedure (or instrument) for measuring some aspect of an individual's personality.

Personal Selling. Refers to the process of making oral commercial representations during a buyer/seller interview situation.

Personal Space. A boundary layer which an individual maintains and which may only be penetrated by a sympathetic person. When two people are able to work closely together they may be said to share personal space.

Personnel Management. Refers to that part of the management function which is primarily concerned with the human relationship within an organization.

Personnel Placement. Refers to process of fitting available personnel as effectively as possible into the available jobs. The converse of personnel selection, it is most likely to occur in conditions of full employment.

Personnel Selection. Refers to the process of selecting the most suitable from a group of applicants for a job, involving both classification of current performance and prediction of future performance.

Personnel Specification. Description of the kind of person needed for a job-in terms of qualification, experience and other characteristics—in the light of the job specification.

Peter Principle. The notion that 'in a hierarchy, every employee tends to rise in the organization until reaching his level of incompetence' when promotion stope.

Phantom Stock Plan. A bonus payment system linking the pay of each employee to the increase in a company's Share price over a period, using a points rating.

Physical Distribution Management (PDM). The planning, monitoring and control of distribution and delivery of manufactured goods, including the use of transpotation, warehousing, agents and retail outlets.

Phantom Stock. Form of bonus in which participants receive partial or complete financial benefit of stock or share ownership without actually owning any stock.

Picket. A person who is posted outside a workplace, as representative of strikers, whose task is to inform people of the objectives of a strike and persuade them to join support it.

Pictorial Chart. A chart readily understood and enjoying widespread use by all management disciplines in charting statistics.

Pictogram. A presentation technique combining the clarity of a diagram with the descriptive quality of a picture.

Pilot Interview. Refers to a dynamic testing program which is intended to check the validity of a full-scale market research program involving interview techniques before the program is actually undertaken.

Pilot Survey. Experimental research survey conducted to test the sample, questionnaire, feasibility to further enquiry, or any other aspect of a proposed full survey.

Pilot System. Refers to a method of testing new procedures by processing a representative sample of data from the operations which are to be covered by the new system, either by sampling historical data or taking a sample from curent operations.

Pioneer Salesman. One who opens up new territory. May be engaged as commando salesman from contract sales force organizer.

Pitch. Make a presentation of an advertising campaign or PR programme to a prospective client.

Placement Test. In such a test, products or packs are delivered to selected usage points for trial to be followed up by interviews collecting information on performance and attitudes towards them.

Placing. Process of selecting, oganizing and implementing a choice between marketing alternatives.

Planned Obsolescence. Refers to a marketing concept that incorporates into the original plan describing or defining the life of a product a finite time interval during which the product will be actively produced and offered for sale.

Planned Order. A shop or purchase order that is planned to satisfy net manufacturing requirements.

Planned Selling. Operating selling activity along predetermined lines with calculated aims and goals, specified strategies and tractics, and monitored against these standards.

Plans. Statements of the things to be done and the sequence and timing in which they should be done in order to achieve a given end.

Plant. A factory of workshop.

Platform. Copy theme of an advertisement. Main selling point Unique selling propostition.

Playing Cards. Give-away advertising medium, artwork and printing provided by playing card manufacturers such as Waddington.

PLC. Abbreviation of Public Limited Company.

Plural Executive. A group of people (*e.g.*, a coommittee or board) who are given responsibility to excercise authority jointly over specified activities of others. A plural executive is often said to carry out 'management by committee'.

Policy Allowance. An addition (other than a bonus increment) to standard time which is made so that a worker can achieve a satisfactory wage for a particular level of performance.

Poilitical Union. Uniting of two or more countries or territories under a common government.

Polyarchy. An organization structure which is characterized by absence of superiors and subordinates.

Polygraph. Machine applicable to advertisement research which measures a number of physiological variables simultaneously.

Popular Price. Pricing technique intended to appeal to a majority of buyers.

Population Dispersal. Movement out of cities such as relocation of industries and offices. Growth of community and neighbourhood societies, housing, shops politics.

Portfolio Planning. Assumes that managing the diversified firm resembles managing a portfolio of investments. Each firm is unique in such things as a growth, cash flow, profits, and tax benefits.

Portfolio Selection. Use of mathematical techniques of the decision theory and risk analysis kind to select new area of business of companies for acquisition.

Port of Entry. A place designated by the government for handling specified import shipment.

Positive Science. A body of systematised knowledge concerning what is.

Post. A position; the job someone is employed to perform.

Postaudit. A critical review of the way in which a project was carried out undertaken when the poject is complete.

Postcall Analysis. Reviewing achievements following sales interview.

Postdate. To affix a date on a document later than the date on which the document is written or executed.

Post-entry Closed Shop. A Closed Shop which accepts new employees on the condition that they join the union immediately upon appointment (*i.e.* new employees need not already be in the union).

Post Panel. Fixed position for poster advertising, usually found in undergound/railway trains and stations or other transportation media.

Poster Site Classifications. Based on type of location, categoy of road, and degree of visibility, for each poster site.

Post Purchase. Refering to arrangements made after a purchase has been completed.

Post-test. Evaluation of a campaign of an advertisement after it has run and has had time to have an effect. Could also apply to a new product launch.

Potential Acquisition Valuation Method (PAV). Systematic approach, involving ten stages, to evaluate investment proposals. Analyzes costs involved and expected return on investment *i.e.* annual net income.

Potential Demand. Desire for a thing as opposed to actual demand.

Power Need. A motivational factor, the desire to control other persons or objects, to obtain their obedience, to compel or influence their actions, to determine their fate.

Power of Attorney. A legal document authorizing a person to act as the agent for the person granting the power.

Pre-coded Question. Multiple-choice question for which an answer is chosen from a number of prepared alternatives, usually by ticking one of them.

Preempt Spot. In television, an advertisement spot bought in advance in a particular time segment at a discount buty which will not be screened if another advertiser offers to take up that time at the full rate.

Preempt System. Method of selling TV air time when prime time is subject to latest bid for time buyer to plan spots economically.

Pre-entry Closed Shop. A Closed Shop which only agrees to the appointment of new employees who are already members of a specified union.

Pre-Entry Closed Shop. A place of employment where no person may be employed unless he is member of a particular trade union.

Preferential Hiring. An agreement or practice under which an employer gives first choice of available jobs to members of a particular trade union. Also known as preferential shop.

Preferential Shop. An agreement whereby an employer gives first preference in hiring to union members.

Prefered Position. Advertisement position in a publication against which a premium charge is made.

Preliminary Expenses. Legal costs and fees paid in connection with the incorporation of a new company. (Also known as 'formation expenses').

Premium Bonus Scheme. A Payment-By-Results scheme in which a Bonus is paid over and above the standad rate, linked to time savings related to Standard Time.

Premium Offer Pre-test. Survey, often postal, to discover which offer consumers prefer. Informal tests sometimes held on a smaller scale.

Premium Pay Plan. Type if measured daywork developed by Philip Industries and using the predetermined motion time system to establish standard.

Press Advetising. Advertising in printed media such as newspapers, maganizes, catalogues, programmes, directories, yearbooks.

Press Council. Set up to establish freedom of Press, and investigate complaints about conduct of the press.

Prestige Advertising. Or institutional advertising. Advertising aimed at promoting the public esteem or corporate image of a company, corporation or other oganization rather than particular products.

Pre-testing Copy. Exploratory research to check the efficacy of a particular piece of advertising copy prior to its being used in an actual advertisement.

Price Discretion. Where a salesman has the authority to vary the price of a product in order to make a sale.

Price, Last. Final price accepted by seller after negotiations or haggling. Last price may often be the market price, as found where there are both bazaars and fixed price shops, and the 'last' price equals the fixed price.

Price-leader. A company which increases its prices first, usually followed by its competitors.

Price Leadership. A situation where a dominant firm supplies a substantial part of total sales.

Price Lining. Policy of charging a standard price for a number of products though their production costs may be very different.

Price Maker. A firm that produces goods and sells them at prices which it can determine itself.

Price Mechanism. System of allocation of scarce resources according to effective demand, expressed through price and price movements.

Price Range. Prices form the lowest to the highest available for a particular type of product. Frequently used to describe the whole spectrum of prices within a company's product range.

Price Relative. An index number which gives the price of a standard quantity of a good at one date as a percentage of its price on an earlier base data.

Primary Employment. Employment provided by investment in physical productive assets.

Primary Labour Market. Workers with narrow Skills, perhaps applicable to one type of work only.

Primary Market

1. A market for a good in which the sellers are the producers of the good.
2. A market for securities in which the sellers are the issuers of the securities.

Prime Time. Those transmission hours in television and radio which attract the largest audiences.

Principal. The individual being represented in a business transaction by an agent authorized to do so.

Principle of Management. The so-called pinciples of management are guidelines on organization structure developed by management theorists such as F.W. Taylor, H. Fayol, L. F. Urwick and J. D. Mooney. The most widely recognized principles are(a) *span of control*—there is an optimum number of subordinates and executive can control; (b) *level of management*—too many levels of management reduce the effectiveness of communication and control; (c) *unity of command*—each man should report to only one manager or supervisor; (d) *delegation*-work must be delegated to subordinates who should be given sufficient authority to enable them to discharge their responsibilities, though bearing in mind that responsibility can be delegated but not relinquished in that the executive who delgates a task remains accountable for its achievement; (e) *rational assignment*—people should be asssigned to tasks rationally and economically so as to ensure full utilization of manpower; (f) *action decisions*—matters requiing a decision should be dealt with as near to the point of action as possible; (g) *line and staff*—it is desirable to separate the control of operations as a management function from the provision of services or advice to operational units.

Prior Analysis. Deciding between alternatives on basis of experience or research material, prior or event.

Proactive Inhibition. Where a person's attitude of mind as a result of previous work learning or experience makes it difficult for him to learn and retain new skills or information. This may happen, for example, where a method of doing a job is changed but it is difficult of employees to learn the new method because it has become instinctive to use the old method.

Probability Theory. In statistical analysis, a mathematical theory concerned with determining the likelihood of the occurrence of a chance event; used to predict the behaviour of a group, not of a single item in the group.

Probable-life Curve. In statistical analysis, a curve deduced from measurement of the frequency distributions of the use and the mortality of equipment.

Probationary Period. A short period at the start of a person's employment with a firm during which the suitability of the person for his job (and of the job for the person) is tested.

Probe. Used to obtain further information when the initial inquiry does not produce a satisfactory response, or to make sure at interview that the respondent has answered the question fully.

Procedure Flowchart. In management, a symbolic and systematic representation of a procedure used to modify, work on, or handle a form or document used in organization activities.

Process Chart. In production analysis, a graphic representation of events that occur during a series of actions or operations on the part of a worker.

Process Consultancy. Activity by a consultant that is intended to help a goup of people to work together more effectively by analysing and improving group processes.

Process Layout. Arrangement of machines in a factory according to functional type so that an item of work may be taken along various routes through the factory according to the operations to be performed on it. The layout is associated with batch production.

Process Production. More or less continuous and capital-intensive manufacture of a product using plant designed to fit the technological requirements of the process (as in production of chemicals, for example) rather than needing to accommodate a large number of successive workers operations.

Product Features. These presented to a customer when promoting the product. Functional features are the quanitiative or quanlitative aspects of a product that either are non-existent in competing products or exist to a lesser extent.

Product Growth. One which entails high cost of development, production, quality control, advertising and selling.

Product Identification. By branding, brand strategy, own brand trade marks, packaging. Major business asset. Reputation staked on brand.

Product Image. Concept which describes what consumers believe the product to be or do, regardless of its liternal accuracy or other-wise. Often their conclusions are made on value judgments without recourse to trial of alternative products.

Production Cost. All expenses which must be met in order to provide the commodity of service, transport it to the buyer and put it into the hands ready to satisfy his wants.

Production Management. Management of all aspects of an enterprises concerned with transporting materials into finished poducts.

Product Management. A method of apportioning managerial responsibility on the basis of products or product goups. The product manager has overall responsibility for all aspects of the product, from design and development, through production, to sales and marketing.

Production Need. Needs of production. The amounts of labour-power, and material means of production, *i.e.,* raw material, auxiliary material, equipment machinery, buildings etc.

Production Schedule. Programme of work necessary to produce promotional or other material.

Production Transfer. Employee mobility within an organization following changes in product, production method and/or technology.

Productive Labourer. Productive labourers are all those whose labours satisfy wants-all those who bring about satisfactions or utilities.

Productive Work. Work which alters the physical or chemical nature of something or is a necessary contribution to the completion of a process that changes the physical or chemical nature of something.

Product Screening. Pre-research techniques to assess characteristics of product and its markets, or to assess competitive products or study comparable markets before undertaking full survey. The screen consists of set of values methodically applied to aspects such as market stability, growth factors, marketability of products, engineering and production factors.

Product Search. Process of looking systematically for new products.

Product Surround. Qualities which enhance value of product, *e.g.*, delivery reputation, after-sales service, superior reputation of product, cash refunds on bottles, corporate image.

Product Test. Test of consumer's reactions to sample products.

Product Testing. Anonymous product testing and product evaluation.

Profile (Personnel). Information on an employee recorded in a company's personnel records system. The information normally includes details of education, experience, current working record and assessment of the employee's potential.

Profiling Systems. Used in job evaluation to grade jobs by analyzing the basic or bench mark jobs and then weighting other jobs in relation to them.

Profit and Loss (P & L) Statement. A business firm's formal statement of revenues, costs, expenses, losses, and profits for a given period, grouped under appropriate headings.

Pro Form a Invoice. Document stating the value of a transaction used to notify the proposed despatch of a consignment of goods.

Prognosis. The third and final phase of research. It means production of future developments.

Programmed Test. Teaching material presented or programmed step by step in a manner that can be adapted to the needs of the individual student or trainee.

Programming. It may be defined as the process by which a set of instructions is produced for a computer to make it carry out a specific activity. The activity includes anything from the solution of a mathematic problem to the production of a company payroll. The instructions ultimately beyed by the computer are the numerical codes which are significant to the computer's central processor.

Programming Language. A set of standard sumbols (and, often groups of symbols) and rules for combining the symbols so that they represent instructions for a computer to carry out specific operations. (Also known as a 'code'). A computer is designed to interpret instructions that are written in its computer instructions code, which is a very elementary language using a very restricted range of symbols.

Progress Chart. Horizontal bar chart of the component bar chart type with the variously shaded or coloured component parts representing the completion of successive stages.

Progress Chasing. Function of department responsible for the satisfactory progress of work through an organization.

Progress Payments. Payments made at stages of a construction or manufacturing program as it moves towards completion.

Project. An activity (or, usually, a number of related activities) carried out according to a plan in order to achieve a definite objective within a certain time and which will cease when the objectives is achieved.

Project Ladger. Comprehensive documentation on the estimates, budgets, modifications and progress of a project.

Project Management (Project Planning). A special type of management activity chiefly concerned with the planning, execution and consolidation of a project of any type within the constraints set by the company and its environment. Project management has recently emerged as a crucially important technique for controlling costs and timescale in projects, in some cases preventing financial failure which might otherwise be experienced. In particular, the value of quantitative planning and control techniques has been realized.

Promotional Games. Prize games and contests for sales promotion schemes, either requiring proof of purchase or no purchase necessary.

Proof of Delivery. Signed receipt showing the date of delivery to the consignee.

Propaganda Selling. Missionary selling.

Property Tax. A tax levied on various kinds of property-personal (jewellery, automobiles, furniture, etc.) and real (land and buildings).

Prosumption. Involvement of the consumer in the production of the goods or services he or she buys, thus removing the distinction between consumption and production.

Protectionism. The view that a government should take action to ensure that domestic procedures of goods do not have to compete with imported foreign good.

Protective Output Norm. Where a work group informally holds down production levels as under productivity restriction, quota restriction, a fiddle, or a work group output norm.

Protestant Work Ethic. The notion that 'to work is good' based upon the teaching that God works and therefore man should too.

Pseudo Product Testing. In which the same basic product is presented in a variety of ways, *e.g.*, different packs, to a test group who are asked to give a preference rating.

Psychic Income. Intangible satisfaction derived from goods of services of some form of economic activity.

Psychodrama. A technique of creative Brainstorming, based upon the unconventional idea of assuming the personality of inanimate objects (e.g., a product, for purpose of improving its design).

Psychogalvanometer. Equipment that measure skin resistance (BSR) and indicates changes in the resistance of the skin through a galvanometric instrument. It is sometimes used as a tool for market research wherein changes in a consumer's skin resistance are measured as the subject is exposed to assorted products or ideas.

Psychographics. A technique devoted to the segmentation of markets using psychological criteria to distinguish between the different segments.

Psychological Inventory. Often confused with psychological test, but in fact, there is a distinction to be made between them. An inventory reflects what the person being tested says he/she feels, while a test measures what he/she known or can do.

Psychological Pricing. Setting selling prices at commonly used amounts (called 'psychological prices or charm prices').

Psychology of Selling. Explanation of the sales process which lays emphasis upon the workings of psychological factors and particularly their manipulation by salesmen to secure, a favourable response to their propositors.

Psychometric Test. Psychological test which seeks to measure particular factors, producing quantified results.

Public Enterprise. Commercial concern whose ownerhip is not exclusively in private hands.

Publicity Manager. Person responsible for managing a company's publicity.

Public Relations. Deliberate, planned and sustained effort to establish and maintain mutiual understanding between an organization and its public.

Public Relations Consultancy. Outside PR unit which advises on PR and conducts PR activities for organizations.

Public Relations Consultant. Individual or firm employed by an organization to advise and/or act on its behalf in the field of public relations.

Public Relations Counseller. PR practitioner who studies communication problems, and makes report and recommendations.

Pullman Advertising. Advertising on tables of Pullman trains. Brochures, folders, book matches, and Travelogue menu-magazine in dining cars of Inter-City trains.

Puppets. In TV advertising, used instead of artists or cartoons. In India and elsewhere, puppet shows used as public relations medium as in family planning campaign.

Purchase Methods. In manufacturing, methods by which purchases are made, depending on the nature of the demand in the plant and conditions in the market in which the goods are to be bought.

Purchase Order. A written order from a firm for goods (and sometimes services) that it wants to buy.

Purchase Probability Decay. In brand choice studies, failure to repurchase same Brand in interpurchase periods.

Purchasing (Procurement). A Materials Management function responsible for buying all items required by a company. Purchasing denotes a strategic, planned approach to the procurement of materials and services, rather than the tactical nature of 'buying'.

Purchasing Agent. An agent who purchases materials for his principals (usually manufacturers).

Purchasing Power. Extent to which an organization, group of people or a geographical area with funds available, whether committed or otherwise, has the ability to make purchases during specified time periods.

Purdue Creativity Test. Psychological test of US origin devised particulary for engineers and engineering workers.

Purdue Hand Precision Test. US test of psychomotor skills.

Purposive Sampling. In statistics, selecting a sample on the basis of its resemblance to the universe as a whole.

Putting-out System. Arrangement, probably most common in the garment and clothing industry, under which outwork is carried out by people working in their own homes.

Putting the Question. Taking the vote on an issue or motion at a meeting or conference. A method of ending discussion on an item on an agenda can be by a motion from the floor 'that the question now be put'.

Pyramid Selling. A system of selling by agents. Each agent is originally a customer, who then buys the rights to sell the items on offer, subsequently selling similar rights to other customers and so on. Each customer thus becomes first an agent and then a managing agent, not selling the product but co-ordinating the selling activities of others.

Q

Q Ratio. The relationship of the market value of physical capital, such as existing plant and equipment or other corporate assets, to its replacement cost. When the Q ratio is low, corporations tend to acquire existing assets rather than build new plants or equipment.

Qualified-circulation Journal/Magazine. Synonym for controlled circulation journal/magazine.

Qualifying Questions. Those which determine relevance of respondents to an enquiry, as in market research and in telephone selling.

Qualitative Analysis. In addition to quantities or numerical assessment it can be useful to consider qualitative concepts such as image held by particular publics of organization or its products or services.

Qualitative Research. Marketing research which seeks information based on reason, opinions perceived images or motives rather than numerical or percentage findings as in quantitative research.

Quality Control and Reliability. Technique for ensuring that during design, production, servicing, etc., both work and material are within limits that will produce the desired product performance and reliability.

Quality Control Chart (or Control Chart). A chart used in tactically quality control to show the performance of a production process.

Quality of Working Life (QWL). Approach to job and organization design seeking to improve the working environment and employer-employee relations.

Quango. A quasi-autonomus non-governmental organization created and funded by a government department or ministry to perform a service independently of a minister of the government.

Qualification or Ideal Method. Advertising appropriation based on scheme produced by advertising agency to show most effective advertising mix to achieve given task.

Quantitative Research. Research in which answers to questions are processed to produce numbers or percentage of people in different categories, according to the make-up of the sample and structure of the questionnaire, giving particular answers.

Quantity Discount. An allowance, in credit, cash, or goods, given by a seller to a buyer because of the size of an individual purchase.

Quarterly. Publication issued four times a year.

Quarto. The original manuscript and letterheadings paper size (10" X 8", 255mm X 203mm) and magazine size (Crown 4 to or quarter or a crown sheet).

Quasi Contract. Not a contract but an obligation imposed by law. It rests on the principle that one should not be enriched unjustly at the expense of another.

Quasi-negotiable Instruments. Certain mercantile documents possess some, but not all, of the qualities of negotiable instruments and are thus called quai-negotiable or semi-negotiable instruments.

Quasi-quality. Minor innovation to boost product in dealing stage of its life cycle, *e.g.*, new packaging different colours, variation in time or casing.

Questel. Interviewing technique developed at Essex University whereby respondent watches computer terminal with back projection film strip projector fitted with keyboard which respondent applies to feed answers on a computerized program.

Questioning Approach. What? How? Where? Who? Key questions which are valid in analyzing methods systems, work study, O & M., etc.

(To) Quit on the Job. To cease putting any effort into work.

Quit Rate. Labour turnover other than dismissals or redundancies created by the policy and decisions of management.

Quorum. Minimum number of people who must be present at a meeting before it can proceed to conduct business.

Quota Sampling. It statistics, a method of sampling in which a scheme of proportionate sample is set up, with the numbers to be interviewed in each class embodying the traits of the overall population.

Quotation

1. A statement, in response to a request by at prospective buyer, of what a firm would probably charge for supplying specified goods or services.
2. A statement by someone trading in a market, especially an organized market, of his prices for buying and for selling specified goods a 'two-way quotation' in response to an enquiry from another trade in the market. (The person giving the quotation is usually supposed not to know whether the enquirer wants to sell or buy).
3. Synonym for listing.

R

RB. Abbreviation of Relaxation Allowance.

Racket. Disreputable, but not necessarily illegal practice, conducted for profit. Usually abuse of trust, sometimes exploriation of vanity.

Racketeering

1. In business, carrying on a dishonest or illegal scheme in order to make money.
2. In organized labour, collusion between union officials and employers in writing contracts, coercion of employers to accept union terms, appropriation of pension and strike funds for private gain by union officials, and similar practices.

Rack Rent

1. A rent equal to or not much less than the annual value.
2. Full commercial rent obtainable.
3. The highest rent a tenant can be compelled to pay.

Racks. Storing equipment used in warehouses and storerooms.

Raiding. Practice or luring employees away from their jobs to take up a job with another employer. (Also known as 'pirating').

Rain Check. Delay in accepting an offer. Thus, 'to take a rain check' is to delay making a decision usually while checking the facts of the matter.

R & D. Abbreviation of research and development.

Random Numbers. In market research probability form of random sample is use, but another method more generally used in scientific studies bases the sample on table of random sampling numbers. Thus, instead of taking every 9th name in list, numbers such as 20, 74, 92, 22, 93 would be extracted from printed table.

Random Sample. Probability research sample in which everyone has equal chance of being selected for interview. Accurate, but more expensive way of surveying a true cross-section of universe.

Random Sampling. In statistical sampling, the process of selection sample units in such a way that all units under consideration have the same probability of being selected.

Random Selection. Systematic selection of sample units so that each possible sample has a definite probability of being chosen.

Random Walk (or Route). Market research technique in which interviewers walk along prescribed routes calling on houses selected on random sampling principles in order to interview the householders.

Ranking Method. Method job evaluation in which all the job to be evaluated are ranked according to some consistent system (*e.g.* by asking somone to put the jobs in order of importance after considering job descriptions).

Rapid Rotating Shift System. A rotating Shift System in which the change from working one type of shift to another occurs at intervals of less than a week.

Rate Buster. A pieceworker who takes advantage of rates to earn high bonus payments and does not join with fellow workers in holding production back to the bogey level agreed on unofficially by the group.

Rate Cutting. Cutting of piece work rates by management when such rates are found to be loose rates.

Rate-for-age Scale. A payment system in which all employees of the same age and doing similar work are paid the same wages.

Rate-of-return Pricing. A method for determining a selling price for an item by adding a mark-up that will produce a target return on investment.

Rate-setting. Term used for establishing payment-by-results or performance-linked pay rates, usually following some form of work measurement though rate-setting is sometimes virtually synonymous with rate-fixing. Rate setting is synonymous for rate-fixing.

Ratio Analysis. Use of financial ratio to assess an enterprise' efficiency and to help to find reason for inefficiency.

Ratio Chart. In presenting statistics, a graph that shows relative rather than absolute variations, that is, percentage changes rather than absolute changes.

Rational Behaviour. Acting in such a way that greatest possible satisfaction is derived from the available money resources. It implies deliberate planning in order to obtain maximum satisfaction with limited resources.

Rational Consumer. Sensible buyer who balances marginal cost against marginal gain.

Rational Management. A management style based on optimizing input/output ratios by the application of quantitative techniques. It is the opposite of Participative Management.

Rational Working Hours. System of German origin under which hours of work are varied according to the work load.

Ratio-to moving-average Method. In statistics, a method of computing cyclical and seasonal fluctuations, so as to get a clear picture of a trend in sales, output, or some other time series.

Raw Score. A score of a testee that has not been converted into a standard score.

Raw Test Score. Basic score produced by an employee or candidate in psychological testing. This score has then to be adapted by the appropriate norm to give a common base according to type of candidate and/or job.

Reader. Someone who has 'read' a publication or periodical as opposed merely to having 'received' it.

Readers Involvement. Copywriting with the aim of gaining the participation of the reader; a particular facet of local newspapers and radio.

Reader Service. Service provided by publishers whereby readers request sales literature, offered by advertisers, on single form or on cards thus avoiding clipping the magazine, or need to write to separate advertisers.

Readership Profile. Classifications of readership of publications expressed in percentage form relative to total readership.

Readership Replication. Extension of the claim period for readership research where a second reading event occurs during or after original claim period, so introducing error into estimated readership figures, leading to overestimation of readership.

Reading and Noting. Readership research index of actual audience for advertisements appearing on particular pages or average pages in specific publication.

Read Most. Term used in assessing the effectiveness of an advertising in the press. Respondents are asked to indicate whether, if they noted an advertisement, they then 'read most' of its copy. This data can then be expressed as a percentage of total readership.

Real Income Per Head Per Annum. Average real income of each member of a nation or community in one year.

Realisation

1. The conversion of any asset into cash.
2. The earning of a return, either through selling goods or services or profiting from an investment.

Real Learning Time. Time taken for a trainee to become capable of working at the speed and quality of the average experienced worker.

Real National Income. Country's total output of final goods and services expressed not in money terms but in real terms.

Rears. Spaces available on the backs of buses for advartisement posters. Especially suitable for certain products, *e.g.*, garages, motor tyres and spares, travel, and driving school services.

Rebate. An adjustment in a charge that has been paid to the supplier of a service or good, resulting in a return of a portion of the payment.

Rebating Commission. Return of commission by agency to client so that a more economic charge or free may be applied.

Rebuy. Suitation where a customer seeks either a replacement or a further supply. This involves the buyer's repeated demand balanced by the suppliers ability or willingness to supply.

Recall Test. As distinct from recognition survey, only prompt given is name of brand. No aided recall in shape of either individual advertisements or copies of publication containing the advertisement under test.

Reciprocal Trading. Arrangement between organizations whereby their roles as seller and buyer are interchangeable, *i.e.*, they buy from and sell to each other.

Reciprocity Treaty. Tariff treaty in which two states grant one another tariff reductions without the intension of allowing other states to share automatically in these reductions.

Recognition Test. Survey to discover recognition of advertisements from which names have been obscured.

Recommended Retail Price. A price for a consumer product that is notified to retailers by the manufacturer of the product as being a suitable price at which to sell it.

Recruitment. Seeking out prospective new employees. Recruitment is undertaken by employment agencies to augment their files of jobseekers, as well as by business themselves, usually through their personnel departments.

Recruitment Advertising. Advertising designed to recurit staff of any kind. Consists mostly of classified and semi-display advertisements.

Recycling. Converting waste into new products as with bottle banks for collecting glass, salvage of waste paper, collection of silver foil, conversion of nuclear waste.

Redemption. Process of trading in or redeeming coupons, voucher, special offers, trading stamps and the like in exchange for a stated product or benefit.

Redeployment. Re-allocation and retaining of labour as change in technology and business situation call for labo(u)r mobility between skills (and perhaps raise danger of structural unemployment).

Rediscounting. Discounting again, that is, selling or discounting a regotiable instrument, such as commercial paper, that has already been discounted once.

Redundancy Payment. A payment that an employer is required by statute to make to an employee who is dismissed because redundancy.

Register. In accounting, a book in which transations are recorded. It may or may not be a Journal.

Registered Trade Mark. A trade mark that has been entered in a publicy available register in accordance with the laws of a country so that only the person registered as the owner of the trade mark is entitled to use it.

Registered Trade Names. Product names which have been registered and should be given a capital initial letter as in Fibreglass, Pop-Rivets, Tannoy, Vaseline.

Registered User. Under trade mark law, only the owner of a registered trade mark is normally entitled to use that trade mark.

Reiteration. Repetition in advertising aimed at reminding by reinforcing memorability, establishing brand names, and implanting pack in consumer mind.

Regional Management Centre. A department of a business school or faculty of management and/or business which pays partiular attention to a particular geographic region.

Relationships Behaviour. The extent to which a leader is likely to maintain personal relationships between himself or herself and members of the group by opening channels of communication, delegating responsibility, and giving subordinates an opportunity to use their potential: characterized by socio-emotional support, friendship, and mutual trust.

Relationship Orientation (RO). In reference to management style, the extent to which a manager has personal job relationships; characterized by listening, trusting and encouraging.

Release of Deposit. A form signed by all parties to an escrow, authorising the distribution of funds deposited in escrow.

Relief Employment. As distinguished from economic or productive employment, it provides employment and income but does not contribute really and independently to the net product produced by the society.

Remedy. The judicial means or court procedures by which legal and equitable rights are enforced; the relief obtained by such means or procedures.

Reminder Advertising. Expenditure devoted to overcoming memory lapse. Accounts for a significant proportion of advertising.

Remittance. A sum of money sent from one person to another, usually as a payment for goods or services. The remittance may be in cash or in the form of a check or other negotiable instruments.

Rendu Price. The delivered price for an imported goods, that is, including all freight, tariff, insurance and other shipping charges.

Rentier. A person whose income is 'unearned', *i.e.* derived from the ownership of capital by way of interest, rent, or dividend, rather than 'earned' in the form of salary, commission, fee or wages.

Re-opener Clause. A there should agreement, though usually prescribing that pay negotiations be re-opened when the cost of living reaches a particular point rather than having a scale or pay directly related to the cost of living.

Repeat Demand. Marketing term for demând cocerned with meeting requirements for frequently purchased consumer goods.

Repayment Guarantee. An arrangement under which a guarantor promises to reimburse a buyer for any downpayment or stage payments made for a contract if the contract is not properly performed.

Repeat Fees. Subsequent fees to performers for repeat showing of TV commercials in which they either appear or provide the voice over.

Repetitive Question. In a questionnaire, the same question put another way. A form of control question. Helps to clarify likely misunderstanding of an earlier question and double checks validity.

Replacement Chart. Chart showing the backup or replacemeent for each key member of management.

Replication. Statistical term referring to repetition of test or drawing of sample to measure test or sampling error.

Reply Card. Used, for instance in a direct mail campaign, in which a card is enclosed, usually perpaid, to encourage a reply.

Reputation Report. Research report on retailer attitudes to manufacturer, his product, distribution methods, advertising, pricing trade terms, complaint handling, after sales servicing.

Requirements Contract. A contract wherein one party to the contract agrees to purchae all his or her requirements of a particular product from another party to the contract.

Resale Price Maintenance. System by which a manufacturer sets a uniform price at which all retailers must sell his product (*i.e.* the price at which a resale is made).

Rescission. The termination of a contract which is then said to be rescinded.

Reservation of Title. An arrangement under which a seller of goods retains the legal title of the goods until they are paid for.

Reservation Price. Also called reserve price, it is the price below which the seller will refuse to sell.

Reserve Price. Minumum selling Price. Most often used at auctions but may occasionally apply when stock is being cleared at a reduced prices.

Reserve Stock. As buffer stock.

Residual Value. The value of piece of equipment at the end of the lease term.

Resource Allocation. Also, distribution theory. The assignment of a society's resources-land, labour, capital—to produce the goods and services it needs.

Response Time. The time needed to answer an inquiry.

Responsibility. Obligation, of a person, to perform some task (or see that others perform it) in a way that satisfies criteria laid down by another person or group of people.

Restricter. A worker who performs or produces at a level considered to be the norm for the group of which he or she is part.

Restrictive Covenant. A clause in a contract that denies the buyer or lessor full rights to the property in question.

Restrictive License. An agreement whereby a patentee permits a licensee to sell a patented product under restricted conditions.

Restrictive Trading Agreement. An agreement between producers or suppliers of goods to adopt a restrictive trade practice.

Results Guide. Synonym for management guide.

Retailer. Person or organization which sells goods to the general public, usually through the operation of a shop or store, *i.e.*, a Retail outlet.

Retirement Allowance. An annuity or pension payable to an employee who has retired from active service.

Retirement Benefit Scheme. As expected provident fund (EPF)

Retrogressive Consumer. Marketing term for a consumer who is keen to economize on an existing product or service.

Revenue. The total income of a unit of government-local, state, or central. The chief source of revenue is taxes.

Revenue Duty. A customs duty or an excise duty that is imposed by a government mainly in order to raise revenue for itself.

Reverse Takeover. A merger between two companies in which the smaller company gains effective control of the larger.

Reverse Take-over Bid. Take-over bid where the company making the bid has the object of having the management of the company taken over run the resulting combined company.

Review Board. Group of committee of senior personal in advertising agency who meet to review critically campaign, produced by another group in the same agency.

Revocation. The withdrawal by the officer or of an Offer, which is then said to be revoked.

Rival Unionism. Where two or more trade unions are competing for members and recognition in the same industry or company. Rival unionism differs from dual unionism in that there is competition rather than acceptance of co-existence between the unions.

Robot. A computer-controlled, multifunctional machine designed to move material, parts, tools, or specialized devices through programmed motions in order to perform various tasks.

Rogby. Personality assessment technique devised by William Isbister. Based on hypothesis that each individual is a 'confused mass of colours' which can be analyzed and broken down into basic colours red, orange, green, blue, yellow, etc.

Rohrschach Test. Or ink blot test. A personality test of the projective technique kind in which a person is presented with ten standard ink blots and asked to say what he or she reads into them. The responses are interpreted by an occupational psychologist.

Role. In management terms, function undertaken and/or position held by an employee etc., within an organization. Role is virtually synonymous with job but is used more executive than, for example, shop-floor jobs.

Role Ambiguity. Frustration felt by an individual who is unclear as to the role required for his position.

Role Conflict. Frustration experienced by an individual who is required to take two roles which have conflicting objectives.

Rol^e Theory. Personality development theory concerned with roles suitable to role positions. Stability of personality structure is fasioned by stability of both social structure or environment and the of person's own habits. Important to accept that people act differently in different role situations.

Routing Salesmen. Designing a calling pattern for salesmen to ensure systematic rather than haphazard coverage.

Rowan System of Bonus. A type of premium bonus system. It is so called because David Rowan of Glasgow first introduced it. In this each unit of work has a standard time assigned to it.

Runaway Shop. A business organization that moves from one location to another primarily to escape unionization of its employees or the aplication of labour laws. It is possible four geographically centered industry to make.

Run of Paper (ROP). Instruction to a publisher indicating that no special position is sought for an advertisement, i.e., it can be placed in any convenient part of the advertising space of the publication.

Run-of-paper Advertisement (RoP advertisement). A display advertisement that is to be inserted wherever the publisher thinks is convenient.

Ryotwari System. A system of land tenure prevailing in India. Ryot means cultivator. Under this system every registered holder of land is virtually its proprietor, and cannot be ejected as long as he pays revenue direct to the government.

S

Sabotage. Any of several illegal tactics used by workers during labour disputes, such as willfully damaging machinery or other property of the employer, wasting or destroying materials, and obstructing or interfering with normal business operations.

Safety Officer. Employee in an organization who is responsible for recommending safe methods of working, educating employees in safe working methods and investigating accidents.

Salary Administration. Activities concerned with fixing and, sometimes, paying salaries in an organization.

Salary Classes. Salary brackets used in calculating entitlements and contributions under certain pension schemes.

Salary Increment. Regular increase in salary, usually annual, written into pay scales and individual contracts of employment. Particularly common in government and other public service.

Salary Roll. The payroll for salaried employees.

Sale. In business law, a transfer of title to goods or tangible personal property in consideration of a payment of money, called the price.

Sale or Return. Colloquial term for practice whereby only goods resoled are charged to a dealer, any unsold goods being return able for full credit.

Sales. The provision of goods or services for which a company or individual receives income.

Sampling Procedure. Practical rules for obtaining a sample from a population.

Sampling Orders. Trial orders for a product by a prospective buyer who may place large orders if the samples meet his requirements for price, quality etc.

Satellite. An enterprise that sells its products to only one or two large firms and is, therefore, dependent on their success for its existence.

Saturation. Point at which additional sales are unobtainable, or beyond which it would be uneconomic to seek them. This may justify introducing a new product or diversifying.

Saturation Point. Level at which any further expansion of distribution in a market is unlikely to be achieved and where further sales are restricted to the potential arising from replacement needs or population growth.

Scalper. A speculator who buys and sells principally to make quick profits.

Schedule of Demand. Demand schedule. It refers to a series of quantity of a good that will be taken by buyers at each of a corresponding series of prices.

Scheme Advertising. Advertising normally of a below-the-line character.

Seal. On a document, a symbol of a person's willingness to be bound by the statements and promises he makes in the document.

Seasonal Discount. Discount offered by media owners to encourage business during what are considered to be slack periods in the year.

Seasonal Fluctuations. Patterns of orders or sales that last for periods of less than one year.

Seasonal Inventories. Inventories whose levels are adjusted to absorb seasonal fluctuations in demand.

Seasonal Rate. Rates in advertising which vary according to the time of year.

Secondary Action. In an industrial dispute between an employer and his employees, secondary action is industrial action taken by the employees against persons who deal with the employer.

Secondary Boycott. Attempts by a union through strikes, picketing or other methods to stop one employer from doing business with another employer.

Secondary Media. Advertising media used to support the primary media in a campaign.

Secondary Picketing. Picketing in furtherance of a trade dispute by individuals or groups not directly party to the main dispute.

Secondary Readership. Indicates readership of a publication by location.

Security of Tenure. The right of an individual to remain in a current position of employment or residence.

Select. To make a choice between alternative courses of action as a result of a test.

Selection Board. A committee that is given the task of selecting new employees from among application.

Selection Interview. An interview that is intended to help the interviewer decide whether to select the interviewee for employment.

Self Cover. Cover of brochure or other print item made of same paper as inside pages.

Self-employed Person. One working on his own, or in business on his own account.

Self-employment. The state of conducting a business activity on one's own behalf as a Solf Trader.

Sell-in. Process of selling goods to the retail trade prior to a consumer promotional campaign.

Selling. Process of persuasion leading to a continuing trading arrangement, initiated and perpetuated at either a personal or impersonal level but commonly confined to oral representation supported by visual aids.

Semi-skilled Work. Work which is related between Unskilled Work and Skilled Work, usually on the basis of a requirement for dexterity but not decision-making or judgment.

Semi-skilled Worker. Generally taken to mean reasonably highly skilled operator/operative though not as highly skilled as a craftsman who has served as apprenticeship.

Semi-solus. Advertisement which appears on a page containing another advertisement but which is not positioned adjacent to it.

Semi-structed. Research conducted by interviewer with guidelines but in which certain key questions may need to be answered.

Sensitivity Training. A group training method intended to develop the ability to see one's self as others do.

Sentence Completion Test. Projective test, subject being asked to fill in blanks in sentences or phrases.

Separation Rate. Ratio of number of employees who leave an employer for any reason during a period to average number of persons employed by that employer during that period.

Service Increments. Increases in pay due after completion of an agreed length of employment.

Service Industries. Suppliers of services not directly involved with manufacturing, *e.g.* travel, entertainment, health, insurance, professional and personal treatment.

Services. Work carried out for others by an individual or organization where no transfer of goods is involved, *e.g.* banking, insurance, travel.

Servomechanism Control. Management information and control system which includes the feedback concept.

Servomechanism Theory. A means for automatically filtering out spurious information on certain types of decision making in management.

Shipper. A middleman who buys in one market or sells in another.

Shoplifting. Stealing from retail stores with intention to evade payment for them leading to stock 'shrinkages'.

Short-time Working. State where shortage of work leads an employer to reduce hours of work to a part-time basis, hopefully temporarily.

Showcase. Cabinet made of glass or clear plastic to display products protected against deterioration and pilferage.

Shut-out. As lock-out.

Sickness Benefit. Payment made to an individual to provide income to compensate for loss of earnings during absence from work as a result of illness.

Sick Pay. Payment by an employer to an employee who is unable to work because of illness.

Signature Slogan. Use of a slogan as a pay-off line, at the end of an advertisement.

Silicosis. Progressive and potentially lethol disease of lungs resulting from breathing in silica in coal mining; quarring, pottery, iron and steel, refractory products and other industries.

Simple Contract. A contract not contained in a deed.

Simulated Training. Training in especially created conditions simulating real working conditions and giving opportunity or formal instruction.

Sinecure. A job or office without regular duties but with regular pay.

Single-life Pension. Pension scheme providing for an employee only not for his wife if she services him.

Single-line Store. A type of retail sales establishment that carries a wide variety of one line of merchandise. The goods handled are related items.

Skilled Labour. Work that requires considerable skill relatively long training and usually also considerable judgment on the worker's part. Also, workers engaged in such jobs.

Skills Inventory. Summary of the skills possessed by employees of an organization.

Skill Testing. Testing for level of attainment in a particular skill, either to assess training required or to assess level attained after training.

Slip Edition. Localized edition to give newspaper special reader interest, as occurs at holiday times when slip editions are prepared for different resorts.

Slogan. Catchwords phrase or sentence associated with a product or company, encapsulating a particularly pertinent selling point in a succinct and sometimes entertaining fashion.

Slowdown. A deliberate slowing of the normal work pace in order to reduce output and force an employer to give in to some particular demand.

Smuggling. The practice of secretly importing goods, either to avoid paying customs duties or to obtain goods that may not legally be imported, such as narcotics.

Social Product. The total of all commodities produced and marked in a community within an economic period.

Socio-group. Those who are associated for work, interest or pay.

Sole Proprietorship. A business venture that is wholly owned by one individual.

Sole Trader. One-man trading concern, representing the simplest and earliest form of business organization.

Solus Position. The placing of an advertisement in the news or editorial section of a publication—away from other advertisements.

Space. Term used to describe pages available for advertising purposes in a publication; constitutes the product available for sale after text matter has been accommodated.

Span of Management. Synonym for span of control.

Specialisation of Labour. The division of tasks into their component operations so that each worker becomes a specialist in one operation.

Special Position. Insertion of an advertisement in what is regarded as a distinctive position in a publication.

Speciality Advertising. Advertising using advertising specialities.

Speciality Shop. A retail establishment selling mainly or exclusively speciality goods; usually offering a large and diverse selection of a very narrow range of goods.

Specification. In marketing, this relates to the specified characteristics and performance required of a product, expressed in quantitative as well as qualitative terms.

Specific Unemployment. Unemployment in particular industries.

Staff Specialist. Member of an organization who provides specialized services or advice to line managers in the organization.

Standard-hour Payment System (or Standard-hour Plan). Synonym for standard-time payment system.

Standard Labour Rate. An employee's base pay, plus any incentives and premiums in money, estimated to be attainable under efficient working conditions.

Standard Labour Time. The time, in terms of man-hours of a specified quality, estimated to be required to produce a specific quantity of goods or services.

Standard of Living Theory. A wage theory which holds that employees should be paid more than a subsistence wage.

Standing Order. A continuing work order that directs the production of an item to meet specified sales objectives.

Statements (of Account). Documents sent to customers, listing all items of account outstanding. They are often treated as the official request for payment.

State Trading. A system of conducting all or some international trade through a government agency.

Static Market. Market which has a pattern over time substantially free from fluctuations, particularly of volume.

Status Agreement. Collective agreement granting staff to manual workers.

Status Group. People who share common life-style, or common social, cultural, occupational or professional interest.

Sticker. An individual who is content to remain in his current position rather than seek promotion.

Storing. The keeping of goods or products over a period of time, usually in a warehouse, a cold storage, plant or other special facility, depending upon the nature of the product.

Straight Lease. A lease for a fixed, agreed-upon price for a specific period, with regular payments of equal amounts. Also known as flat lease.

Strike Pay. Or dispute benefit. Paid by a trade union to its members to compensate for loss of income during a strike or other industrial action.

Striker. Person participating in a strike.

Structural Unemployment. Unemployment which is accepted by a government as part of the economic balance of the country.

Structured Interview. One in which questions are determined in advance and set out in a questionnaire.

Sub-editor. Journalist who prepares copy for press, cutting, amending and marking up with typesetting instructions, *i.e.*, subbing.

Subsistence. The minimum food, clothing, and shelter a person or family needs for survival.

Supervisory Training. Courses and planned experience for supervisors/foremen.

Supplements and Features. Special sections or extra pages in newspapers or magazines devised to attract advertisements.

Supplier. Also, Vendor. In business and industry a person or firm that regularly sells its goods or services to another. In the retail business a supplier is also called a resource or source.

Supply of Labour. The number of workers or the number of man-hours of services or (where payment is made by results) the actual amount of work performed.

Supportive Leadership. Management emphasis on the building up of good social relations within an organization, a feature of the human relations school of thought.

Subscription. An agreement to purchase a periodical, a series of theater or concert tickets, or some other item to be used over a period of time.

T

TA. Transactional Analysis.

Tabloid. Small page newspaper, opposite to broadsheet and printed lengthwise on the web.

Tabular Standard. A monetary standard in which the standard is not the price of a single commodity, but it is based upon the price of a representative list of commodities.

Tachistoscope. A device used in planning advertising techniques such as subliminal advertising. An image is displayed for a brief controlled time and the viewer's response is used to judge the best exposure to be used in practice.

Tactical Pricing. Short-term variations, usually reductions in price, to stimulate sales.

Tailor-made Panels. Diary panels set up by market research company (*e.g.* Mass Observation) for individual clients to observe, measure, and check what is happening to clients' brands.

Tainted Goods. Or blacked goods. Products or supplies that have been blacked by a trade union.

Tare. The weight of the packaging, wrapping, containers, or other materials used in shipping goods. Tare weight plus Net weight make up gross weight.

Target. Quantified aim or result to be achieved or bettered within a stated period of time.

Target Audience. Audience to whom marketing, selling or advertising copy platform is aimed, derived from either demographic or psychological market profile or both.

Tax Avoidance. The management of financial matters so as to lower taxes as much as is legally possible.

Tax-cab Advertising. Advertising medium consisting of advertisement panels fitted to the nearside cab driver's door.

Tax Return. A document containing details of an individual's income and expenses and his claims for personal reliefs that is used to assess his income tax.

Taylorism. A synonym for Scientific Management, or the linking of remuneration to output through a Payment-By-Results scheme.

TCD. Management technique of total cost approach to distribution.

Technological Progress. Quite frequently it refers to the construction of more and better instruments of production and to the utilization for this purpose, of a great share of the existing store of technical knowledge.

Technology. The body of knowledge concerned with applying science to the production of goods and services.

Techno-marketing Synergy. To overcome longer gestation periods in technology and its effect on marketing the forecasting, technology and marketing are brought together with use of computer to forecast introduction of new products. Uses technique such as Delphi time scaling.

Television Producer. Advertising agency executive who takes strategy and approved storybook produced by creative group and converts this into TV commercial, selecting production company, TV director and cast.

Television Shopping. Direct response marketing using television as advertising medium. Orders phoned in and computer print-out supplied to advertiser.

Television Studio Tests. Closed-circuit studio tests of commercials at TV studio, with depth interviews of specially recruited sample to measure comprehension of advertising message. As undertaken by British Market Research Bureau.

Teller. A bank employee or officer who actually handless money, receiving deposits and paying out withdrawals. In large banks there may be separate tellers for different transactions, such as paying, receiving, collecting notes, etc.

Termination. Also, separation. The process of leaving a job, either voluntarily (in cases of resignation or retirement) or involuntarily.

Terms of Trade. The relationship between the prices of exports and imports. It may be expressed as an index. This index is expressed as appropriation of the price index of exports to the price index of imports as follows:

$$\frac{\text{Price Index of Exports}}{\text{Price Index of Imports}} \times 100$$

The price index or exports measures changes in the aggregate value of a representative selection of exports as compared with the corresponding value in a base year.

T-group. A small group of people that meets, with a trainer, for the purpose of improving members' skills in interpersonal behaviour by talking and thinking.

Theme Advertising

1. Another term for above-the-line advertising.
2. Advertising, normally of an above-the-line character.

Third-party Selling. As is computer industry, manufacturer sells box to service company which adds software and sells complete package.

Three-shift System. A system of shiftwork in which three shifts are worked in each period of 24 hours in most or all of each week.

Three-two-two Shift System. Synonym for continental shift system.

Threshold. In retailing, minimum number of customers per location and hinterland to justify existence of store.

Threshold Worker. A new employee who has not previously been employed.

Thruster. Manager (or organization) which acts aggressively, is dynamic, positive and exploits opportunities.

Tickler. Jargon for reminder. A tickler file is maintained by some managers as a matter of style. Items may be entered into the file according to a specific date, time, or subject and accessed for use on the appropriate occasion.

Timelength. Time of a commercial spot in television or radio.

Time Note. Promissory note or similar document which specifies a date or dates of repayment.

Time Rate. A rate of payment for an individual's work based on the amount of time spent at work. (Also known as a 'day rate' or 'timework rate'.)

Time-saved Bonus Scheme. Synonym for premium bonus scheme.

Time Served Worker. Skilled craftsman or worker who has completed a formal apprenticeship.

Time-span of Discretion. The maximum time for which the holder of a specified job would normally work on a task without being reviewed or checked by his superiors.

Time Ticket. A report of time spent in performing a labour task usually in the form of a handwritten report or a punched card. Also known as job ticket.

Time Wage. The reward paid to labour by hour, day, month or year.

Time Wage Rate. A system of wage payment based on the number of hours or other time period spent working.

Time Worker. Work that is paid for by a time rate. (Also known as 'daywork.)

Title (or Credit Title). List of executives and performers in a television or film programme.

Time Token. Money whose face value is greater than the value of the material from which it is made.

Tommy Shop. Formerly employer owned shop providing goods for employees in place of cash wages.

Top Hat Pension Scheme. Or discretionary endowment pension scheme.

Top Management. Loosely, the chief executive of an organization and managers close to him in the organization's structure.

Trade Advertising. That aimed at distributors, using media such as trade press, direct mail, exhibitions.

Trade Credit. Facilities by which firms who purchase industrial goods, or the intermediaries in any channel of distribution, are permitted to delay payment for goods they have bought.

Trainee. A person who is receiving training.

Training. Systematic development and improvement of an individual's ability to perform a specific task or job.

Training Officer. Takes central advisory and executive responsibility for implementing the training function.

Training Scheme. A series of activities planned to provide a specific type of training.

Training Specification. A detailed statement of what a trainee needs to learn based on a comparison between his job specification and his present level of ability, training or experience.

Training Transfer. Extent to which effectiveness of training on a simulator or in training situation transfers to effectiveness on the job. Also known as positive transfer, transfer of training or training benefit.

Transient Statement. Remark by interviewer to more respondent on to next topic or question.

U

UDC. Universal Decimal Classification.

Ultimate Consumer. Person or persons who actually consume or use a product or service, as distinct from the shopper or buyer who may be no more than a purchasing agent, such as housewife.

Unaided Recall Method. Refers to the technique for assessing the effectiveness of advertisements in which an interviewer asks someone which advertisements he remembers having see or heard.

Uncertainty Bearing. Responsibility for risks which cannot be standardised and insured against.

Unclaimed Wages. Wages earned but not claimed by employees, although cash is available to make the payment. Also, wage checks not yet presented for payment.

Unconstitutional Strike. Strike called, with or without official trade union backing, in branch of an agreed procedure or procedural agreement.

Uncontrollable Costs. Those affecting a manager or management's budget and area of activity but outside his or its discretion and ability to affect.

Uncontrolled Media. Media in which the PR practitioner has no control over what shall be published or broadcast.

Uncontrollable Variable. A variable in a system which is not under the control of the managers of the system.

Under Bond. Also, in bond. Describing goods which are being stored in a bonded Warehouse.

Under-development. Refers to the failure to utilize fully the potential economic output warranted by existing technological knowledge.

Undermining. Where a plant is manned or a job performed by too few employees for it to operate at a high level of efficiency. Opposite of overmaning.

Under-Population. Refers to a condition when the marginal product of labour is greater than the existing average output per-head for the country as a whole.

Underwriting Commission. Commission paid to someone who underwrites a public offer of securities.

Unearned Income. Income which does not arise from work of one sort or an other.

Unemployed Person. Refers to one who is seeking work of wages but is unable to find any suited to his capacities and under conditions which are reasonably judged by local standard.

Unemployment Benefit. Payment which is made to a person available for employment to compensate for the fact that he is unable to obtain work and a regular income.

Unfair Dismissal. A dismissal which is judged to be unfair by a tribunal. The case is usually brought against an employer by the individual concerned, supported by a Trade Union.

Unfair House (or shop). Where wages and / or working conditions are inferior to those in the industry or locality generally. A term originating in the printing industry.

Unfair Labour Practice (US Spelling: unfair labour practice). US equivalent of an unfair industrial practice.

Unilateral Arbitration. A situation in which one side in an industrial dispute decides unilaterally to go to an arbitration body to seek a solution to the problem.

Union Reference. Where a trade union or its representative seek to use a disputes procedure or a grievance procedure. Such a step by an employer is known as an employer reference.

Unit, Case, Sales Ratio, Standard Cost or Sale Volume Method. Basing the advertising appropriation as percentage of total cost of production, distribution and profit per unit.

Unlimited Company. A company having no limit on the liability of its member is an unlimited company.

Unloading. Disposing of goods in a market at a low or concessionary price.

Unmanned Manufacturing. The technology of operating entire manufacturing facilities without the need for human operators (*e.g.*, with the use of robots).

Unpaid Work. Work carried out within the household for the benefit of its members, and difficult to assess in terms of a national real income.

Unproductive Labour. In some accounting procedures, the same as indirect labour.

Unproductive Wages. Wages paid for Unproductive Labour.

Unskilled Work. Work that consists of simple manual operations that can be learned in a short time and which requires the exercise of little or no independent judgement.

Unskilled Worker. Someone who performs, or can only perform, unskilled work.

Upgraded Training. Training to give supplementary skills and knowledge to increase versatility mobility of labour. Sometimes known as supplementary training.

Upgrading. Improving something without making major changes. Especially, giving an employee more money and/or status and/or responsibility and usually a different title without significantly changing his job.

Upstanding Wage. As guaranteed working wage.

Utility Theory. One of the decision theory techniques for calculating acceptable risk taking in business and project planning.

V

Vacillating Customer. Customer unwilling, or unable, to determine own needs when presented with positive proposition.

Value Satisfactions. Marketing term for the satisfactions or reasons that leads consumer to purchase a particular product or service.

Van Testing. Form of consumer panel using a mobile shop where product tests are conducted in different areas.

Variable Working Hours. Virtually as flexible working hours although sometimes used to describe a less formal system which allows employees even greater freedom of choice in working hours.

Variance Ratio. Refers to the ratio of one sample variance to another sample variance when both samples are taken from a normal population. The ratio is usually denoted by F.

Variety Store. A store carrying a wide range of relatively inexpensive goods for the household.

Vendor. The seller, but especially the seller of small items, *e.g.* street newsvendor who sells newspapers.

Vendor Rating. Classifying of distributors by volume of sales, with preferential trade terms for different grades of vendor.

Vendor's Lien. An unpaid seller's legal right to maintain possession of property until the purchase price has recovered.

Verbal aptitude or Intelligence Tests. Used in personnel selection etc. to test facility in the use of works in oral and written communication.

Vertical Market. Selling of a product or range of products restricted to one type or classification of market.

Vertical Marketing System. As one of the chains or channels of distribution, consists of suppliers, co-ordinators, retailers, consumers in store or in-home.

Vested Right. A right entitled to government protection and belonging so absolutely and unconditionally to person that it cannot be defeated by the act of any private person of organization.

Vesting. The conveying of an irrevocable right to a benefit usually after a specified number of years of continuous employment have been accrued within the same company; most prevalent in Pension and profit-sharing plans.

Vesting Day. Date public authority takes over the nationalized industry.

Vicarious Liability. The liability of an employer for the actions of employees while working under instructions.

Video Casstte Advertising. Commercials on home video cassettes sold or hired out for showing on domestic VCRs.

Videodisc or Videodisk. Means of recording sound and vision on a disc like a small gramophone record, which can be played back on a special recorder and shown on a TV screen.

Video Magazine. PR medium. House Journal produced on video cassette and supplied to organization's locations for showing on television sets to employees.

Videophone. Marriage of telephone and television facilities so that caller and called can see each other.

Vigilance Men. Trade union members who are responsible for reporting to their unions the emergence of any grievances or potential grievances at the work place.

'Vikalpa, Quarterly publication of the Indian Institute of Management, Ahmedabad (India).

Visible. (or visible transaction). A sale, by a resident of goods (rather than services). For the buyer's country such a transaction is a 'visible import, for the seller's country it is a 'visible export'.

Visible Imports. Imports of physically visible goods appearing as payments in the current account of a country's balance of payments statement.

Visual. Drawing or illustration of an advertisement or other piece of promotional material, finished to an adequate standard for presentation to a client.

Visual Abilities Test. Type of personnel selection test designed to test such visual abilities as acuity of sharpness of vision at various distances and the ability to perceive depth.

Visual Perception Time. The time it takes to 'read' a picture.

Vital Statistics. Facts and figures relating to the essential matters of a company, person or economy.

Vocabulary Test. Sometimes used in psychological testing to discover a person's store of understood words. Such a test often consists of a standard list of words which the subject is asked to define.

Voluntary Group. A number of retailers of similar goods who are associated with a single wholesaler and adopt a common policy on promotion.

Voluntary Unemployment. A description given by Keynes to unemployment directly due to the withdrawal of their labour by a body of workers because they do not choose to work for less than a certain real reward.

Voucher. Any written document that serves as proof that money has been paid or received, such as a cancelled cheque, pettycash receipt, receipted bill etc.

Voucher Index. An alphabetical list, in card-index or carbon-copy form, of persons or firms that are payees of the company.

Voucher Register. A journal or record, usually in columnar form for the entry of vouchers.

W

Wage. Also, wages. Refers to any regular payment to an employee of a business for his or her labour by the hour, week, month, or some other period, or by units of output.

Wage Administration. Activities concerned with fixing and sometimes, paying wages in an organization.

Wage Drift. The gap between nationally negotiated wage rates and actual earnings which tend to be much higher.

Wage-offer Curve. A curve which shows the different amounts of hours of work which a worker will offer or work for different amounts of wage rates.

Wage-price Guideposts. Conditions or standards set by the government in an effort to control the behaviour of wages and prices.

Wage Rate. The amount paid to the worker per hour or per normal working day or for performing a certain job.

Wages and Salaries. A term for remuneration paid to employees of a business or other organization. Both are fixed by contract and are usually determined by a trade union or national agreement.

Wait Time. The time a job spends waiting to be moved or waiting to be worked on in the factor area. Also known as queue time.

Wants. Desires which may not yet be apparent. They may be converted eventually into needs. New wants have to be anticipated by the marketeer and satisfied with new products or services.

Warehouse-keeper's Certificate or Receipt. A document issued by a warehouse-keeper stating that certain goods are held in his warehouse at the disposal of the person names. Such a certificate on receipt is not transferable, and the goods are not deliverable upon its production. It is simply an acknowledgement of having received certain goods.

Wash Sale. A bogus transaction which is said to have taken place at an artificially price in a Commodity market used by a seller to boost prices.

Wastage. Proportion of employees, actual or predicted, leaving an employing organization or type or category of employment.

Wastage Rate. Percentage of particular kinds of employee leaving an employing organization during a particular period, usually a year.

Waste Circulation. Parts of a circulation which are of no value to the advertiser but which he nevertheless has to pay for in his campaign.

Waybill. A receipt showing list of the goods accepted for shipment/despatch issued to shipper/consignor by a common land carrier. It is a transportation document prepared by the carrier company at the point of shipment.

Wealth. The wealth of an individual can be defined as his stock of tangible or intangible assets which have a market value.

Water-out. Research problem or weakness that informants, may be unable to sustain prolonged questioning, or may fail to respond to tests which place unrealistic demands on their ability to respond.

Weber's Law. For a salary structure to have uniform incentive value the salary levels should increase in geometric proportions.

Weighted Sample. Market research etc term for a sample with a specific bias, rather than random sampling.

Welfare Capitalism. The concept that workers will be discouraged from joining labour unions if employers create sufficiently favourable conditions.

Welfare State. A social system based on the government's assumption of responsibility for providing unemployment compensation medical care, old-age pensions, and income for families unable to participate in the productive process.

Wharfinger. A person who maintains a wharf at which goods are stored for compensation.

Whip. A fast worker introduced by management as a pacesetter for other workers on a production line.

White-collor. Of, relating to, or performing clerical or supervisory work.

Wholesaler. A person who deals in large quantities of goods. He generally specialises in the purchase and sale of only one commodity.

Widget. In general discussion on production and selling etc., a standard product, obviating the need to relate the instance to a particular product type.

Wildcat Strike. Strick of workers, especially a small but important section of a factory's work force, that lasts for a short time, is not backed by a union and of which the employer is given very short notice.

Will. A written document that provides for the distribution of the writer's property after his or her death.

Windfall. An unanticipated sizable profit or other gain, such as unexpected inheritance, rise in stock prices, etc.

Window-dressing Service. Service provided by manufacturers who send window dressers to their distributors and arrange window displays of their products.

Wink. An interval of 0.0005 minute (0.03 second) employed in method study.

Wink Counter. A timing device, graduated in winks, which is photographed by a movie camera at the same time as the performance of a task for purposes of method study. A wink counter gives a digital display (c.f. microchronometer.)

Wish Image. How company wishes to be seen by outsiders.

Withdrawal of Labour. See strike.

Wondering Personnel Test. General learning ability test that is particularly widely used by industry and business in the USA. Development in the 1960s, it is derived partly from the Otis self-administering test of mental ability.

Women's Bureau. An agency concerned with promoting the welfare if wage-earning women improving their work conditions, increasing their efficiency, advancing their opportunities for profitable employment and similar efforts.

Workplace Layout. Space, facilities and conditions provided for a worker in the performance of a specified job.

Work Simplification. Concerned with simple techniques of analyzing any aspects of work or systems with the object of cutting out all unnecessary effort. May involve eliminating, combining, rearranging simplifying work.

Work Staff. Office, supervisory or other white-collar workers whose occupations are closely involved with the manufacturing or production processes in a factory.

Written Down Value. Value of an asset after depreciation has been taken into account. Written down value virtually synonymous with net book amount.

X

X-efficiency. It refers to the efficiency with which an entrepreneur uses the inputes, solves the organisational problems and perform his firm's activities at least cost.

Xerographic Printer. A page printer (*i.e.* a printer in which the character pattern is set for a whole page before printing, which uses principle of xerography.

Xerography. The technique upon which photocopiers are based—dry powder deposition and fixing.

X-Y Plotter. Means data plotter.

Y

Yardage. Amount of space allocated to a brand on a supermarket shelf.

Yardstick. The rates charged by one business used as a measure for setting other rates.

Yellow-dog Contract. An agreement to the effect that a new employee would refrain from joining a union, which employers fighting unionization forced workers to sign.

Yellow Journalism. Sensationalized an exagerated journalism.

Yesterday. Refers to previous period.

You Approach. Personalized form of copywriting which directs message at individual reader.

Young-helmoholtz Theory. Three-colour theory of colour vision which assumes a three-colour mechanism of the retina which responds maximally to red, green and blue/violet respectively.

Young Persons. Legislation re-advertising.

Youth Training Scheme (YTS). A programme of work experience and education followed by 16-year-old school-leavers in Britain, financed by government grants and administered by the Manpower Services Commission.

Yuppies. (young, upwardly-mobile professionals). A mildly derogatory reference to successful but status-conscious business (or other professional) people.

Z

Z-chart. A graphical method employed in time series analysis to compare observed periodic (monthly) values of a variable, their cumulative total and the moving annual total.

Zemindari System. The land tenure system in which land is owned by the landlord who holds responsible to the Government for the payment of land revenue.

Zero-based Review. A zero-based budgeting technique, developed into a formal management planning process.

Zero-order Model. Stochastic model used in brand choice research, assuming that brand of product last bought does not influence the purchase to be predicted.

Zero Price Advertising. Distribution of advertising at price which does not cover its costs *i.e.*, a zero money price, while the advertised goods are marked up to finance the advertising.

Zone. Tading area or area to which product launch is temporarily limited, a zoned campaign or one that is zonal.

Zoned Campaigns. Advertising campaigns and marketing strategies may be limited to a particular zone or area of the country, perhaps to a television region. This may be to boost sales in a certain area, or to launch a new product on a zonal basis spreading to other zones as sales develop or production capacity is increased.

Zone Circles. A version of the problem solving technique, Quality Circles in which employees are grouped into self-regulatory teams in order to improve motivation and benefit from a joint approach to operating difficulties.